A Strategic Vision for Africa

A Strategic Vision for Africa

The Kampala Movement

Francis M. Deng

I. William Zartman

BROOKINGS INSTITUTION PRESS
Washington, D.C.

Copyright © 2002
THE BROOKINGS INSTITUTION
1775 Massachusetts Avenue, N.W., Washington, D.C. 20036
www.brookings.edu

Library of Congress Cataloging-in-Publication data
Deng, Francis Mading, 1938–
  A strategic vision for Africa: the Kampala movement / Francis M. Deng
and I. William Zartman.
    p. cm.
Includes bibliographical references and index.
  ISBN 0-8157-0264-7 (cloth : alk. paper) —
  ISBN 0-8157-0265-5 (paper : alk. paper)
  1. Conference on Security, Stability, Development, and Cooperation in
Africa. 2. National security--Africa. 3. Africa--Foreign
relations--1960- 4. Sustainable development--Africa. I. Zartman, I.
William. II. Title.
  DT30.5 .D464 2002
  327'.096--dc21   2001004710

            9 8 7 6 5 4 3 2 1

The paper used in this publication meets minimum requirements of the
American National Standard for Information Sciences—Permanence of Paper for
Printed Library Materials: ANSI Z39.48-1992.

Typeset in Minion

Composition by Oakland Street Publishing
Arlington, Virginia

Printed by R. R. Donnelley and Sons
Harrisonburg, Virginia

Foreword

This book is an account of the efforts by Africans, both the leadership and at the grassroots, to develop a strategic vision encompassing security, stability, development, and cooperation for the continent. According to Francis M. Deng and I. William Zartman this initiative—the Conference on Security, Stability, Development, and Cooperation in Africa (CSSDCA)—was originally inspired in 1989 by Olusegun Obasanjo, now president of Nigeria, under the institutional framework of the Africa Leadership Forum. Between November 1990 and May 1991, scholars and political leaders from across Africa met four times. The fourth and principal conference, held in Kampala, Uganda, in May 1991, resulted in what became known as the Kampala Movement. Two basic assumptions grounded this movement. First, the Organization of African Unity (OAU) had failed to meet the aspirations of the African peoples. Second, in the post–cold war era, Africa would be marginalized by the strategic withdrawal of the major powers and left to fend for itself. Africa, therefore, had to put its house in order, guided by the principles of an appropriate policy framework, to re-engage the international community.

The CSSDCA's proposed policy framework—which initially inspired Africans in all circles, governmental and nongovernmental—proved too ambitious and threatening to African governments, and they shelved it by requesting more studies and further considerations. During the mid-1990s the movement became dormant though not extinct, especially during Obasanjo's unjust imprisonment, which started in 1995. In 1999, in the wake of political reform in Nigeria, Obasanjo gained his freedom and rose to power as the country's elected president. On the moral high ground and with an influential stature in Africa and the international community, he again introduced the initiative and reactivated its eventual adoption by the OAU. What is needed alongside the OAU adoption, according to the authors, is the reinvigoration of a civil society movement, such as the one that fostered the Kampala Movement, to keep the intergovernmental process on track.

By providing a historical record of the CSSDCA, its substantive contents, the lessons learned from other regional experiences outside of Africa, including the Organization of American States (OAS), the Association of Southeast Asian Nations (ASEAN), and the Organization for Security and Co-operation in Europe (OSCE), and the present status of the initiative, this book helps to facilitate the evolution of a policy agenda for Africa. Its prospects for success largely depend on the role that scholars, policymakers, practitioners, and activists play in collaboration with civil society to hold the OAU and individual governments accountable for their performance in accordance with the agreed principles of the policy framework.

Francis M. Deng is the UN secretary general's special representative on internally displaced persons, and I. William Zartman is professor and director of the Conflict Management program at Johns Hopkins University. They would like to express their profound gratitude to several scholars who prepared the initial drafts for various chapters. Abdelwahab El Affendi provided the draft for the Horn section of chapter 2, and Gilbert A. Khadiagala provided the draft for the southern Africa section of the chapter. Jannie Leatherman drafted all of chapter 3, and Anne-Marit Austbo provided the draft for chapter 4. Mehri Madarshahi contributed information on the use of CSSDCA principles by the OAU, subregional organizations, and individual governments in chapter 5. Beth Elise Whitaker revised and edited the materials contributed by the research scholars mentioned above, developed them into a draft manuscript, and helped frame the introduction and conclusion in chapter 5.

At Brookings, Theresa Walker edited the manuscript, Inge Lockwood proofread the book, and Robert Elwood provided the index.

The Brookings Institution acknowledges with deep gratitude the generous support that the Carnegie Corporation of New York has provided over the years for the Africa Project activities, of which this is the concluding volume.

The views expressed in this book are those of the individual authors and should not be attributed to the people whose assistance is acknowledged above, to the organizations that supported the project, or to the trustees, officers, or other staff members of the Brookings Institution.

MICHAEL H. ARMACOST
President

January 2002
Washington, D.C.

Contents

Preface by Olusegun Obasanjo   xiii

1 *Introduction*   1
    Elements of the African Condition   2
    Kampala Initiative: Negotiations toward a Normative Framework   5
    Kampala Principles   6
    Consideration and Negotiation   9
    Organization of the Book   13

2 *The African Context*   14
    West Africa   16
    The Horn of Africa   26
    Central Africa   38
    Southern Africa   48
    Conclusions   61

3 *Regimes in Other Regions*   66
    ASEAN and Asia Pacific 68
    The Americas and the Organization of American States   78
    Europe, North America, and the Organization for Security and
      Cooperation in Europe   88
    Conclusions   98

4 *An Evolving Framework*   104
    The Roots of the CSSDCA Proposal   105
    Evolution of the CSSDCA   111
    Principles and Implementation   117
    Implementation   122
    Conclusions   136

5 *Beacons and Benchmarks*   139
     Norms and Africa   140
     Security   144
     Stability   147
     Development   149
     Cooperation   151
     CSSDCA Principles in Recent Initiatives   154
     Recent Revival   157
     The Next Steps   158
     Strategies for the Future   160

Appendix: Specific Principles of the Kampala Document   164

Notes   170

Index   188

Preface

This book is a record of the dedicated efforts of many people, both Africans and Africa's friends, concerned with the extreme challenges confronting the continent in the urgent quest for security, stability, and development, within a framework of regional and international cooperation. These efforts have resulted in the formulation of a vision and the measures needed to realize it as a Conference on Security, Stability, Development, and Cooperation in Africa—CSSDCA. And while there have been severe constraints, and even setbacks, Africa's quest for human dignity is an imperative that might be impeded but can no longer be reversed.

Perhaps a balanced perspective of the African pursuit of human dignity is to see it as an evolutionary process that has witnessed spectacular achievements, disheartening setbacks, and relentless commitment to forging a better future. The liberation struggle against colonialism was a most ambitious project, and Africa, supported by the lofty principle of self-determination, with the backing of powers equally motivated by the ideals of common humanity, was able to achieve victory. However, the euphoria of freedom, the desire to focus undivided attention on economic and social development, the fear of diversity and pluralistic democracy as potential sources of disunity, and not least, the corruptive lure of power, soon resulted in one-party rule, authoritarianism, and centralized state monopolization of political and economic power. The jealous guard over myopic concepts of state sovereignty militated against continent-wide cooperation and unity, which some visionary leaders advocated, and even led to the dismantling of regional and federal arrangements, which the colonial powers had put in place as effective mechanisms for administering their territories and fostering coordination and cooperation across boundaries.

All this was a recipe for a second wave of liberation struggle, this time against internal domination. However, the bipolar ideological divide of the cold war and its global control mechanisms stood against this liberation from within, bolstering regimes and shielding dictators on the basis of where they stood ideologically. Although this state of affairs ensured a degree of global stability, it also fueled proxy confrontations between the superpowers and their ideological allies within and between states. A number of countries in Africa suffered severely from armed conflicts with ideological overtones during the cold war.

While the end of the cold war was initially expected to usher in a higher level of security worldwide, it only improved the relations of the former ideological camps, removed their strategic involvement in many parts of the world, marginalized certain regions, foremost among them the African continent, and permitted the previously dependent and weak states to fall victim to internal contradictions and internecine warfare. Many parts of Africa rapidly descended into chaotic conditions involving tensions, unrest, violence, and even state collapse.

It was in anticipation of these post–cold war developments that the normative framework of a Conference on Security, Stability, Development, and Cooperation in Africa (CSSDCA) was conceived by the Africa Leadership Forum (ALF), under my direction as the founding chairman of the forum. Indeed, the ALF was created not only to facilitate the role of incumbent leaders but also to develop the capacity of young and mid-level leaders to deal with the unfolding crises of the continent. The CSSDCA process itself was also envisaged as a means of enabling the Africans to rise to the challenges confronting them, while, at the same time, building on the European experience with the Helsinki process that led to the Conference on Security and Cooperation in Europe (CSCE) and eventually culminated in the Organization for Security and Cooperation in Europe (OSCE). It was hoped that the ground would be prepared for international cooperation, especially with the countries of the OSCE.

Initially, the CSSDCA process, leading up to the Kampala Conference, was viewed with a great deal of optimism, even euphoria, in Africa as a framework for a new beginning that would foster security, stability, development, and cooperation for the continent. Incumbent and former heads of state and government who attended the Kampala Conference praised it as the most important development on the continent in recent years. It was a truly promising initiative.

For the same reason, it threatened the status quo and especially the power positions of a few governments whose domestic hold on unscrupulous power rendered them vulnerable and insecure. They became the most vocal in their opposition to the initiative, and others caved in through the usual deference to the need for consensus within the Organization of African Unity (OAU). Since the opponents could not oppose the initiative in principle, they resorted to diversionary tactics of requesting further studies and response from governments. The bottom line was that they shelved the initiative.

Developments in my own country, Nigeria, have been both representative of the negative trends in Africa and, more recently, a source of encouragement for positive change. With independence, Nigeria, like most African countries emerging from colonialism, adopted a Westminster model constitution that enshrined principles of parliamentary democracy and fundamental freedoms. Regional cleavages and divisive leadership soon made democracy a laughing stock, prompting a series of military coups aimed at placing the country onto a more constructive course of nation building. It was through one of these military actions that I first rose to a position of national leadership and became head of state when my senior colleague, the leader of our revolution, Murtala Mohammed, was assassinated. I kept our erstwhile promise to lead the country toward a more sustainable democracy and, despite pressures to the contrary, restored parliamentary democracy. However, the failure of the politicians to effectively address the serious problems confronting the country, in particular the ethnic and regional diversities and disparities in the sharing of political and economic power, soon led to more coups and countercoups, culminating in the worse military dictatorship Nigeria had ever witnessed, the dark years of Sani Abacha. On the basis of fabricated allegations, I was accused of conspiracy in a coup attempt and sentenced to fifteen years imprisonment. The intervention of Providence led to Abacha's sudden death and brought Nigeria back to the democratic course that culminated in my return to the leadership of my country, this time as a popularly elected civilian president.

I used the opportunity of my position and the good offices of my country to reintroduce the CSSDCA process to my colleagues in the Organization of African Unity. Developments since the CSSDCA was first introduced had vindicated the urgent need for the initiative, and the Organization proved more prepared to accept it than had been the case a decade earlier. From an initial endorsement by the Assembly of Heads of State and Government, through a series of ministerial meetings that developed modalities of implementation, to the final adoption by the assembly, the CSSDCA process can now be said to have been fully integrated into the OAU system.

There are those who suspect that this integration may indeed be a disguised containment and that the ambitious vision initially envisaged for the process may have become significantly compromised. They may be right. On the other hand, the potential for incremental development of the CSSDCA within the system can no longer be ruled out. Only time will tell whether the process is being contained or institutionalized to develop in a constructive and least disruptive manner within the OAU system. But in addition to adoption and implementation on the continental level, the Kampala principles need to be an active cause for civil society organizations, from whence they came, and a prominent guideline for Africa's subregional organizations, to which they are also addressed.

One thing is clear: African leadership cannot claim legitimacy without courageously confronting the plight of the African peoples and their urgent quest for the universal ideals of human dignity. Africa is a continent endowed with material and human resources. There is no justification whatsoever for the peoples of Africa to be the leading recipients of outside humanitarian assistance that can only sustain life at a minimum level of survival. Africans are fleeing by the millions within their countries as internally displaced persons or across international borders as refugees. Most of them are destitute, depending only on international charity. National sovereignty can only be meaningful if it discharges a certain level of responsibility in providing adequate protection and assistance to citizens and all those under state jurisdiction. Otherwise, failure to do so exposes a country to international scrutiny and maybe intervention on humanitarian grounds.

Africa's quest for human dignity has become an urgent imperative and it is time to hold the leadership accountable for its dismal record of achievement and the prospects for forging a better future for the peoples of Africa. I warmly welcome and commend this book as a significant contribution in that direction.

OLUSEGUN OBASANJO
President of the Federal Republic
of Nigeria

March 2001
State House
Abuja, Nigeria

1

Introduction

This is the story of a grassroots movement, told in midcourse, after the movement swept a continent, won and lost in high places, and now hangs on the cusp of success or exhaustion. It is a lesson in the power politics of an idealistic search for a strategic vision. It is a memorial to lofty aspirations grappling with corruption and lust for power. And it is a road map for attaining those aspirations, to decide whether the last of the third world gets caught up or left behind by globalization. The lesson, the memorial, and the road map begin in Africa, but their importance goes beyond Africa and around the world.

Any appraisal of the African condition must inevitably be ambivalent. On the positive side, the 1990s witnessed a renewed hope about the prospects for peace and development on the continent. Several factors contributed to this optimism, including the end of the cold war, the movement away from state-controlled economies, the increasing strength of internal struggles for democracy, the end of apartheid in South Africa, and the wave of competitive elections that have been held in nearly thirty countries. Despite the positive rhetoric, however, Africa remains a continent in crisis, and the beginning of the new millennium appears to accentuate its gravity. Violent conflicts, human rights violations, economic mismanagement, incompetent governance, and flawed development policies are among the manifestations of this crisis. Although some countries have enjoyed greater growth and freedom in the past decade, others have experienced economic stagnation, instability, and violence.

Rather than looking to the outside world to resolve these problems, some Africans have turned inward in light of the changing international and domestic dynamics. With the end of the cold war, internal and regional conflicts are now being seen in their own context rather than as episodes in the global confrontation between the superpowers. This is a positive development. At the same time, however, the strategic withdrawal of the major powers has also contributed to the marginalization and even neglect of Africa. The international community remains engaged primarily on humanitarian grounds and, to a lesser extent, in defense of human rights, as well as through economic attempts to revive the decline in development. Unfortunately, crises of grave magnitude are now generally met with reluctant and belated responses. The time has been seen by some as ripe for a new approach.

Elements of the African Condition

In the 1990s, two factors combined to provide the context for the creation of a normative framework for Africa: the breakdown of world order and the increasing marginalization of Africa. From the outside, the end of the cold war meant the collapse of a system of world order that had shaped perceptions, restrained as well as focused conflict, and maintained state order for the half century after World War II. While the defeat and disappearance of one of the parties in the bipolar confrontation left international relations without any clear shape and purpose, it also eliminated the remaining superpower's concern for many regions and their issues, lifted restraints on previously submerged conflicts, and removed support for governments held in power by more foreign than domestic backing.

The major tenets of African political systems were removed in the cold war victory: the centralized party-state was undermined by competitive notions of democracy and loyal opposition, the centralized economy was subject to austerity and competition through imposed structural adjustment, and the ideological commitment to African socialism was shattered by notions of accountability, political and economic competition, and privatization. Some of these developments worked against their stated purpose, only to provide further causes of grief for Africa: privatization was applied by warlords and rulers to state revenues, competition was used by rebel movements to contest legitimate governments, and the end of cold war patronage left governments and rebels alike to fend for themselves on the informal arms market.

The increasing marginalization of Africa was gradually becoming more and more apparent to observers outside Africa and to some African leaders. The sobering fact was that most of the hopes and aspirations that had provided the spur for independence were not realized. Politicians and intellectuals succumbed to the tendency to find ready-made scapegoats for African problems. African nations seeking self-determination only reached half their goal, since the passage of power from foreign to national rule had left nationalist rulers firmly ensconced with seats of power in the name of the people but without the obligation of turning to their people for authorization and accountability.

At the same time, Africa's position in the global system was gradually slipping, not only in regard to political justifications but also economically. The development myth and dream had vanished. Per capita national product dropped by a third, food production fell by 20 percent during the 1970s and 1980s, external debt equaled more than three times total exports and more than three-quarters of GNP, and Africa's share of the world national product dropped from nearly 2 percent to slightly more than 1 percent, while holding more than 9 percent of the world's population and growing (despite AIDS and genocide).

There were occasional African responses to this multileveled problem. At the highest level, the members of the Organization for African Unity (OAU), baffled by their own inability to handle the recurrent politico-military security problems of the continent, turned in the 1980s to take on economic challenges, despite the founding agreement that left economic matters to the United Nations (UN) Economic Commission for Africa (ECA). In 1980 an extraordinary summit formulated the Lagos Plan of Action, a self-reliance program for economic revival. When it proved unrealistic, a new Priority Program for Economic Recovery was launched in 1985 with the United Nations (UN), aimed at reinserting rather than removing African economies from global interactions. This was followed by more specific declarations: the Common Position on External Debt (1987), the Khartoum Declaration on Human Centered Development (1988), the Mauritius Declaration on

Education (1989), and the African Charter for Popular Participation in Development (1990). All contributed general principles to the struggle for development, but they remained unconnected and unimplemented. Then, at the beginning of the 1990s, the breakdown of internal security frustrated development, and the OAU turned back to its security functions, leaving its economic and social principles unfulfilled.

In security matters, the target changed just as the continent refocused its attention. Instead of facing interstate conflict among OAU members, which required collective security responses, Africa entered an era of state collapse under the combined breakdown of governmental functions and the rise of domestic rebellions. The outbreak at the end of 1989 of the second internal revolt in Liberia after Samuel Doe was fraudulently elected in 1985 called for an internal collective security response that was picked up by the regional organization, the Economic Community of West African States (ECOWAS), rather than by the OAU. The collapse of the Siad Barre regime in Somalia at the same time escaped African attentions completely and fell to the United States and the UN to handle, badly. The discriminatory regime of Juvenal Habyarimana in Rwanda was challenged in 1990 by (and then locked in a stalemate with) the Rwandan Patriotic Front (RPF) in the name of the excluded Tutsi minority. As Africa and the larger international community stood by and watched, 800,000 people were killed in the genocide of 1994.

Domestically, Africa in the early 1990s faced a rising call for democratization to complete the promise of self-determination through independence. The most explicit form of this wave was the Sovereign National Conference, one of the most extraordinary political developments in the postwar era, known by its French-ordered acronym, CNS, because it occurred almost exclusively in French-speaking countries. In twelve countries, beginning with Benin in 1990, self-constituted representatives of civil society took sovereignty away from autocratic single-party rulers, put it into their own hands, rewrote constitutions, opened up political systems, and held new elections for more accountable governments. Other non-French-speaking states imitated the movement in their own ways. By 1997 nearly thirty African countries held competitive elections for national office.

These nonviolent revolutionary reforms represented a comprehensive effort by African bodies politic to meet some of the current problems at a basic level, but they did not always stick, and in half the cases were reversed by entrenched autocrats better versed in politics than their opponents. Despite the positive rhetoric and the wave of optimism, something more would be needed to resolve the challenges to economic and political development in Africa.

Kampala Initiative: Negotiations toward a Normative Framework

In 1989, after some years of retirement and more years of private discussions and public speeches, former Nigerian president General Olusegun Obasanjo launched the Africa Leadership Forum (ALF) as a vehicle for his efforts to confront the African crisis. The ALF organized several conferences, drawing on the civil society and state sectors in various locations and some development seminars at Obasanjo's farm in southwest Nigeria. One such meeting, in Paris in April 1990, drew the conclusion that Africa would remain in its multileveled crisis until a comprehensive solution producing stable conditions for development was found from within. A broad conference to examine such solutions was recommended, and, for the following six months, the director of the ALF, Felix Mosha, toured the continent, contacting leading African public and private personalities about the feasibility of the project.

In the following six months, between November 1990 and May 1991, four preparatory conferences were held to shape the ideas behind the conference and to cultivate support. The first two meetings, in Addis Ababa, worked on the procedures and the contents of the effort. Obasanjo brought the general secretaries of the Addis-based organizations—the OAU and ECA—to join in convening some thirty politicians and scholars and spoke of a triad of security, pluralism, and economic cooperation, each encompassing a number of basic principles. A steering committee comprising about half of the conference participants met again in February 1991 and restructured the principles into four goals: security, stability, development, and cooperation. The committee envisaged a final document signed by African states, which would then adopt its principles through national legislation. The document, which would emerge from a civil society movement, would then be made official and enacted by the states.

Preparations also emphasized contacts with relevant sectors of support, abroad and domestically. A third meeting, in Cologne in March, brought the leaders of the ALF movement in contact with officials in the movement that had produced the Helsinki Document for Europe and North America in 1975 and created the ongoing Conference on Security and Cooperation in Europe (CSCE). It was recognized that the European movement started as a private initiative that took time to develop, that the African movement needed to rest on its own roots, and that Africa might need to make use of, or supplement, its existing organization, the OAU. The fourth meeting sought to develop those roots by bringing together African nongovernmental organizations (NGOs) in April in Ota, where it was recommended that NGOs be included in all aspects of the evolving process.

The principal conference of this movement was convened in Kampala on May 19 and 20, 1991, by the ALF, ECA, and OAU and brought together 500 participants, including five current heads of state, three former heads of state, and diplomats, scholars, business executives, and representatives of students' and women's organizations. Diplomatic gloves were off, people spoke frankly, and not all supported the general idea. After initial speeches, participants broke up into working groups on each of the four issue areas and emerged with new drafts, which were then adopted with consensus and enthusiasm by those assembled. The result of this process was a statement of principles known as the Kampala Document.

Kampala Principles

The Kampala Document included a statement of seven basic principles, a longer declaration of more than forty norms and policies, and a recommendation to African leaders to inaugurate a Conference on Security, Stability, Development, and Cooperation in Africa (CSSDCA) to lead to the adoption of a new and comprehensive politico-economic regime. The agreed principles were as follows:

I. Every African state is sovereign. Every African state respects the rights inherent in the territorial integrity and political independence of all other African states.

II. The security, stability, and development of every African country are inseparably linked with those of other African countries. Consequently, instability in one African country impinges on the stability of all other African countries.

III. The erosion of security and stability in Africa is one of the major causes of its continuing crises and one of the principal impediments to the creation of a sound economy and effective intra- and inter-African cooperation.

IV. The interdependence of African states and the link between their security, stability, and development demand a common African agenda based on a unity of purpose and a collective political consensus derived from a firm conviction that Africa cannot make any significant progress on any other front without creating collectively a lasting solution to its problems of security and stability.

V. A conference on Security, Stability, Development, and Cooperation in Africa (CSSDCA) should be launched to provide a comprehensive framework for Africa's security and stability and measures for accelerated continental economic integration for socioeconomic transformation. CSSDCA shall encompass four major areas henceforth called calabashes: security, stability, development, and cooperation.

VI. A new order embodied in the framework of CSSDCA must be created in Africa through a declaration of binding principles and a commitment to ideological independence, which will guide the conduct of governance in individual African states as well as the imperatives of intra-African and inter-African relations. The implementation of the new order should seek an active partnership and positive involvement of the rest of the world.

VII. The fulfillment in good faith of all the CSSDCA principles must be adhered to by all participating states within the context of any other obligations each participating member may have under international law.[1]

The Kampala Document rests on the premise that peace and security are necessary for the other three goals of stability, development, and cooperation. Lack of democracy, denial of personal liberty, and abuse of human rights are all causes of insecurity. The key to security, therefore, is the responsible exercise of sovereignty, in the absence of which cooperation among neighbors is required to deal with internal problems and conflicts. Measures are required to ensure the security of states and people, creating a security community among African states where war is no longer envisaged as a tool of national policy and where the basic necessities of life are ensured for their citizens.

The concept of security is seen in its totality, transcending military considerations, including conflict prevention, containment, and resolution, and culminating in common and collective continental security. It also embraces all aspects of the society, including economic, political, and social dimensions of the individual, family, community, local, and national life. By this definition, the Kampala Document posits that the security of each country and of the continent depends on the ability of people to live in peace with access to basic necessities of life, while they fully and freely participate in the affairs of their societies.

The management of security has tremendous implications for the stability component. The stability of every country in the years ahead may hinge on the effective institutionalization of democracy and good governance. The current clamor for democratization is equally a clamor for economic redemption, which is more achievable in the context of good governance. The security component may also become all the more of a necessity while democratization takes shape. It is to be expected that conflicts could intensify as different approaches to issues such as governance, identity, resources, and stratification become more apparent.

Stability is equally important to Africa's political and economic development. Promoting political and social stability in individual countries is, therefore, a second key component of the CSSDCA process. Under the stability principles of the Kampala Document, all African states are to be guided by strict adherence to the rule of law, popular participation in governance, and full protection for human rights and fundamental freedoms. Political organizations should not be based on religious, ethnic, regional, or racial considerations. There should be accountability and transparency in public policymaking and execution, and absence of violent and destructive fundamentalism in religious practice.

For the purpose of economic development, African states are to subscribe to certain fundamental principles under the CSSDCA process. Development calls for an open, competitive economy to ensure the satisfaction of basic human needs and the full growth of the African human potential. One of the major causes of Africa's present economic crisis is its failure to utilize earnings from commodity exports to diversify economic activity and invest in value-added production. A time has come for effective diversification, horizontally by broadening the production base and vertically by processing and marketing. Popular participation and equal opportunity and access must also be promoted and sustained as a crucial basis for the realization of development objectives. Finally, regional economic integration is indispensable for Africa's socioeconomic transformation and survival and for its competitiveness with the rest of the world in the twenty-first century.

The last item, cooperation, is the culmination of the previous three and is seen as necessary to achieving lasting stability, security, and development. The Kampala Document provides a framework for collective action and for cooperation among African states bilaterally, regionally, and internationally. It also advocates economic integration in the African Economic Community, joint development of common natural resources, interdependence based on beneficial cooperative relations with other developing and industrialized nations, and supranationality based on the need to devolve certain key responsibilities to continental institutions. Overall, then, the Kampala Document charted an invaluable course and framework for Africa's development based on self-reliance and diversification, effective and responsive governance, regional integration, and international cooperation.

Consideration and Negotiation

The Kampala Movement is a process in motion. In the years following the Kampala meeting, the OAU took several looks at the Kampala Document, selected from it some small pieces, and tabled the rest. Most devastatingly, Obasanjo's home state, Nigeria, under its dictator, Gen. Sani Abacha, turned against the father of the document, sentenced him for conspiracy, and put him under house arrest, then tried, convicted, and sentenced him to fifteen years in 1995 at the time he was planning to revive the campaign for a CSSDCA.

The reaction of the OAU and its membership in the early 1990s was cool and selective, since their interests were being challenged by the proposed regime. Already at the Addis Ababa preparatory meeting in November 1990, the OAU secretary general challenged the foreign nature of the document because of its connection with the Helsinki Document for Europe and North America and recalled that Africa already had a security regime in the OAU, despite its frequently noted insufficiencies. The OAU Council of Ministers, meeting in Abuja in June 1991 under the presidency of Nigerian general Ibrahim Babangida, two weeks after Kampala, deferred consideration of the document to a later Council session, to the Secretariat, and to member states, and therefore did not submit it to the OAU summit. Subsequent submissions to the Council in Abuja in February 1992 and in Dakar in July 1992 and February 1993 resulted in successive deferrals.

There is no doubt that the CSSDCA would have had some relationship to the OAU, either parallel in competition, superior in surveillance, internal in subordination, or simply in replacement. It could therefore be conceived as a threat to the organization as constituted. Personal rivalry among the principal personalities, both from pivotal governments and the OAU, also prevailed.

However, the OAU at the time of the development of the movement to promote the CSSDCA was also developing its own program of conflict management, and that process gained from the ideas exposed at pre-Kampala meetings. The eventual Mechanism for the Prevention, Management and Resolution of Conflicts, which comprised a new department in the Secretariat (a body like a Security Council capable of action between summits) and an ad hoc institution of Special Representative of the Secretary General (SRSG), was adopted at the Dakar summit in July 1993 and immediately put to use. Imitation was the best form of opposition to the CSSDCA.

Opposition also came more broadly from member states. Some of the heads of state in attendance at Kampala, notably Sudan's Omar Hassan Ahmed al-Bashir and Zambia's Kenneth Kaunda, found the source of Africa's problems abroad and in the past. According to this viewpoint, there was no need for a new regime, such as the CSSDCA. In the OAU Council of Ministers, Libya was also vocally opposed.

Besides the active "derailers," other states played different roles in the OAU discussions. A larger group were simply "brakers," seeking to slow the process of considering the Kampala propositions because of their vulnerability to its provisions, particularly on democracy, sovereignty, free enterprise, and cooperation. Most of the rest of the states were "riders," uninspired by the document and waiting to go along with the majority. No favorable majority ever formed, and relevant governments came to forget about the initiative.

Contrary to the entrenched official reactions, the post-Kampala period and then the period of Obasanjo's incarceration were not times of inaction in the civil society, however. The ALF continued to discuss the Kampala principles at conferences on related subjects in September 1991 and March 1992. Further publications disseminated the document. It also received the attention of Africanists and their publications. During the incarceration period, interim leadership of the ALF kept working at the project through a series of publications supported by the Carnegie Corporation. An ALF secretariat continued to function in Accra, and in New York, Hans d'Orville, president of the African Leadership Foundation, organized a succession of publications with numerous testimonials in support of the incarcerated general Obasanjo; and in Washington, Francis Deng, former Sudanese foreign minister, was designated by General Obasanjo to head the ALF in his absence. Toward the end of the period, a new strategy was being planned, which would enlist academics and political figures in key African countries, working through regional research organizations, to bypass the continental level and press for adoption of the Kampala principles by subregional organizations, which could then put pressure on the OAU. At the same time, other organizations grew up in civil society to press for some of the same principles. Human rights and pro-democracy organizations grew, sometimes even under government auspices. Although the period was undoubtedly one of dormancy for the official process, attention within civil society was maintained, and the Kampala Movement was kept alive.

Even on the state level, some of the principles have been put into practice in individual countries. Plural—hence opposition—political parties developed, often under difficult circumstances, but at least more frequently than in the previous decades. Aid offered primarily through the National Endowment for Democracy in the United States helped parties learn the ropes of organization and elections, and foreign and foreign-trained domestic election observers monitored the results.[2] Combined domestic and international pressure for democratization brought competitive elections in Kenya, Ghana, Ivory Coast, Zimbabwe, Zambia, Liberia, Tunisia, Senegal, Cameroon, Gabon, Sierra Leone, Uganda, Burundi, and even Nigeria beyond the CNS states, where, arguably, there otherwise would have been none. Together, this does not eliminate the need for a comprehensive set of principles, nor does it even outweigh the worse examples of their breach. But it does indicate that the spirit of Kampala moved on at the grassroots level.

Events in Nigeria in 1998–99 once again revitalized the CSSDCA process. In June 1998, Abacha, then the sole candidate for president, suddenly died, struck down by a heart attack. He was immediately replaced by Gen. Abdulsalami Abubakar, a principled military figure with no ambition except to return the country to elected civilian rule. A month later, Chief Moshood Abiola, a weak but symbolic figure elected president in 1993 in an annulled election to a now-expired term, also died suddenly of a heart attack. The leading candidate in the new elections was Obasanjo himself, who emerged from prison and retirement to win election in February 1999 to the position he had relinquished twenty years before.

The new Nigerian government made the revival of the Kampala process a major point of its foreign policy. This attention has brought a resurrection of the movement and given it major impetus. As a result, CSSDCA was endorsed at the 1999 OAU Extraordinary Summit in Sirte and handed to a steering committee to prepare. The organization eventually adopted the Kampala Document as a statement of its own record of activity, with review conferences envisaged to evaluate its progress, thus bringing the movement under its protective wing. In the process, the state action became separated from the civil society movement, and the Kampala effort hopped along on one leg instead of walking on two—state and civil society. No state has included its principles as such in its national legislation, although many of the tenets were scattered throughout constitutions, declarations, speeches, writings, and occasional practices. The business as usual of African conflicts, authoritarianism, underdevelopment, and selective cooperation continued, as has Africa's marginalization in a globalizing world. The challenge of the time is to implement African states' commitment to the moment while broadening its base throughout civil society to provide dynamic, multileveled support for a new framework.

Organization of the Book

This book is a comparative analysis of the Kampala Movement in midstream. It is an account of the efforts that were exerted toward the CSSDCA and a background to the renewal of those efforts since the election of General Obasanjo as president of Nigeria. Chapter 2 is a review of the need for a new regime seen through four of the regions of the continent—West Africa, the Horn of Africa, Central Africa, and Southern Africa—under the four components or "calabashes" of the CSSDCA—security, stability, development, and cooperation. Chapter 3 examines the experience of other parts of the world in their search for an appropriate normative and institutional framework and the lessons which Africa can build upon in promoting the CSSDCA process. The organizations covered in this chapter are the Association of Southeast Asian Nations (ASEAN), the Organization of American States (OAS), and the Organization for Security and Cooperation in Europe (OSCE). Each of the sections deals with the particulars of the region, the process by which its normative framework was developed, the principles enshrined in the framework and the mechanisms for their enforcement. Chapter 4 documents the evolution of the Kampala Movement: its origins, justifications, principles, progression, obstacles, and ongoing challenges. Chapter 5 analyzes the normative assumptions behind the CSSDCA, elaborates the principles of the four calabashes, and then restates them in the form of concise Guiding Principles. Chapter 6, the conclusion, restates elements of the past experience with the evolution of the CSSDCA, including impediments and accomplishments, and lays out the prospects for the evolution of the regime.

2

The African Context

The creation of the modern African state as the framework for a system of governance was the result of a dialectic struggle between African nationalist movements and the colonial empire. In the outcome, the vanquished empire swallowed up the victorious movement, and the new African state emerged as the colonial creation manned by Africans. The social contract that is generally associated—if only mythologically—with the creation of a new state was skewed toward the anticolonial confrontation, and the nationalist movement was emptied of its normative content as a guideline for the new rulers.[1] Self-determination became a truncated, incomplete process.[2] In the early 1990s, with the cold war over and self-government achieved throughout the continent, Africa again resumed its search for normative guidelines.

Nationalist movements throughout Africa, seeking to achieve self-determination for their people, became the driving force of African politics after World War II.[3] These movements confronted a colonial state that had lost its aura of omnipotence and sense of legitimacy in the war but which sought to hold onto maximum privileges for itself and for its remaining citizens as it bargained to divest itself of colonial sovereignty.[4] As a result, the social contract normally drawn up between citizens and rulers was instead negotiated between the new and the departing sovereign, with the citizens excluded from the bargain. Absent were documents that have had a defining role in other countries' political evolution, such as the Declaration of Independence or the Bill of Rights in the United States, the Declaration of the Rights of Man in France, or the Magna Carta in England. Constitutions were established as programs, not charters, and even the agreements with the metropole at the time of independence became an object of delegitimization and revision as African states sought to buy back and revise the residual privileges accorded to the departing colonial powers.

If this state of affairs had a cause in the decolonization pact, it also had a purpose. The goal of African politics was to consolidate the new, fragile African state against its external and internal challenges. When, after several tries, independent African states set up their own regional organization in 1963, only three years after the independence date for most members, the principal purpose of the new Organization of African Unity (OAU) was to defend the sovereignty of its members.[5] Conflicts between states were covered by very few norms as guides for settlement, but rather by an "I'm-alright-you're-alright" spirit that would leave no one offended. The norms that existed consecrated the status quo, as seen in the strongest of them, the freezing of colonially inherited borders in order to keep the Pandora's box of boundary conflicts closed.[6]

In their cooperative relations, African states left little leeway to the OAU beyond its function as a club for chiefs of state. In its pale shadow, subregional organizations grew up, initially for purposes of economic cooperation, but increasingly for security and conflict management purposes. Yet their activities were also constrained by jealous concern for the sovereignty of their members.

When the new governments were created, they became the possession of the national movement turned single party, institutionalizing itself as the incarnation of the nation. Self-determination was arrested in its first stage, the removal of non-Africans as governors and their replacement by some Africans declaring themselves to be representative of all Africans. As a hangover of the spirit of the nationalist struggle, any competing movements and parties became treasonous, any competition including multiparty elections was divisive, and contests of succession to the founding father of the nation were subversive. When the only way to retire a repressive and incompetent chief was the military coup, the same norms protective of the state were carried over from single party to military government and were strengthened.

The same spirit governed economic relations, where the party state was seen as the source of economic power and direction, the only legitimate font of investment capital against foreign or private investors viewed as illegitimate profiteers. Colonial economic holdings were taken over in the name of the people, but by the state, and parastatal corporations were created as national economic ventures and as employment bins and political payoffs. As a result, productivity dropped, scarce government revenue was drained into loss-making enterprises, health and social service failed, and economic decline ensued.

By the end of the third decade of independence (less for some countries), Africa began to be taken by a widespread feeling that norms governing the distribution and exercise of power needed to be instituted, the process of giving government into the hands of the governed needed to be completed, and accountability and competition needed to be restored to politics and economics to keep activities honest. A wave of democratization swept the continent, in part fueled by the installation of national democracy in South Africa, and in a dozen countries, civil society seized sovereignty from the reigning chief in a sovereign national conference (CNS) and established its own social contract.[7] The OAU repeatedly searched for an appropriate task to take on as its major orientation and adopted a new executive organ called the Mechanism for the Prevention, Management, and Resolution of Conflicts among its members.

Yet the search for guiding and legitimizing norms of the early 1990s was scarcely an unmitigated success. Most of the CNSs were overturned by wily rulers adept at hanging on, several democratically elected heads of state adopted the monopolizing practices of their predecessors, and state collapse continued to occur. Domestic conflict increased, often turning into proxy interstate wars, with no rules of the game to govern legitimate intervention (and nonintervention), domestic reconciliation, and state reinstitution.

West Africa

West Africa had enjoyed three decades of independence when the Kampala meeting that produced the Conference on Security, Development, and Cooperation in Africa (CSSDCA) document took place. Although the meeting and document were the products of the former head of state of Nigeria, Gen.

Olusegun Obasanjo, other West African leaders were not in evidence at Kampala. Yet West Africa was emerging from a long period of nationalist (civilian) or military single party rule and grasping at new forms of political and economic relations that often approximated principles found in the Kampala Document. The tragedy accompanying these efforts has been that the ensuing decade of the 1990s was blotched by one of the continent's worst multistate conflicts, and many of the valiant attempts at returning government to the hands of the people were sabotaged by authoritarian rulers.

In the broadest sense, West Africa continued to be free of interstate wars in its fourth decade of independence, as it had generally been in the previous years. Indeed, the interstate relations of the region are characterized by institutionalized cooperation of the entire region since the mid-1970s, when the Economic Community of West African States (ECOWAS) was established. Even within ECOWAS, subregional groups also developed their own patterns of cooperation. If these did not produce a highly integrated region that continually met its goals of increasing economic unification, it did establish forums and routines of cooperation in economic and security matters. When conflicts threatened to break out, mechanisms for conflict management were readily available to handle them.

However, the search for responsible government in one state, Liberia, at the beginning of the decade turned in the opposite direction from the rest of the region, into state collapse and internal war. The conflict from the beginning reflected fissures and rivalries among the states of the region, and in the end spread to neighboring Sierra Leone, which also collapsed into vicious civil war, and Guinea-Bissau, and involved many neighboring states, either in an ECOWAS peace-enforcing operation known as the ECOWAS Monitoring Group (ECOMOG) or in supporting the rebels. The Liberian civil war in West Africa foreshadowed the broader War of Zairean Succession, which engulfed Central Africa at the end of the decade, and underscored the need for standards and accountability for governance and sovereign responsibility, as well as development and cooperation in the region.

Security

West Africa is the home of enormous contrasts in the personal and state security referred to in the Kampala Document. The region is practically a security community in that war for the conquest of one state (or even a part of it) by another is not a likely option. The last interstate war was the 1985 War of the Poor between Mali and Burkina Faso over a somewhat worthless piece of territory and much pride. It ended in a tired draw, a cease-fire mediated by neighbors, and an International Court of Justice Solomonic settlement. It was the only actual war for territory in the region since independence. Wars of state conquest have been totally absent.

Even so, governments in the region do not always feel secure, but the source of insecurity is their own armies. The region introduced the military coup as a means of succession to the continent south of the Sahara in 1963 when Togolese police and veterans overthrew their government and have clung to power ever since. The frequency of military coups peaked in the mid-seventies and then trailed off as military governments became civilian in appearance but kept tight security control. Yet coups and attempted coups in the 1980s occurred in Nigeria, Liberia, Guinea, Niger, Burkina Faso, Ghana, Mauritania, Chad, Central African Republic, and Sierra Leone, and even the military rulers that these coups brought in were not secure from their own medicine. In the 1990s, seven of the seventeen states in West Africa changed their governments by violent, extraconstitutional means.

In the beginning of the decade, in Mali (1991), Guinea-Bissau (1991), and Sierra Leone (1992), the military overthrew entrenched single party regimes, but only in Mali did the army under Gen. Amadou Toumani Toure then proceed to join the CNS movement and introduce democracy. Indeed, in Sierra Leone, a series of military rulers threw one another out before elections finally took place in 1996, and then again thereafter. Elsewhere, the threat of losing perquisites to an elected regime led the military to intervene. The king-maker of previous Nigerian coups, Gen. Sani Abacha, overthrew a civilianizing government in November 1993 and put himself in power. In Niger, the deadlock in the elected CNS government led Gen. Ibrahim Bare Mainassara to remove the civilians in 1996; four years later, Mainassara was assassinated by his bodyguard, and a new civilian government was elected. Even the paragon of stability and development, Ivory Coast, "lost its virginity" in the coup of 1999.

In most of these cases, individual security among the population was not endangered by the coups. In Liberia and Sierra Leone, however, civil wars wreaked disastrous damage on the population, with a third of Liberia's 3 million people displaced and as many as 250,000 killed and half of the 5 million Sierra Leoneans displaced and 100,000 killed during the decade. While the war in Liberia began as an externally backed insurgency against the narrow and illegitimate government of Sgt. Samuel Doe, it soon spread into a regional conflict between the French-speaking and Nigeria-led blocs of the region over control of Liberia, and then spilled over to destroy the elected government of Sierra Leone and to weaken the regimes in Guinea-Bissau and Senegal. In all five countries, and during the Ivory Coast reversals, citizens' as well as governments' security was damaged.

The 1990 New Year's Eve attack of Charles Taylor's National Patriotic Liberation Front (NPFL) on Liberia was launched from Ivory Coast and supported by Burkina Faso and, more distantly, Libya. In response, President Ibrahim Babangida of Nigeria, a personal friend of Doe, mobilized the Economic Community of West African States (ECOWAS) to authorize ECOMOG to support Doe and end the war. Although the NPFL overran most of Liberia, ECOMOG did prevent the capture of Monrovia but not the assassination of Doe in the ECOMOG compound by a breakaway rebel group. The war continued through a dozen broken truces for six more years, ravaging the country, spawning more splinter groups, spilling over into neighboring countries, and in the end resulting in the election of Taylor as president in 1997.

In Sierra Leone, the five-year civil war between the largely urban elected government of Ahmed Tejan Kabbah and the rural rebellion of Corp. Foday Sankoh's Revolutionary United Front (RUF) ended in 1999 with a power-sharing agreement that brought the RUF into the government, despite its hideous terrorist tactic of amputating the limbs of civilians. When soldiers of the RUF broke their own truce, a UN force of 10,000 growing to 15,000 intervened, strengthened by a temporary intervention of the British Army in early 2000.

Stability

The most positive development at the beginning of the decade was the sovereign national conference (CNS) movement, invented by Robert Doussou of Benin to meet the problems of the tired, failing fifteen-year-old regime of Mathieu Kerekou. Representatives of civil society met to take sovereignty into their hands, rewrote the constitution, held new elections, and sent the political system off in new, responsible, accountable directions. The movement took hold primarily in the French-speaking African countries of West and Equatorial Africa over the next three years but also was felt in Ghana, where the military regime gradually opened itself to free and fair multiparty elections, and in Nigeria, where the increasingly repressive military regime was finally replaced by the election of General Obasanjo and the beginning of a full transition to responsible civilian rule. In half of the ten CNS countries, a new president in a multiparty system was elected, according to a new constitution. However, in the other five countries, the incumbent authoritarian was able to tame the movement and use it to reaffirm his own power and incumbency. Even more unfortunate, in the successful five, by the end of the decade, the elected president was overthrown by a military coup in two, and threatened by an army revolt in one.

The CNS movement put into practice some of the ideas of accountability and responsibility found in the Kampala Document. Whether individual countries had their own CNS or not, the movement was bound to have its effect as the most powerful expression of the second wave of democratization in Africa, assailing the bastions of single party and single ruler system of governance.[8]

The two major English-speaking states of the region spent the last two decades of the century trying to square military and civilian aspects of governance in a stable system.[9] When Nigeria's second republic, introduced in 1979, turned heavily corrupt, the military took over in 1983 under Gen. Muhammadu Buhari, replaced two years later by Gen. Ibrahim Babangida. Under pressure from within and without, Babangida's Armed Forces Ruling Council painfully weighed constitutional options and in 1989 ratified a new constitution that mandated a two-party system with restrictions, lest it institutionalize a North-South or Muslim-Christian confrontation. State elections in 1991 and then national elections in 1993 proved the success of the efforts, but Babangida canceled the victory of his hand-picked candidate, Moshood Abiola, and then was replaced by his chief of staff, General Abacha. Only after the heart attacks of Abacha and Abiola in 1998 was there an acceptable transition to civilian rule, and the hope of stability, with the election of Obasanjo in February 1999.

The first coup of Flight Lt. Jerry Rawlings in 1979 ended a decade of military rule in Ghana, but the civilians to whom the coup leaders handed over power lasted an even shorter time. On New Year's Eve 1981, Rawlings staged a second coup and installed a populist military regime. As in Nigeria, internal and external pressures for a return to civilian rule gradually produced moves toward pluralism and even, in 1991, debates over the possibility of a national conference. Relatively free and fair competitive elections held in 1992, and again in 1996, confirmed Rawlings in power, but the opposition created a vigorous multiparty system and finally, in the election of 2000, when Rawlings could no longer run, his hand-picked successor was defeated by the opposition.

In other leading states of the region, stability has been ensured by a single party that remained the dominant force in a new multiparty system, sometimes using the power of incumbency to maintain its position. The Socialist Party of Senegal (PS) and the Democratic Party of Ivory Coast (PDCI) maintained their hold over the legislature and the presidency after the founding presidents, Leopold Sedar Senghor and Felix Houphouet-Boigny, respectively, had left the scene. In both cases, not only a handpicked successor—Abdou Diouf and Henri Konan Bedie, respectively—but also a cohesive political class ensured continuity and contained an active opposition. However, in Senegal, the PS monopoly on authority was broken by the election of Abdoulaye Wade to the presidency in March 2000, and in Ivory Coast, the PDCI monopoly was broken by a military coup in December 1999 and then by the election of the opposition to power in October 2000.

Stability in a situation of enhanced responsibility and accountability was achieved in two notable CNS experiences, in the original state of the movement, Benin, and in Mali. Free and fair elections in 1992 and 1998 in Mali brought and kept President Alpha Oumar Konare in power and left the opposition is disarray. In Benin, the new democratically elected president, Christophe Soglo, of the original CNS movement was roundly trounced by the former dictator, Mathieu Kerekou, now a born-again Christian and democrat and a better ruler in his new persona. The two states were lone survivors of the democracy movement, but their records have been a positive example.

Stability without responsibility or accountability has been the more frequent pattern, particularly among the smaller states. Gnassigbe Eyadema in Togo and Blaise Campaore in Burkina Faso successfully outwitted their CNS movements and were unfreely and unfairly reelected in 1993 and 1998, and

1991 and 1998, respectively. Gen. Maaouya Ould Sid'Ahmed Taya in Mauritania and Gen. Lansana Conté in Guinea made sure that they faced no CNS at all and were reelected in 1992 and 1993, respectively. In many of these cases, instability is only postponed unless autocratic rulers make immediate plans to initiate processes leading to fully accountable and responsible governance.

Development

Three major events marked the economic fortunes of the West African countries: the decline in their terms of trade and per capita incomes over the 1980s; the 50 percent devaluation of the CFA (African Financial Community) franc in January 1994; and the international financial institutions' (IFI) insistence on structural adjustment. The states of the region made up the poorest part of the world. Only one (Ivory Coast) had a per capita income of more than $600 ($660 in 1996, and falling precipitously after the 1999 coup), and Burkina Faso, Guinea-Bissau, Mali, Niger, Nigeria, Sierra Leone, and Liberia were in the $200 range.[10] Per capita income growth in the post-1988 decade was positive for Benin, Mauritania, Cape Verde, Guinea, Guinea-Bissau, and Ghana. It also turned positive for Burkina Faso, Ivory Coast, Mali, Niger, Togo, and Senegal in the mid-1990s, as these countries took advantage of the CFA devaluation.[11] Both real agricultural and industrial growth in the decade after 1988 was between 1 and 4 percent in the countries of the region (except for the countries of conflict—Liberia and Sierra Leone), essentially keeping pace with population growth, although both tended to increase in Ivory Coast, Benin, Mali, Senegal, and Togo in the later years. Per capita food production in the mid-1990s was well above both world comparator and all African countries in Benin, Ivory Coast, Ghana, and Nigeria, and well below in Burkina Faso, Guinea, Guinea-Bissau, Mali, and Senegal. No West African country except Sierra Leone and Burkina Faso saw anything but a drop in terms of trade between 1987 (already a bad year) and 1996.

In social terms, poverty was felt by the population in the 1990s.[12] The infant mortality rate was at, or above, the African average in all states but Ghana, Cape Verde, and Senegal, and 50 percent higher for Gambia, Guinea, Guinea-Bissau, Mali, and Niger (and double for Liberia and Sierra Leone). Life expectancy was below the African average in all states but Togo, Cape

Verde, Ghana, and Ivory Coast, and, of course, lowest in the countries of conflict. Primary school enrollment was below the African average in all states but Cape Verde, Ghana, Nigeria, and Togo.

Despite these statistics, the region contained the material for far greater development, based on two advantages. One is market size, as particularly embodied in the more than 100 million Nigerians but then extended through the regional economic cooperation agreements to the entire sixteen-state area. The other is oil, again concentrated in large reserves in Nigeria but extending offshore in the Bight of Biafra westward to a yet undetermined extent. These advantages can be a drain, to be sure: a large population is no market if it does not produce and consume, and oil is the cause of corruption and inflation. Nigeria has excelled on all counts, leaving the region with an enormous undeveloped potential.

While many of the economies followed a state centralized model in previous decades, most moved to clean their houses, balance their accounts, reduce social expenditures, privatize parastatals, and open their economies to competition. These changes were not without cost. They led to social protests in Nigeria, Togo, Ghana, Ivory Coast, among others, and refusal to reform led to state collapse in Liberia and Sierra Leone, as governments simply could not provide the services and reward the followers as their populations had come to expect. Yet the fact that most states were able to ride out the austerity and even, in the case of the CFA countries, to tighten belts and benefit from their new export price advantage to rebound economically and socially showed that structural adjustment could be practiced without serious political disruption when the government showed a clear plan and direction.[13]

Cooperation

West Africa was born to independence in the bed of cooperation through the effects of its two major colonial rulers. The eight French-speaking states that were granted independence in 1960, plus Guinea, which broke away in 1958, were part of French West Africa (AOF), an essentially federal area that enjoyed common services, a common currency, and a common metropolitan security system. The independence movement took the form of a large regional confederation of proto-parties, the African Democratic Rally (RDA). Independence naturally severed or strained some of these ties, and states broke away from the inherited cooperation on occasion as their political orientation demanded.

The three main cooperative activities have remained throughout the ensuing forty years, with appropriate changes. The West African Monetary Union lost Mauritania, Mali, and Guinea over time but gained Guinea-Bissau from its lonely Portuguese heritage. In 1972 most of the former AOF states reformalized their ties in the West African Economic Community (CEAO). They added to their economic cooperation a Non-Aggression and Defence Accord (ANAD) in 1977, which also benefited from a continuing commitment from France to provide back-up security through a series of bilateral defense treaties.[14] The CFA devaluation of 1994 brought new order into these arrangements. The previous cooperation agreements were replaced by a new West African Economic and Monetary Union (UEMOA) of Senegal, Mali, Guinea-Bissau, Ivory Coast, Niger, Burkina Faso, Togo, and Benin. The group has achieved a modicum of customs integration and cooperation around its common currency and has also served as a conflict management mechanism.

British West Africa was a far looser arrangement, since its four territories were not contiguous, its independence came over a span of eight years, and Nigeria alone is its own federation. In the mid-1970s, however, Nigeria joined the campaign of the Economic Commission for Africa (ECA) to promote a common economic cooperation organization for all sixteen states of the region, the Economic Community of West African States (ECOWAS), created in 1975. The ECA's purpose was to bridge the colonial divide and promote trade integration, toward which ECOWAS has made only minimal progress in its quarter century of existence. Nigeria's purpose was also to overcome the French-speaking cooperation and to replace the security role of the distant metropole, through a Pact of Mutual Assistance in Defense Matters (PMA) signed among ECOWAS members in 1981. This agreement was the dubious basis of the ECOMOG intervention in Liberia, Sierra Leone, and Guinea-Bissau throughout the 1990s, leading to a tightening of the ECOWAS security mechanism in 1999.

Thus cooperation and competition run hand in hand in West Africa, with only mixed results. The two organizations run a turtle's race to achieve economic integration, their members remaining too strongly attached to their weak sovereignty to give up much of it for the cause of joint economic gains. In security matters, the CEAO has focused on conflict management within its family, whereas ECOWAS, benefiting from the military capacity of Nigeria, has concentrated on security assistance. The CEAO efforts have not been frequent, and the ECOMOG experience essentially delayed Taylor's victory for seven years, made him more radical, and spawned a number of competing factions and unintegrated militias, in Liberia and in neighboring Sierra Leone and Guinea. The value of the effort lay in experience gained in providing a West African solution for a West African problem, but experience can be costly.

Cooperation rises and falls. With the election of Taylor in Liberia in 1997, and the election of Obasanjo in Nigeria and the signing of the peace agreement in Sierra Leone in 1999, Nigerian troops have been gradually withdrawn from the two countries. However, the collapse of the peace agreement in Sierra Leone and the resumption of hostilities led to the return of foreign troops from the region and beyond, including British troops to restore security and stability. Guinean troops, a smaller part of the ECOMOG contingent, had also been provided to maintain security in Sierra Leone in the previous decade under the Mano River Union, now defunct. Other smaller economic cooperation agreements have also operated with some success in the area. The Council of the Entente, the region's oldest organization, dating from 1959, provides compensation payments to Ivory Coast's poorer hinterland neighbors from the eastern part of the former AOF. The Organization for the Development of the Senegal River (OMVS) groups the states of the western part of AOF in cooperation about a natural resource, but its work has been slowed in the 1990s by the effects of the Senegal-Mauritanian race riots of 1989. The broader effort within the Permanent Interstate Committee for Drought Control in the Sahel (CILSS) galvanized a sustained response to the drought cycles beginning in the mid-1970s. [15]

More than anything, West Africa suffers from a lack of commitment to its cooperation efforts. Goals of economic integration remain unmet, security cooperation is uncontrolled by collective standards, and state sovereignty and group competition over the British-French colonial divide overcome collective action among all the states of the region. Yet regional cooperation remains a strong, if imperfect, force in West Africa, more developed than in any other region of the continent.

The Horn of Africa

The greater Horn of Africa is a constellation of conflict around the core state of Ethiopia, involving Sudan, Eritrea, Djibouti and Somalia, plus Kenya and Uganda formerly from East Africa, all members of the Inter-Governmental Authority on Development (IGAD) established in 1996 as a successor to the Inter-Governmental Authority on Drought and Development (IGADD) formed ten years earlier. The region was home to one of the earliest and most ambitious experiments in regional cooperation in Africa (the East African Community [EAC], 1967–77). The dramatic collapse of the EAC and the weakness of IGAD illustrate how ingrained conflict patterns impeded security, stability, and development, the Kampala Document's goals.

Security

Developments in the Horn offer a textbook illustration of the classical security dilemma, in which one party's efforts to achieve security merely increase the insecurity—and hence the countervailing security efforts—of its neighbors. Obsession with the security of fragile states, which tended to increase insecurity for all, were built on traditional animosities that justified both insecurities and efforts to overcome them. The first flash points in regional conflict were the international tensions in the early 1950s over the status of Eritrea in 1952, the crystallization of Somali nationalism over the British return of the Haud grazing region to Ethiopia in 1954, the outbreak of civil war in southern Sudan in 1955, and the rise of Kenyan Somalis' concern over their status at the end of the decade.[16] As the conflicts intensified in the early 1960s, refugees began to flood neighboring countries, and dissident exile groups and rebel factions established bases there as well. Leaders of the rebellions sought to mobilize historical animosities to secure regional support.[17]

Very soon, the conflicts became entangled with one another, starting with the Sudanese and Eritrean rebellions. The Eritrean Liberation Movement (ELM) and the Eritrean Liberation Front (ELF) were formed by Eritrean exiles in Sudan in 1958 and 1960–61, respectively.[18] The civilian government that took power in Sudan in 1964, following the overthrow of the military regime of Gen. Ibrahim Abboud, allowed the Eritrean rebels to open offices in the country and even permitted arms shipments.[19] In turn, the

Ethiopians supported the Anya-nya rebels in Sudan. The two countries' agreement in 1967 to each stop support for the other's rebels was not fully implemented. Similar agreements between Sudan and Uganda in 1966 also achieved very little, and support from Israel to the southern Sudanese rebels through Uganda was stepped up after Idi Amin came to power in 1971.[20]

Ethiopian support was crucial in negotiating an end to the civil war in Sudan in 1972. The Ethiopians expected Sudan to reciprocate by helping to contain the Eritrean rebels, but Sudan had limited leverage on them.[21] Haile Selassie's imperial regime in Ethiopia collapsed within less than two years of achieving peace in Sudan, and its new Marxist successor was hostile, giving no incentive for Sudan to cooperate. Instead, the new Ethiopian regime's alliance with Libya and South Yemen was seen as a threat by Sudan and its American and Egyptian allies.[22] In 1983 Ethiopian support was crucial in turning an army mutiny into a full-fledged rebellion in southern Sudan, determining the leadership and course of the rebellion, and giving shape to Sudan People's Liberation Army (SPLA) under the leadership of Col. John Garang.[23] Sudan in turn increased support for the Eritrean (EPLF) and Tigrean (TPLF) Peoples Liberation Fronts, which was crucial in toppling the Marxist regime in Ethiopia in 1991.

As Uganda began the slide into conflict in turn, the turmoil in that country and neighboring Sudan began to reinforce each other. In 1971 refugees fleeing the fall of Ugandan president Milton Obote established guerilla bases in southern Sudan. These were closed in 1972 when Uganda broke with Israel and ended support to the Sudanese rebels, but following the ousting of Uganda's Idi Amin in 1979, and again after the collapse of the Tito Okello regime in 1986, refugees again poured into southern Sudan to set up guerrilla camps. Uganda's continued support for the SPLA led to Sudanese support for Ugandan rebels from the mid-1990s.

The other major cause of regional instability came from Somali irredentism. The notion of Greater Somalia comprising the Ethiopian Ogaden (including the Haud), northwest Kenya, and Djibouti, was the driving force of Somali politics since before independence. These claims led to insurrections in the Ogaden and northeast Kenya, a brief war between Ethiopia and Somalia in 1964, and then a disastrous Somali invasion of the Ogaden in 1977–78.[24] Djibouti , described as a paradox of vulnerability and stability in the region, received waves of refugees from both Somalia and Ethiopia. [25]

Stability

After independence (Sudan 1956, Somalia 1960, Uganda 1962, Kenya 1963, Djibouti 1977, Eritrea 1993), political developments in several of the region's states followed a similar trajectory. Parliamentary democracies, characterized by fierce and divisive competition among the elite, corruption, neglect of the wider public concerns, and lack of progress in solving major problems, were followed by brutal, corrupt military dictatorships.

In Sudan, a military regime led by conservative senior army officers took over in November 1958, achieving relative success on the economic front. But its failure to resolve the conflict in the South and its increasing authoritarianism led to its overthrow in a popular uprising in October 1964. Elections produced a succession of weak and short-lived coalition governments until a group of radical army officers took over in a bloodless coup in May 1969. After a series of violent conflicts among rival factions within the regime, a moderate faction under President Gaafar Nimeiri emerged victorious by mid-1971. In 1972 Nimeiri signed the Addis Ababa peace agreement that brought autonomy to the South, but a further deal five years later, which brought the major northern opposition groups into the government, began the process of undermining southern autonomy. Peace was achieved in the South but not democracy in the North.

Economic and political blunders by an increasingly autocratic and isolated Nimeiri alienated the bulk of his internal and external supporters and caused the whole system to unravel. Unilateral moves to rotate southern troops and redivide the South in violation of the 1972 agreement led to the resumption of the civil war in May 1983. A decision to impose Islamic law in September 1983 also increased tensions. Nimeiri was toppled in April 1985 when the army abandoned him in the face of a popular uprising. But war in the South continued unabated. Democracy was restored in the North but not peace in the South.

Another succession of weak coalition governments attempted to grapple with a wide array of problems as the war intensified but made little headway. In June 1989, a coup by army officers with links to radical Islamists ended Sudan's third democratic experiment. But the war intensified, the economy deteriorated even further, and the population began to be subjected to unprecedented human rights violations. By the late 1990s, international and indigenous pressure forced the regime to make a verbal concession of self-determination for the South and a form of multiparty politics for the North. However, the conflict in the South was not resolved, and after January 1997, armed conflict spread to the east of the country as well. Both peace and democracy were wanting.

In Somalia, the corrupt and inefficient multiparty system turned into single party regime was replaced in 1969 by the military coup of Gen. Siad Barre to an initially enthusiastic welcome. But disappointment was soon to follow. Although officially campaigning against tribalism and promoting scientific socialism and Greater Somalia as unifying ideologies, Siad Barre built his power by manipulating clans and playing them off against one another.[26] The break with the Soviet Union in 1977 and the disastrous defeat in the Ogaden war with Ethiopia in 1978 deprived Barre of the two ideological pillars of his regime and left naked oppression and manipulation of differences as the only tactics left. This set in motion a chain of events that would lead to the simultaneous collapse of the regime and the state in early 1991.

In Uganda, the crisis in the parliamentary system came in the mid-1960s, and it took the form of a clash between the prime minister, Milton Obote, and the Baganda king, the Kabaka, who was the constitutional head of state.[27] The new centralized presidential republic was then overthrown in 1971 in a coup by Gen. Idi Amin, whose rise to power was also welcomed at first but soon descended into brutal chaos.[28] After Amin was toppled by a Tanzanian invasion force in 1979 in retaliation for his own invasion of Tanzania, a succession of civilian and military regimes came and went against the background of continued conflict, ending only with the takeover by the rebel National Resistance Army of Yoweri Museveni in January 1986. Museveni was praised for restoring peace and providing the country with its best and most effective government since independence, and for presiding over credible economic reform. But he was also criticized for his refusal to allow multiparty politics and for his aggressive foreign policy toward his neighbors.

Kenya and Djibouti followed a different trajectory, characterized by the relatively stable rule by conservative, staunchly pro-Western civilian regimes. But here it is the civilian authorities that performed the task undertaken by the military elsewhere: the elimination of multiparty politics and the centralization of power in the hands of an authoritarian head of state. In Kenya, the party-state was constructed through elaborate coalition-building strategies, coupled with repressive policies targeting opposition groups and civil society organizations.[29] The process accelerated following the death of Kenya's first president, Jomo Kenyatta, and the assumption of power by Daniel arap Moi in 1978. A constitutional amendment passed in 1982 to make Kenya a de jure single party state under the Kenya African National Union (KANU) was reversed a decade later following strong internal protests and heavy international pressure, including suspension of foreign aid. However, in the multiparty elections held in 1992 and 1997, the ruling party under President Moi succeeded in maintaining power in the face of a fractured opposition.

Djibouti also maintained a single party system under former president Hassan Gouled Aptidon and his Rassemblement Populaire pour la Progrès (RPP). But opposition pressure, which led in 1991 to a rebellion among the Afars, one of the two major ethnic groups in the country, forced the passage of constitutional amendments permitting a restricted form of multiparty politics.[30] The ruling party won all seats in the parliament in 1992 and secured the presidency against four other candidates the following year. Although the main armed dissident group, the Front pour la Restoration de l'Unité et de la Démocracie (FRUD) signed an agreement in December 1994 to end the insurgency, the opposition remained split and suspicious about the government's intentions.[31] In April 1999, the ruling party's candidate and Gouled's chosen successor, Ismail Omar Guelleh, was elected head of state, in a relatively fair election.

Ethiopia's imperial system was unique in the region. Emperor Haile Selassie attained immense international and regional prestige, but his autocratic style faced growing internal opposition. Protests in Eritrea erupted into civil war in 1961, and the Ethiopian-Eritrean federation was canceled the following year, a decade after its adoption. A disastrous famine in 1974, to which the government showed marked indifference, brought the protest to the heart of the system. The emperor was toppled in September 1974 by a revolutionary military committee (Dergue) of radical officers. Power struggles in the following year led to the emergence of Col. Mengistu Haile Mariam, a ruthlessly ambitious officer advocating a radical Marxist program, as the strong man of the regime.[32] However, even though the main faction in the Eritrean rebel movement had already espoused Marxism, no peaceful resolution to the conflict was achieved. Instead, other conflicts erupted, in Tigray in the North, in the Ogaden and among the Afars in the East, and the Oromo in the center. A major famine in 1984 exacerbated matters. By the time the events in eastern Europe came to deprive the regime of its main foreign backing, the Ethiopian empire was unraveling at a precipitous pace.

The Eritrean rebel movement experienced internal struggles, which quickly took on a sectarian/ethnic character, as Muslim pastoralists in the lowlands supported the ELF, while Christian highlanders joined in 1976 to form the Eritrean People's Liberation Front (EPLF). The ELF was completely routed by the mid-1980s. At the end of the decade, a new radical Islamic group, the Islamic Jihad Movement, was founded with support from Islamic groups in Sudan and Saudi Arabia, but it too failed to shake EPLF dominance. The EPLF and the Tigray People's Liberation Front (TPLF) then forged a broad-based alliance, the Ethiopian People's Revolutionary Democratic Front (EPRDF), with movements representing other ethnic groups.[33]

The success of the EPLF and the EPRDF in taking power in Addis Ababa in May 1991 signaled the start of a new era in the region's history. Eritrea's right to self-determination was recognized, and it proceeded to a friendly divorce and EPLF single party rule in 1993, through an internationally supervised referendum. On the Ethiopian side, the EPRDF regime reorganized itself into a federal state, with regional autonomy and the ostensible right for self-determination for ethnically delineated areas. Still, a number of groups, including former allies of the TPLF, such as the Oromo Liberation Front (OLF), renewed their conflict with the Ethiopian state, as did the EPLF itself, in a two years' vicious and costly war that began as a border dispute in 1998, leaving the two countries poorer and bitter.

Development

The 150 million people of the greater Horn of Africa depend largely on agriculture or pastoralism, with the exception of Djibouti's service-oriented economy and some input from services and foreign remittances in Eritrea. Between 70 and 80 percent of the labor force is engaged in agriculture, which also provides the bulk of exports.[34] But agriculture contributes only half the GDP in Ethiopia, Somalia, and Uganda, between 20 and 33 percent in the other countries, and 3 percent in Djibouti. Unemployment is very high, often upward of 40 percent. Drought and conflict have meant that life is precarious for large parts of the population. Millions have been displaced within their own country or across borders by war and famine, and emigration of skilled labor inhibits development. National economies are heavily indebted and dependent on foreign aid.

Except for transit trade between Uganda and Kenya and between Ethiopia and Djibouti, and temporarily between Ethiopia and Eritrea, intraregional trade is low, and intraregional communications and transportation networks are severely underdeveloped. A moment of cooperation in the early 1990s brought some important gains in regional exchanges, and growth rates rose sharply (except in Djibouti), but the return of conflict began to reverse the gains by the end of the decade. During 1998 alone, Eritrea and Ethiopia spent hundreds of millions of dollars on arms, and their border war between 1998 and 2000 set their economies back years (although Djibouti appears to have benefited from the shift in transit trade).

Uganda's economy has shown the most dramatic recovery from its earlier periods of conflict. Structural reforms advocated by the international financial institutions have helped rehabilitate and stabilize the economy, control inflation, boost production and export earnings, and attract foreign aid and investment. Uganda is held up as a model for African economic revival. Similar, if less dramatic, successes had been registered in Ethiopia and Eritrea before their war. Ethiopia has benefited from foreign aid and investment, but Eritrea has been more cautious in accepting either. Economic competition over markets and resources, and then over currency, flared up after Eritrea's independence. Its adoption of its own currency in 1997 was the culmination of a process of disengagement between the previously integrated economies, a process that harmed both countries and eventuated in war. The economy in Djibouti, based on services and foreign aid, endured a severe and prolonged recession after the 1991 Gulf War reduced export markets and transit traffic was worsened by political violence at home. The GDP growth rate was a mere 0.5 percent in 1998. The economy has little room to maneuver, given limited natural resources and severe underdevelopment.

Kenya's economy is the most advanced and dynamic in the region, benefiting from peace and security, and from consistent adoption of free market policies and openness to investment. Kenya has also served as the regional headquarters of international organizations and major foreign businesses, and its position as a transportation hub for most African destinations

and relatively developed infrastructure have brought huge economic benefits. However, the economy suffers from corruption, mismanagement, and
political instability. In the early 1990s, the government began to implement
new policies of economic liberalization and reform at the insistence of
the international financial institutions and Western donors. The reforms
enabled it to reverse the trend of negative economic growth of recent years
and turn growth rates of 5 percent in 1995 and 4 percent in 1996. However,
after that, growth slowed down again, and donors complained about the
same problems as before, compounded by an extremely high population
growth rate and urban unemployment.

Sudan is a special economic case because of its chronic half-century of
civil war and international isolation. It has received little development aid
since 1990, and its foreign debt from previous commitments, at more than
$20 billion, is higher than that of the rest of the countries of the region com-
bined. It has also suffered from high inflation, falling foreign remittances,
and a precipitous deterioration in the value of its currency. Threatened by
expulsion from the IMF, the government agreed to implement fiscal reforms
and resume debt payments. The reforms succeeded in containing inflation,
producing healthy growth rates on paper, and winning IMF praise, but they
brought little improvement to the lot of the average consumer. Famine again
struck in the war regions at the end of the decade. In mid-1999, a Canadian,
Malaysian, Chinese, and Sudanese consortium took over an oil concession
abandoned by Chevron, with plans to export up to 150,000 barrels per day
(bpd) to fuel the escalation of the conflict with the South.

With the state still collapsed in Somalia, the economy has gone into free
fall.[35] The worst of the disastrous famines of the mid-1990s, which led to
hundreds of thousands of deaths, returned at the end of the decade, and
most Somalis continued to lead a precarious existence. Humanitarian aid
keeps starvation at bay, if one is lucky.

In theory, all countries agree that peace and cooperation are vital if development—or even existence—is to be achieved. Most broadly, all countries
of the region are among the twenty-one members of the Common Market
for Eastern and Southern Africa (COMESA), which was created in 1993 as
successor to the decade-old Preferential Trade Agreement (PTA) and aims at
economic integration in some form. But there must be economic activity
within national economies for integration to take place.

Cooperation

In contrast to competitive alliances to conduct conflict in the region, comprehensive regional cooperation for development has been rare. The first attempt was the Desert Locust Control Organization (DLCO-EA), established in 1962 among all the IGAD members plus Tanzania. But the laxness that followed initial success, coupled with economic and political deterioration during the 1980s, led to the degradation of regional capacity to deal with infestations and the need to call in international organizations such as the Food and Agriculture Organization (FAO).[36]

The other initial experiment in regional cooperation was the East African Community (EAC) of Kenya, Uganda, and Tanzania. The three countries did not start independent life as separate economies that then proceeded to integrate but rather were part of an integrated economy that witnessed progressive differentiation and finally breakdown. At Tanganyika's independence in 1961, the East African Common Services Organization was set up to manage their common market and shared services. However, tensions arose over the differential benefits accruing from the economic union, with Kenya, the most industrialized of the three, gaining more from trade with its partners, who also lost vital customs revenues.

Compensatory measures, such as a common fund, did not go far enough to allay the concerns of the disadvantaged countries, and so provisions to deal radically with the problem of unequal benefits were the basis of a treaty setting up the East African Community (EAC) in December 1967. But Tanzania and Uganda developed cooperation on the basis of common socialist policies, which was subsequently undone by the 1971 military coup in Uganda. The breakdown in Ugandan relations with Tanzania paralyzed the East African Authority of the three heads of state, although it was Kenya whose withdrawal ended the EAC in 1977.[37] The EAC countries started in the 1960s from where Europe was trying to move in the 1990s: with a common currency, a single market, coordinated central banking, a redistribution mechanism, and even a shared university. However, unequal benefits and burdens, and the failure to reach political union, led to the disintegration of the project. "East African Cooperation" was established in 1996 and is starting to make gradual headway.

Beginning in 1980, following the relative success of the West African Interstate Committee for Drought Control in the Sahel (CILSS), donors and international agencies urged the states of the Horn to form an intergovernmental authority to coordinate the fight against drought and famine. Somalia, Sudan, Uganda, and Djibouti initiated negotiations, which Kenya and Ethiopia joined in early 1982. Eventually, the Inter-Governmental Authority on Drought and Development (IGADD) was launched at a summit in Djibouti in January 1986.

During its early years, the organization made little progress in fostering effective regional cooperation, even in the limited area of fighting famine. A famine early warning system depended entirely on data provided by the governments, yet previous famines proved disastrous precisely because governments tended to ignore warning signals and even hide and manipulate information.[38] Although the organization constituted a forum for dialogue that was credited with managing the conflict between Ethiopia and Somalia, this action was indirectly responsible for the collapse of the Somali state.

IGADD's lethargy was blamed partly on its first executive secretary, Makonnen Kerbit.[39] However, it is more plausible to find its causes in the persistent conflict in the region. In addition, Western donors were not enthusiastic about offering aid to the brutal Marxist regime in Ethiopia, the brutal Somalian clan dictatorship, or the ethnically repressive regime in Sudan. A donors' conference in 1987 produced funds for food security and antidrought projects representing only 10 percent and 5 percent, respectively, of the total members' requests of $1.073 billion.[40]

The year 1991 ushered in a rare moment of cooperation, based on domestic power shifts that brought Ethiopia out of hostility with its neighbors. Sudan, Ethiopia, and newly independent Eritrea, joined by Djibouti, began to hold frequent summit meetings to forge close relations of cooperation, based on guarantees of noninterference and mutual support. Economic cooperation was stepped up, the free movement of people and goods across borders was instituted, and agreements were signed on security and political cooperation.[41] Ethiopia and Eritrea continued to use a single currency, while the Sudanese currency was also made official tender in Eritrea. A new general secretary, David Muduuli, was appointed, also in 1991.

The result was a new regional cooperation formula that called not only for noninterference and nonsupport for neighboring dissident groups but also positive cooperation—a "mutual suppression pact" against the regional rebellions. Sudan was rewarded for its support of the new Ethiopian government by the expulsion of the SPLA rebels from Ethiopia, bringing an end to the thirty-year-old Sudanese-Ethiopian cold war. Sudan proceeded to curb the activities of remaining Ethiopian and Eritrean rebel factions, such as the Eritrean Islamic Jihad group and the Oromo Liberation Front. Following tension on the Ugandan border in 1990, Sudan initiated a non-aggression pact with Uganda in April 1991, which allowed for a joint monitoring force on the border. Ugandan President Museveni visited Khartoum in 1992 and in February 1993 helped broker the first meeting ever between the SPLA leader John Garang and Sudanese government representatives at Entebbe in Uganda. This encounter enabled the resumption of the talks in the Nigerian capital, Abuja, in April that year.

The new cooperation formula extended IGADD's mandate of fostering environmental cooperation, giving it a more comprehensive role in promoting peace, security, and stability in the region and raising its international profile. As a result, a new international donor group, the Friends of IGADD, was formed in early 1995 at the behest of the Netherlands with the United States, the United Kingdom, Norway, Italy, and Canada to support IGADD's peacemaking mission and to promote cooperation for development.

It appeared that all the requisites of successful and effective regional cooperation were in place: political will, appropriate institutions, and enthusiastic international support. But unmistakable danger signals could be detected, indicating that the momentum was failing. The first regional question to be faced was the succession crisis in Somalia. Djibouti took the lead, organizing a conference to bring the warring Somali factions together in July 1991, while Eritrea and Sudan proposed sending in peacekeeping forces.[42] The efforts were without effect.

Another challenge occurred in 1993, when Sudan accepted proposals for IGADD to take over from Nigeria the task of mediating the Sudanese conflict. But at the same time tensions began to reappear among members. Sudan's curbs on the Muslim dissident groups in Eritrea and Ethiopia ran against its sympathies, while Uganda and Kenya, and to a lesser degree Eritrea and Ethiopia, were favorable to the demands of the SPLA against the

Sudanese Islamist government. The IGADD mediation initially made major progress in the peace process by taking the Declaration of Principles, but by late 1994 the agreement broke down. None of the countries was prepared to accept regional mediation in its own conflicts, and none of the parties could be expected to cooperate wholeheartedly in suppressing groups to which it was sympathetic.

Given this situation, the conflict structure re-emerged and internal conflicts spilled over again into neighboring countries. Attacks by Islamic Jihad in Eritrean territory intensified in 1992, and by December 1993, Eritrea lodged a complaint with the UN Security Council against Sudanese provocations.[43] Sudan pronounced Uganda responsible for the continuation of the conflict in the South. Eritrea severed diplomatic relations with Sudan in December 1994. Uganda followed suit in April 1995. In June 1995, Eritrea hosted a meeting for the Sudanese National Democratic Alliance (NDA), the main opposition coalition of the SPLA and major northern parties. The NDA vowed to topple the Khartoum government by force, and about half a dozen armed groups, all based in Eritrea, were set up. The closed Sudanese embassy in Asmara was handed over to the NDA.

In September 1995, Ethiopia accused Sudan of complicity in the June assassination attempt against Egyptian President Hosni Mubarak as he was visiting Addis Ababa for the OAU summit. Ethiopia scaled down diplomatic relations with Sudan, cut air travel between the two countries, and reversed their visa-free travel arrangements. When the newly established OAU conflict resolution mechanism failed to resolve the matter, Ethiopia and Egypt took the case to the UN Security Council, where sanctions were imposed on Sudan in April 1996. Thus, when the region's leaders met in Djibouti in 1996 to celebrate the revitalization of the organization as the Inter-Governmental Agency on Development (IGAD), the atmosphere that generated the optimism of the early 1990s had all but disappeared. A new regional cold war was in full swing. And in the spirit of cold wars, the United States was involved. In the summer of 1993, the United States had placed Sudan on the list of countries supporting terrorism, given full support to the anti-Sudan measures, and increased military assistance to its three neighbors. By early 1997, this cold war had become extremely hot. The SPLA launched attacks near the Ugandan, Ethiopian, and Eritrean borders. Although the offensive was largely unsuccessful, Sudan accused three of its neighbors of direct involvement and threatened retaliation. Regional cooperation became a remote possibility in such a charged atmosphere.

Worse was to come. In the summer of 1998, Uganda and its close neighbor and ally, Rwanda, became involved in a conflict with the neighboring Democratic Republic of Congo (formerly Zaire). Uganda's interest was in eliminating various rebel groups that operated from Congo and Sudan, in retaliation for Ugandan support for the SPLA. Eight African countries were involved militarily in the War of the Zairean Succession, and the ensuing conflict was dubbed "Africa's first world war," although the world appeared largely unconcerned.

At the same time, another ominous development took place closer to the heart of the region. A simmering border dispute between Eritrea and Ethiopia, aggravated by economic and political differences, as well as personal animosities, erupted into armed conflict. The unraveling of the core alliance was the most serious blow yet to regional cooperation in May 1998. Not until two years later were the OAU and the United States able to achieve an agreement on a peace process. The recently instituted conflict resolution mechanism of IGAD had not even been invoked.

Clearly, failures of stability, security, and development have marked attempts at cooperation in the Horn of Africa to date. The regional pattern of competitive cooperation to pursue conflict was broken only by one brief period in the early 1990s. Then the regimes of the regional states joined forces on the basis of common sympathies to overcome their rebellions and underdevelopment. But eventually the conflict pattern prevailed, again undermining development in the region.

Central Africa

Central Africa at the end of the millennium was about as far from the principles of the Kampala Document as any part of the continent, and it reached that position on a path marked by some of Africa's worst potholes of state decline and collapse. The Kampala principles presuppose a responsible and accountable state, interacting with a healthy civil society. Multistate intervention in the War of the Zairean Succession was the result of a power vacuum in the middle of Africa, but in its midst several attempts emerged to establish basic principles of the type found in the Kampala Document that could help contain future conflicts and establish a basis for sound relations.

Congo, the giant and potential core state of the region, was born in 1960 out of the collapse of the colonial state rather than through an orderly process of the transfer of powers.[44] A state (later renamed Zaire) was installed only through the efforts of Gen. Mobutu Sese Seko during his first decade in power after 1965. But in the subsequent fifteen years, he privatized his creation, alienated his population, bought off his opposition, and left a growing vacuum around his operation. Since government agencies were providing no local services and were only conducting predatory activities, communities were forced to get by on their own resources.

When Mobutu, under pressure from the United States, called for expressions of public participation in 1990, he was surprised to see the sovereign national conference (CNS) movement spring to life in Zaire and seize sovereignty in the hands of civil society. Mobutu was able to undermine the CNS and hold onto power in a reduced position often referred to as "Mayor of Kinshasa and Gbadolite" (referring to the capital and his home town palace). However, a local resistance movement rose up in the East with support from neighboring Rwanda and Uganda in 1996 and by May 1997 had swept across the country and overthrown Mobutu. Ill with cancer, he died four months later in exile. Instead of incorporating the work of the CNS, however, the new government of the Democratic Republic of Congo (as it was renamed) under Laurent Kabila regarded civil society as the opposition and the CNS as Mobutist. Kabila tried to roll the clock back to 1965 and located his power base first in the Banyarwanda areas of the East and then in the Balubakat area of the South—his home area. His assassination in January 2001 brought in his son Joseph as his successor and new steps toward the liberalization of the regime.

Several other states in Central Africa experienced similar processes of collapse and were then sucked into the vacuum that Congo had become. Despite Uganda's better preparation for its independence in 1962, it was not until 1979 that Idi Amin's murderous regime was removed, with support from neighboring Tanzania. As discussed earlier in the chapter, the collapse of the hollow state was completed by an interregnum of civil war until Yoweri Museveni's National Resistance Movement took power in 1986 and began state restoration.

In two small but overpopulated neighbors, Rwanda and Burundi, conflicts alternated with repressive dominance by one of two ethnic groups—the majority Hutu or the minority but privileged Tutsi. Rwanda had its revolution in 1959, when the Hutu majority took over, whereas Burundi continued to be controlled by Tutsi-dominated governments. In 1990 the largely Tutsi Rwandan Patriotic Front (RPF) launched an attack into northwestern Rwanda with support from neighboring Uganda. This created a complex climate of fear and tension in Rwanda that ultimately resulted in the genocide of 800,000 Tutsi and moderate Hutu in 1994, before the RPF was able to complete its takeover.[45] Similarly in Burundi, after uninterrupted Tutsi control, the assassination of the first elected Hutu president in 1993 led to a reasserted Tutsi rule in the midst of civil war, rebel insurgencies, and renewed efforts to prepare for elected civilian rule.

The experience of the formerly French states of Equatorial Africa (plus Equatorial Guinea) was characterized by single party regimes for the first three decades after independence in 1960, including those of two more egregious dictators—Jean-Bedel Bokassa in the Central African Republic and Macias Nguema in Equatorial Guinea. The CNS movement swept across many of these states between 1991 and 1993, with results varying from authoritarian reassertion in Chad and Gabon to the collapse of the state into civil war after a democratic interlude in the Central African Republic and Congo-Brazzaville with intervention from neighboring Angola.

The two "hinge states" of the region—Cameroon to the west and Kenya to the east—have navigated between stability and collapse under the repressive tutelage of dominant party regimes, maintaining the appearance of multiparty pluralism despite ethnic tensions. The most notable case of evolving political pluralism and stability has been Tanzania, which has shown a constant improvement of economic and political openness and welfare during its four decades of independence since 1961.[46]

Security

In Central Africa, degenerating security conditions for states and their citizens have characterized the 1990s. Ordinary citizens, targeted ethnic groups, and whole populations have become the victims of violence emerging from a struggle for scarce resources, status, and power. The culmination of this struggle has been the War of the Zairean Succession—drawing involvement from Uganda, Rwanda, Burundi, Zimbabwe, Angola, Namibia, Chad, the

Central African Republic (CAR), Congo, Libya, and Sudan into Congo—and its spillover into internal conflicts in Congo-Brazzaville, CAR, Uganda, Rwanda, Burundi, and Angola. Minorities, defined not by their numbers but by their exclusion from power, are at risk, but so are individual citizens.

Genocide returned to the political agenda with the massacre of nearly a million Rwandans, largely Tutsi targeted for deliberate and vicious extermination, but violence was also practiced against ethnic groups in Kenya, Uganda, Burundi, Congo, Congo-Brazzaville, and CAR. In unequally divided societies such as Rwanda and Burundi, a self-proving security dilemma of genocide was installed whereby the minority Tutsi, fearing a loss of power to the majority Hutu under democratic conditions, took measures to defend themselves, which effectively ensured their loss of life as well as power if the majority should ever take over. Similar cycles took place, under different situations, in the two Congos, where there was no ethnic majority but where shifting minority domination and alliances prevailed. As a result, large refugee movements and internal population displacements were created; of the 6 million refugees in sub-Saharan Africa in the middle of the decade, about a third were in the Central African region. Many of them were reduced to permanent migrancy, while others were actively asserting a political right of return.

Thus states themselves have been at risk, either in parts of their territories or in the eyes of their regimes. Little more than a year after he came to power, Congo's Kabila faced a spreading rebellion, supported by invading armies from neighboring Uganda and Rwanda. By early 1999, the regime lost control of half its territory. Because of the presence of Rwandan *génocidaires* and Ugandan terrorist groups in eastern Congo, Rwanda and Uganda treated the region as a security zone, and the Rwandan president suggested a relocation of boundaries. The Angolan army overthrew the government of Pascal Lissouba in Congo-Brazzaville in 1997 and maintained Kabila in power in Congo in 1998, while trying to hold off the growing threat to the security of its own regime from the National Union for the Total Independence of Angola (UNITA) of Jonas Savimbi.

Former Burundian strongman Pierre Buyoya overthrew the regime of Sylvestre Ntibantunganya in 1996 and then faced the insurgent efforts of the National Council for the Defence of Democracy of Leonard Nyangoma and Jean-Bosco Ndayikengurukiye. The state-building regime of Museveni in Uganda faced a motley group of insurgents enjoying the support of various neighbors, including the Lord's Resistance Army with the support of Sudan and the Alliance of Democratic Forces with the support of Congo. The elected regime of Ange Patassé in CAR confronted the repeated efforts of various dissidents, including a dissatisfied army. Such, of course, has not been the condition of all states in the region, but the exceptions represent a minority among their peers.

Practices and institutions of conflict management have generally proved inadequate to the challenge facing them. As in 1964, when an OAU ad hoc committee was unable to handle the second Congo crisis, no regional or continental institution was capable of managing the fifth (1996–97) and sixth (1998–) Congo crises that constitute the War of the Zairean Succession.[47] In the sixth round, mediation was undertaken by the Southern African Development Community (SADC), to which Congo had been admitted the previous year. However, because three SADC members were the major military supporters of the government, and the two major supporters of the rebellion were not SADC members, the mediating agency was also a participant in the conflict it sought to manage, and the Lusaka Agreement it produced in the fall of 1999 marked a truce of fatigue, punctuated in the coming year by renewed fighting.

As a first test of the new mechanism adopted by the OAU in 1993 (as a borrowing from the Kampala Document), Mohamed Sahnoun was sent as special representative of the secretary general (SRSG) to Congo-Brazzaville to mediate the first round of civil war that accompanied the country's first democratic elections. Working with President Omar Bongo of neighboring Gabon, he was able to bring the conflict under control. In the second round of elections four years later, however, the same parties failed in the same attempt, and Denis Sassou Nguesso ousted Lissouba before the vote, with the support of neighboring Angola. In 1992–93 the OAU—along with Western countries—cosponsored a mediation effort at Arusha in the midst of the Rwandan crisis, but the ensuing agreement proved the trigger for the 1994 genocide. The OAU was also able to send in a small Neutral Military Observer Group (NMOG), and Sahnoun was also SRSG of both the UN and the OAU, but all efforts were without avail.

In the absence of institutional capabilities for conflict management, the most imaginative and effective effort was the initiative of former president Julius Nyerere of Tanzania, beginning in 1996, with the support of the East

African states, the Carter Center, and the interested world community, which gradually opened avenues of reconciliation in Burundi.[48] This peace process in Arusha also incited the launching of a domestic process of reconciliation between the presidency and the parliament, and the two processes have paced each other to provide a complementary conflict management effort. After Nyerere's death in late 1999, former president Nelson Mandela of South Africa took over as the mediator for the Burundi conflict and immediately brought international attention and influence to that process. Thus the region has produced some innovations in conflict management, at the same time as it has produced much insecurity for people, groups, and regimes.

Stability

Central Africa was one of the two parts of the continent where the CNS movement brought sovereignty back into the hands of the people in a truly extraordinary exercise of democratic control of governance. However, democratization and popular sovereignty did not bring stability; instead, their introduction was the occasion for re-emergent conflict that swiftly moved from political to violent, and then the reassertion of authoritarian rule.

In two CNS countries, Congo-Brazzaville and CAR, a new leader was elected, although in neither place did the election open the way to democratic responsibility and stability. In Congo-Brazzaville, in fact, the former single party dictator returned in a coup in 1997 with support from neighboring Angola. Only in Tanzania has there been regular party competition and presidential succession, producing the third duly elected president since independence, even though the Chama Cha Mapinduzi (CCM) has remained the dominant party. Uganda's experience under NRM dominance has been one of gradual evolution toward pluralism, owing principally to heavy international pressure. Museveni, like Nyerere before him in Tanzania, viewed political parties as divisive and was supported in this view by a referendum in 2000, but he was constrained to allow some measure of political organization and openness.

Elsewhere, the single party held sway. In Chad, Gabon, and Congo (then Zaire), a CNS arose, but the ruler was able to bring it to heel and maintain himself in power, despite the appearance of opposition parties; in the latter two cases, this was Bongo and Mobutu, entrenched leaders since the 1960s, whereas in Chad it was Idris Deby, victor in 1990 of the fourth military coup since 1975. Paul Biya of the Cameroonian National Union (UNC) staved off the CNS movement in his country and won his presidential elections despite opposition. Although Rwanda has known no pluralist elections since independence in 1963, the RPF government began the local round of a competitive election cycle in 1999 and is expected to dominate the political scene. In Burundi, the first competitive elections in 1993 led to the election, and then assassination, of the first Hutu president, Melchior Ndadaye. After returning to power through a coup in 1996, the military leader who scheduled that first attempt at elected rule, Buyoya, seems committed to trying again.

Thus the experience of the region has been stability only at the hands of authoritarian rule, with the assumed representativity of the nationalist movement-turned-single party often replaced by the assertion of stability through repression by a military ruler. In most cases, courts are constrained and parliaments are powerless. There are few measures to protect human rights or to ensure the rule of law in this type of system.

Development

The effects of insecurity and instability (or repressive stability) on development have been predictable. Between 1988 and 1996, the only states that maintained a positive per capita GNP growth figure were Uganda and (barely) Equatorial Guinea and Tanzania.[49] The region included some of the lowest per capita GNP figures in the world—Tanzania $102, Chad $110, Congo $166, Burundi $176, Rwanda $199[50]—as well as sub-Saharan Africa's highest—Gabon $4628. Only the other oil economies besides Gabon such as Cameroon ($772) and Congo-Brazzaville ($925) plus Uganda ($555) and Kenya ($374) were above the sub-Saharan African average of $334. In mid-decade, only Congo, and (barely) Uganda, Tanzania, and Gabon showed an above-African-average production of basic food over 380 kg per capita, and in all countries per capita food production dropped during the1980s and 1990s, in most cases by a third. Industrial growth during the 1988–96 period exceeded the sub-Saharan African average of 0.6 percent only in Gabon, Tanzania, Kenya, and Uganda. Neglect and violence caused negative growth of more than 10 percent in Rwanda, Burundi, Congo, and (the following year) Congo-Brazzaville.

In these conditions, life expectancy for Uganda, Rwanda, Burundi, Chad, CAR, and Equatorial Guinea was less than 50 years at mid-decade, but was 55 in Gabon and 58 in Kenya, the rest of the region being around the African average of 52. Primary education enrollment was over the sub-Saharan African average of 75 percent of the relevant age population in Kenya, Uganda, Cameroon, and Gabon, the most developed countries of the region, whereas the rest attained much lower levels. Obviously, life expectancy, education, and production are affected by civil violence but also by state consolidation, governance, and leadership.

The world context has not always been favorable to Central Africa's development. Terms of trade over the 1988–96 period were less than 90 percent of the 1987 figures in CAR, Chad, Congo-Brazzaville, Gabon, and Uganda, although they were well over 100 in Cameroon (480), Rwanda (170), and Kenya (124). The states of the region received between a half (Rwanda) and a twentieth (Cameroon, Congo, Gabon, Kenya) of their GNP in official development assistance (ODA) in 1996, with several countries (Burundi, Tanzania, CAR, Chad) at about a fifth. But only Cameroon, Gabon, and Chad received 3 percent of the GNP in foreign direct investment (FDI) in the same year, Rwanda 1 percent, and the rest less than 1 percent. And the debt service ratio the same year was equal to more than 5 percent of GNP in a number of cases—10 percent for Congo-Brazzaville, 8 percent for Gabon, 7 percent for Kenya, 6 percent for Cameroon, 3 percent for Uganda, 2 percent for Burundi, and the rest 1 percent or less.

The initially presented figures for per capita development summarize much of the story of the region. The more developed economies of Gabon, Congo-Brazzaville, Cameroon, Kenya, and Uganda provide better living conditions for their people, but most of the other countries of the region are among the world's least developed. However, the raw figures are not always directly translated by governing capacity into personal welfare. In the oil countries, per capita income is generally an unreal statistic relating to the oil economy, not the national economy. Exceptions to higher levels of development in regard to basic food production, life expectancy, and education among the more developed countries testify to the inequitable or ineffective application of resources. Nor do higher levels of development ensure stability and security, anymore than the reverse effect; Congo-Brazzaville collapsed in savage violence in the 1990s, and Cameroon, Gabon, and Kenya maintained a shaky repressive stability that did not ensure universal security, whereas Tanzania could show security and stability along with the lowest level of development.

Cooperation

Unlike the rest of the continent, Central Africa is a battleground among regional organizations and a graveyard for the efforts of continental and universal organizations of cooperation. Since its first foray into the continent, with the United Nations Operation in Congo (ONUC) in 1960, the United Nations has shown its inadequacy in dealing with African conflicts. As a result, it has adopted the principle of subsidiarity, looking first for African solutions to African problems. In the 1980 episode of the Chadian conflict, the UN Security Council refused to cooperate with the OAU and left the first Inter-African Force to its own confused devices. In 1994, after sending a limited force to Rwanda armed with restrictive instructions, the Security Council refused the appeal of the force's commanding officer, Gen. Romeo Dallaire, for reinforcements and a new mandate to stop the genocide. As the War of the Zairean Succession developed, the United Nations pressed a belated inquiry into possible civil rights abuses against the perpetrators of the genocide, which Security Council members then held up as a precondition for assistance to the new Kabila government. As a result, many of the countries of the region express hostility to the world organization in any form, yet they continue to call for UN troop deployment.

Since the 1970s, the ECA has been pressing African states to regroup into economic cooperation regions that cross the artificial colonial divisions. Central Africa constitutes the least obvious natural region, and its institutional history reflects this basic fact, compounded by political strains, tugs, and rivalries. There are two major geographic features of the region. The Congo river basin is divided into two areas of different sovereignties, one state of Congo uniting the south basin, and Congo-Brazzaville, eastern Cameroon, and the CAR dividing the north basin. The other feature is the mountainous backbone of the continent, itself rent by the Great Rift Valley, divided among Kenya, Uganda, Tanzania, Rwanda, and Burundi.

At the time of independence, this area was grouped into three postcolonial organizations: the East African Community (EAC), Common Services

Organization (EACSO), and Common Market (EACM) of formerly British Kenya, Uganda, and Tanzania; the Customs and Economic Union of Central Africa (UDEAC) of the former French Equatorial African (AEF) states of Chad, CAR, Gabon, and Congo-Brazzaville, plus Cameroon; and the Economic Community of the Great Lakes Countries (CEPGL) of former Belgian Congo, Rwanda, and Burundi. Poaching in UDEAC territory, Mobutu in 1968 drew Chad and, briefly, CAR into a Central African Economic Union (UEAC), which soon withered away. In 1994, with the devaluation of the CFA franc, UDEAC (including the recently added Equatorial Guinea) became the Economic and Monetary Community of Central Africa (CEMAC), united by a common convertible currency.

The answer of the ECA to these partial unifications was to sponsor an Economic Community of the States of Central Africa (CEEAC) combining the UDEAC and CEPGL members and uniting the Congo basin into one organization of cooperation (still divided by different monies). The result was ineffective. On the other side of the mountains, tripartite East African cooperation fell apart amid distributive inequities and political animosities in 1972, and in 1975 the ECA arranged an oversized trade cooperation agreement among the states of the continent that were not yet organized by identifiable region—the Preferential Trade Agreement of Eastern and Southern Africa (PTA). When southern Africa developed its own organization (SADC) and overcame its conflict with South Africa, now transformed from an apartheid state, the PTA turned into the Common Market of Eastern and Southern Africa (COMESA) in 1994, comprising all the states of the Horn of Africa, East Africa and Southern Africa (except South Africa and Botswana). The unwieldy COMESA grouping conflicted with SADC, which also contained nine of its members. In addition, in 1996 the former EAC states decided to revive East African Cooperation, also in competition with COMESA, and to include Rwanda and Burundi among its members.

The result has been economic incoherence and political competition.[51] None of these groups that purport to foster development through integration in their region have been able to make significant strides in lowering internal tariffs, coordinating a common external tariff, providing for free labor movement, fostering convertibility (East African Cooperation achieved this in the year 2000), promoting equitable project allocation, and stimulating regional trade, all of which are necessary to pave the way for the common market, which all of them declare to be their goal at various times between 2000 and 2020. Instead, the groups become either vehicles for the personal leadership ambitions of one head of state against another or else the arena for personal rivalries among competing member presidents. The crowning example is the struggle for Congo's body and soul among a number of competing regions. To SADC, Congo is a hunting ground for Robert Mugabe's Zimbabwe and Mandela's and then Thabo Mbeki's South Africa in pursuit of economic big game of copper, cobalt, diamonds, and gold. To some EAC members, it is a rebel sanctuary that needs to become a security zone and lebensraum for excess populations. To CEEAC, it is a French-speaking hinterland, a potential ally of weight. When the regional organization of the core of Africa is finally decided, economic cooperation for development, security, and stability will be able to move ahead.

As part of the process of regional integration, isolated stabs have been made at the elaboration of a set of principles like those of Kampala. On May 15, 1998, Kabila called a conference of his neighbors from both east and west to celebrate the anniversary of his takeover of power and to establish principles of security, stability, and cooperation by which to resolve the conflicts of the region. Unfortunately, no one came to the party and the demarche failed. Ambassador Aldo Ajello, special envoy of the European Union for the Great Lakes region, focused his activities in late 1998 and 1999 on the convocation of a regional conference for conflict resolution, a long-standing proposal of France, and the elaboration of principles of constructive interaction on which to base regional conflict solutions. Such initiatives testify to the deep-felt need of the Central African region for standards to serve as benchmarks and goals toward which to progress.

Southern Africa

The articulation in 1991 of the CSSDCA's four calabashes of security, stability, development, and cooperation coincided with profound transformations in southern Africa. Of note were the emergence of South Africa from the clutches of apartheid, the rising popularity of democracy as an avenue for national stabilization, and the reinvigoration of the Southern African Development Community (SADC) as a mechanism for security and economic collaboration. For a region that had been plagued by decolonization conflicts since the 1960s, the four calabashes seemed to offer the institutional prescriptions for regeneration.

While the rest of Africa was decolonizing in the 1960s, southern Africa remained the domain of minority settler regimes battling the progressive advance of African nationalism. South Africa, a society divided by the apartheid ideology, provided the legitimacy and protection for colonial regimes in Angola, Mozambique, South West Africa, and Rhodesia. On the other side of the battleline were national liberation movements and their supporters, the Frontline States (FLS). The independence of Angola and Mozambique in 1975, after a decade of stalled decolonization, was a momentous event in southern Africa's liberation that added to the pressure of the FLS on Rhodesia and then on South Africa itself.[52]

Most southern African states retained strong traditions of administrative capacity and effective governance stemming from the congruence of frontiers with precolonial political boundaries.[53] Monarchical traditions in Botswana, Lesotho, and Swaziland furnished symbols of institutional continuity and legitimacy in the face of postcolonial challenges, although often based on narrow interests. In Lesotho, a mostly monarchist party, the Basotho National Party (BNP), won the preindependence election in 1965, suspended the Westminster constitution in 1970, and ruled in an authoritarian style until splits among the elite in the mid-1980s ushered a phase of military coups and instability. Similarly, the Swazi state based its legitimacy on the authoritarian monarchy of King Sobhuza II, who experimented with limited pluralism in the late 1970s by nominating a cabinet and a parliament.[54] Malawi under President Kamuzu Banda's Malawi Congress Party (MCP) instituted thirty years of personal rule that promised national integration and economic prosperity. Botswana differed from the authoritarian trend, constructing a participatory democratic model with representation of opposition parties in the national legislature. Botswana's diamond-based economy enabled Presidents Seretse Khama and Ketumile Masire to strengthen pluralism at home and withstand external pressure when Botswana became a member of the FLS.[55]

Unlike the more geographically vulnerable states with strong economic links to South Africa, the FLS, under the initial leadership of Tanzania's Julius Nyerere and Zambia's Kenneth Kaunda, defied the South African military incursions and transportation monopolies, providing logistical and

material support to liberation movements at enormous costs on their stability and security.[56] Before these experiments faltered amid external debts,
increasing poverty, and bureaucratic paralysis, Tanzania and Zambia sought
alternative development patterns anchored on egalitarianism under a single
party regime. Angola and Mozambique extended the radical tradition by
instituting Marxist-Leninist regimes in a bid to overcome socioeconomic
dislocations of colonialism. Yet while endowed with substantial mineral and
energy resources, severe internal and external challenges stymied meaningful
transitions to socialism in Angola and Mozambique. Support for Zimbabwe's
decolonization from the ruling Front for the Liberation of Mozambique
(FRELIMO) compounded the latter's state-building tasks, especially after
the hasty withdrawal of Portuguese personnel and the prolonged support
from South Africa for the Mozambique National Resistance Movement
(RENAMO). State reconstruction in Angola was bedeviled by a vicious civil
war pitting the National Union for the Total Liberation of Angola (UNITA)
against the ruling Popular Movement for the Liberation of Angola (MPLA)
and by an external war waged by South Africa against the South West Africa
People's Organization (SWAPO) on Angolan soil.[57]

The problems of postcolonial reconstruction in the former Portuguese
colonies provided lessons to the newly independent states of Zimbabwe
(1980) and Namibia (1990). Robert Mugabe's Zimbabwe African National
Union-Patriotic Front (ZANU-PF) could make only a rhetorical commitment to socialism since it had inherited a diversified economy with a vibrant
agricultural sector, and the end of the cold war interrupted Mugabe's scheme
to institute a de jure one party state.[58] The participation of the United
Nations and Western countries in Namibia's transition to statehood in April
1990 led to a multiparty constitution that tied the hands of President Sam
Nujoma's SWAPO.[59]

Decolonization conflicts galvanized efforts toward regional cooperation
through the political and diplomatic interaction of the FLS. In 1980 the FLS
created a broader economic grouping, the Southern African Development
Coordination Conference (SADCC) to address regional cooperation and
reduction of dependence on South Africa. The SADCC bridged the political and ideological divides that had prevailed in the region since the 1960s
and attracted substantial external resources to alleviate some of the economic weaknesses of member states. But its potential remained stunted by

regional conflicts and South Africa's absence. The transformation of SADCC into the Southern African Development Community (SADC) in 1992, and the entry of South Africa in 1994, signaled the start of a new era of regional stability and peace.[60]

Security

The CSSDCA's conception of security distinguishes between the security of peoples and of governments: the former derives from the satisfaction of social, cultural, economic, political, and human rights needs, and is an essential precondition for the latter. It also recognizes the links between national and regional security in its prescriptions of a "common security" and "good neighborliness."[61]

When the SADC was formally launched in Windhoek in 1992, its article 5 was explicit on the goals of promoting and defending peace and security: "The region needs, therefore, to establish a framework and mechanisms to strengthen regional solidarity; and provide for mutual peace and security."[62] These efforts culminated in the establishment of the SADC Organ for Politics, Defense, and Security, in June 1996. Its objectives are to safeguard against instability from within and without, promote political cooperation and common political values (including the promotion of democracy and human rights), develop a common foreign policy, establish security and defense cooperation through conflict prevention, management, and resolution, peacemaking and peacekeeping, and a mutual defense pact; and address extraregional threats to peace and security in southern Africa. While Zimbabwe and South Africa have conflicted over the relation between the Organ and the SADC proper, most regional leaders seem to prefer separate mechanisms operating at the level of heads of states, ministers, and technical committees. Currently, the most important institution of SADC is the Inter-State Defense and Security Committee (ISDSC) in which ministers meet regularly to discuss state and regional security issues.[63]

There has been significant progress in joint military exercises and training for peacekeeping, best exemplified by two SADC multinational military peacekeeping exercises in Zimbabwe in September 1997 and South Africa in April 1999.[64] Even though SADC has not formally created a peacekeeping force, observers have hailed these exercises as precursors to the region's indigenous capacity for peacekeeping, and the ISDSC has proposed to set up a brigade-size multilateral force.[65] The SADC heads of police created the Southern African Regional Police Chiefs Cooperation Organization (SARPCCO) in August 1995 to foster strategies to reduce cross-border crime, resulting in a SARPCCO Committee to combat the cross-border movement of stolen vehicles and the 1996 SADC Protocol on Illicit Drug Trafficking.

In the era that SADC's executive secretary, Kaire Mbuende, has described as forging a "common value system in politics and economics,"[66] security collaboration confronts the specter of internal conflicts that have replaced South Africa's destabilization campaigns. A mutiny by a faction of the Royal Lesotho Defense Force against the elected government in January 1994 and a subsequent constitutional rift between Prime Minister Ntsu Mokhehle and King Letsie III led Mokhehle to request military intervention by South Africa, which then associated Botswana and Zimbabwe in a tripartite SADC mediation task force.[67] By threatening to use military force and impose economic sanctions, the task force enabled the parties to restore constitutional rule in August 1994. Instability reappeared after three opposition parties demanded the annulment of the May 1998 election results, accusing the ruling party of massive electoral fraud. Four months of election protests led to the complete collapse of civilian order, and when sections of the Lesotho military again joined the opposition protests in September, the beleaguered government again requested South African military intervention, later joined by forces from Botswana. The operation unexpectedly met intense resistance from the rebellious military and culminated in massive property damage in Maseru. Nevertheless, the SADC forces paved the way for the civilian opposition and the government to settle their differences in October and to prepare fresh elections in eighteen months; the troops withdrew in April 1999.

Insecurity for peoples and states in southern Africa has been most pronounced in the civil war in Angola. Building on regional and international changes, Portugal negotiated a peace agreement, the Bicesse Accord in 1991, that tried to end the conflict between the MPLA and UNITA through unification of rival armies and an elected government. When, in September 1992, UNITA lost the presidential elections, its leader, Jonas Savimbi, refused to accept the results and plunged the country back into a bloody war.[68] Renewed UN and regional efforts produced another agreement, the Lusaka

Protocol in November 1994, but that too collapsed in four years. UNITA's control over diamond mines has enabled its army to occupy a growing third of the country and control the borders with Congo and Zambia. A new phase began in December 1998 with the failure of UN-organized dialogue, the government's expulsion of UNITA from the national assembly and the unity government, and then the withdrawal of the UN mission from Angola in March 1999. Angolans were left to their own devices to deal with continued human suffering in a land with more than 10 million landmines, a devastated infrastructure, and an economic crisis.

The SADC's foray into the War of the Zairean Succession has highlighted problems of evolving regional security mechanisms. President Laurent Kabila's decision to join the SADC in 1997 expanded Congo's economic and security options, but in exchange he brought with him all the baggage and insecurities of the Great Lakes region. When his initial allies, Uganda and Rwanda, turned against him in August 1998, Angola, Namibia, and Zimbabwe intervened militarily, invoking SADC security arrangements. Mugabe then initiated a binding defense pact for mutual military assistance among the three intervenors and Congo in April 1999.[69] South Africa and the rest of SADC, however, saw the war primarily as a civil conflict to be resolved by negotiation, and Zambia was designated by the SADC to mediate, producing the Lusaka Agreement that took eleven months to negotiate, three more months to sign, and years to implement. What thus began in 1992 as a collective dialogue on institution building for security has exposed new regional fault lines that will take time to bridge.

Stability

The Kampala Document conceived of Africa's stability as a balance between state and civil society underwritten by the rule of law, popularly elected governments, transparent public institutions, and respect for human rights. Political pluralism has made serious progress in the region, although its most democratic systems—in South Africa, Botswana, Mozambique, and Namibia—are characterized by a dominant party, and its most striking exercise of alternance—in Zambia—is characterized by the same repressive measures no matter which party is in power.

South Africa's successful transition to a multiracial democracy was a model for a region striving for stability through democratic evolution. The inauguration of the Government of National Unity (GNU) in April 1994 began an era of undoing the legacy of apartheid within the framework of national reconciliation and power sharing. The new constitution defined the powers between the central and nine regional governments, granted universal suffrage, and subordinated executive and legislative institutions to a presidentially appointed constitutional court. In four years of majority rule, the framework of unity persisted as the African National Congress (ANC) and its allies have dealt with the myriad transitional issues such as the Reconstruction and Development Program (RDP) and the Truth and Reconciliation Commission (TRC). The leadership change from Nelson Mandela to Thabo Mbeki in 1999 furnished both institutional continuity and policy stability in South Africa's transition.[70]

Before the momentous changes in South Africa, Namibia had southern Africa's most liberal democratic constitution. SWAPO won the April 1989 elections with a convincing victory but had to share power with other parties in an environment of social and political pluralism. In neighboring Zimbabwe, the dominant ZANU-PF had to compete with a weak opposition party, the Zimbabwe Unity Movement (ZUM), in the 1990 elections.[71] It was, however, in Zambia that Frederick Chiluba's Movement for Multiparty Democracy (MMD) initiated the most far-reaching crusade for pluralism and good governance that became popularly identified with Africa's "second liberation." Starting in 1990, the MMD led protests for change that culminated in multiparty elections in October 1991, which ended Kaunda's twenty-seven years of authoritarian rule.[72]

No less significant for the region was the successful transition to multiparty politics in Mozambique following years of civil war between FRELIMO and RENAMO. Mozambique's settlement, achieved through international mediation and implemented through international generosity, ushered a period of stability rooted in tolerance and mutual respect. In contrast to Angola, FRELIMO and RENAMO shifted their conflicts from the battlefield into the regularized institutions of state and civil society.[73] Democratization in Mozambique contributed to the pressures for constitutional reforms in Malawi. In 1993 President Kamazu Banda reluctantly agreed to hold a national referendum on the reintroduction of democratic pluralism in which an overwhelming 64 percent voted in favor. Subsequently, Bakili Muluzi's United Democratic Front (UDF) won the presidential and parliamentary elections of May 1994. Four years later, Muluzi was reelected as fifteen political parties competed to choose a president and legislators.[74]

Similarly, the forces of regional contagion have decisively affected the demands for constitutional reforms in Swaziland. Since 1995, students and trade unions have organized strikes and mass actions demanding that King Mswati III relinquish his absolute powers and repeal the 1973 decree that banned political parties and suspended the constitution. SADC states have tried to mediate the constitutional crisis by invoking the regional consensus toward multiparty democracy. To address these issues, the king appointed a twenty-nine-member Constitutional Reform Committee (CRC) in 1996, but its deliberations have been slowed by opposition from the conservative traditional chiefs who control parliament.

In terms of institution building, Botswana is the only country in the region with a long experience with democratic institutions, a competent civil administration, and electoral competition. In April 1998, Festus Mogae became Botswana's third president, in another smooth leadership transition, and was reelected along with his dominant party, the Botswana Democratic Party, in October 1999.

Most of southern Africa, however, is replete with fragile and unconsolidated democracies, straining under the weight of popular pressure and inadequate channels of representation. The promise of democracy has waned as constitutional amendments, clamp-downs on press freedoms, human rights abuses, and political intolerance have reappeared.[75] Part of the reason is that both old and new regimes assumed that multiparty structures and elections were the end, rather than the start, of democratization. Moreover, there has been a tendency to implant democratic structures without supportive liberal and independent institutions that guarantee the circulation and competition of ideas, in what Stephen Chan correctly depicts as "troubled pluralisms."[76]

SWAPO in Namibia began to roll back the democratic gains in 1997 when its party congress endorsed a constitutional amendment to allow Nujoma a third five-year term in defiance of popular opinion. Although purported to be an exception made only for the "father" of Namibian democracy, this amendment set an unfortunate precedent for a region in search of institutional certainty. In Zambia the goodwill that marked Chiluba's election was squandered in practices reminiscent of the dictatorships of the 1960s. In a cycle of insecurity witnessed in the 1990s, Chiluba has muzzled the press, barred former president Kaunda from running in the 1996 presidential elections, and detained opponents, measures that have invited coup attempts and international condemnation, finally leading him to accept the constitution and not run for a third term in 2001. Equally tarnished is Mugabe's ZANU-PF which, through countless constitutional amendments, has reduced the meaning of multiparty democracy. Mugabe is allowed to nominate his own members of parliament, making a mockery of electoral processes that are already staked in favor of the ruling party. In a political climate where the opposition has been intimidated, press freedoms eroded, and the judiciary cowed by threats from the executive, strikes, rioting, and looting have emerged as the only avenues for political dissent. Yet these measures so alienated his population that Mugabe's constitutional amendment to increase his power was defeated in a referendum in 1999, and nearly half the legislature was occupied by the opposition Movement for Democratic Change (MDC) in elections in 2000.

SADC has reiterated the value of democracy and pluralism for regional stability, but these norms are embattled and contested. They have met selective enforcement, as in SADC's military intervention to check military insurrection in Lesotho, but only protests before egregious violations of the rights of opposition groups, the judiciary, and the press in Zambia and Zimbabwe. It is partly for this reason that several national civic associations have tried to mobilize into regional networks for the advancement of pluralism and human rights since the mid-1990s. Regional institutions such as the African Center for the Constructive Resolution of Disputes (ACCORD) and the Southern African Human Rights and NGO Network (SAHRNGON) reflect the determination of nongovernmental organizations to have a permanent imprint on matters of regional security and stability.

Development

The development calabash of the Kampala Document is predicated on intrinsic links between economic growth and democracy: development sustains stability, creating political stakeholders, just as growth is dependent on a stable political environment. Southern Africa has embraced market forces in a bid to become part of the global economy, but the development record is mixed, and the impact of globalization has been decidedly uneven. Generally, however, most of the states still confront the socioeconomic strains that dominated the 1980s: economic disparities compounded by poorly implemented World-Bank and IMF-imposed structural adjustment programs, low domestic savings, dependence on declining and scarce foreign capital for investment, heavy debts, and weak financial and physical infrastructures. Consequently, almost all southern African economies have witnessed increasing poverty, rising unemployment, and falling standards of living.[77]

SADC's 1998 annual report noted that the average growth rate of all SADC economies was around 4 percent in 1996, compared with the 6.4 percent average for developing countries. Of SADC's twelve member countries, seven—Congo, Namibia, Angola, Seychelles, South Africa, Swaziland, and Tanzania—recorded growth rates of less than 5 percent. In 1997, owing to the Asian financial crisis and poor weather conditions, the region's growth rates plummeted to 2.2 percent, below the 5.9 percent average of developing economies. More important, the report noted that over the medium and long term, most SADC economies will continue to experience constraints in their balance of payments and external debt burdens. The Food and Agricultural Organization (FAO) and SADC Regional Early Warning Unit have also warned of severe shortages of food in the region at the turn of the century as a result of decreasing cereal production.

South Africa's new government sought dual transformations from an isolationist economy into a global economic actor and from an agriculture- and mining-based economy to one based on exports of manufactured goods. But the external environment has been less than benign, as emerging market economies suffer the consequences of unregulated capital mobility and constrained global markets. Internally, the Reconstruction and Development Program (RDP) and Growth, Employment, and Redistribution (GEAR) plans were grand experiments in redressing apartheid's socioeconomic disparities while providing institutional assurances for local and foreign investment.[78] But the economic recession since 1998 postponed the promise of postapartheid prosperity predicated on economic growth. As the rand fell precipitously and foreign direct investment shrank, the GDP growth rate for 1999 was 1.8 percent and projected to be only 2.8 percent in 2001. In addition, South Africa's unemployment has been estimated at 38 percent, contributing to escalating crime rates that have dampened investments and business confidence.

Botswana is southern Africa's economic success story, with economic growth at 7 percent and foreign reserves estimated at $5.7 billion in 1996–97. Central to Botswana's growth is the lucrative diamond sector, which constitutes 33 percent of GDP and 80 percent of trade in goods. To reduce dependence on diamonds, the government has tried to diversify the economy by expanding manufacturing. Yet half of Botswana's 1.5 million residents live in poverty, and the unemployment rate is estimated at greater than 20 percent. The International Monetary Fund has recommended improvements in income distribution, poverty reduction, and employment creation. In Malawi, while increased agricultural production boosted the economic growth rate by 9.7 percent in 1996 and 8 percent in 1997, the government has performed dismally on poverty alleviation. In 1997 the Muluzi government sought to reverse this trend with a program to broaden income and employment opportunities by strengthening the private sector.

Of all southern African states, Mozambique has made the most remarkable economic recovery, with a GDP growth rate of 6 percent in 1997. After the 1994 elections, the government shed its image as one of the world's poorest nations by adopting a rigid privatization program to lure foreign direct investment and rebuild its decaying infrastructure. In recognition of Mozambique's heavy debt (estimated at 60 percent of the budget), the World Bank granted it the Heavily Indebted Poor Country (HIPC) status in April 1998, enabling it to use only 20 percent of export earnings to pay principal and interest on its outstanding $15 billion foreign debt, but living standards have not improved.[79] In contrast to Mozambique, Zambia's request for HIPC status to ease its crippling $7.1 billion debt was rejected because of its failure to comply with the Structural Adjustment programs. After adoption of the constitutional amendment barring Kaunda from running again, donors halted balance of payments support, estimated at $140 million in 1996. As a result, the Chiluba government has been unable to meet its development goals in the face of the decline in copper prices and lack of major foreign investment.

Similar woes confront Zimbabwe, which started the 1990s with a 15 percent drop in real incomes, 40 percent inflation, over 50 percent unemployment, and more than 60 percent of workers living below the poverty line. With the growth rate averaging 1 to 2 percent a year, foreign reserves depleted, and private capital inflows drying up, Zimbabwe set up export processing zones to lure investors in labor-intensive manufacturing. Since the mid-1990s, however, the proliferation of violent protests by students, workers, and ex-freedom fighters against economic mismanagement and soaring inflation have hampered Mugabe's implementation of austerity measures mandated by external donors, further diminishing the prospects of economic and financial assistance. In 1996 the IMF suspended financial support to Zimbabwe for missed targets and high deficits. Shortly thereafter, the government's controversial scheme to resettle poor black farmers on white-owned farmland without compensation became a sticking point in the release of $53 million of a $176 million IMF standby facility required to prop up Zimbabwe's battered economy; the aid suspension continued after Zimbabwe decided to commit more than 6,000 troops to Congo at heavy cost to the economy.

In the rest of southern African economies, conflict, corruption, and poor governance have affected meaningful economic activity. In Swaziland, for instance, while a twenty-five-year national development strategy seeks to boost the private sector, industrial strikes and social unrest have deterred foreign investors. As a result, economic growth since the mid-1990s has hovered at 2.5 percent and unemployment at 40 percent. Civil wars and instability have all but erased economic growth in Angola and Lesotho, confirming the inextricable relationship between security, stability, and development.

Cooperation

The economic advantages of interdependence in industry, agriculture, and labor migration formed the functional basis for regional cooperation. Southern Africa has a long tradition of integration schemes starting with the 1953 British colonial experiment, the Central African Federation of Northern Rhodesia (Zambia), Southern Rhodesia (Zimbabwe), and Nyasaland (Malawi). Created partly to blunt the growth of African nationalism, the federation reflected the inexorable economic interdependence among the colonial territories.[80] The Southern African Customs Union (SACU) was created in 1910 and renegotiated in 1969 among South Africa, Botswana, Lesotho, Namibia, and Swaziland to foster trade among members and provide compensations to the weak economies in exchange for dependence on South Africa. After 1994 SACU members have been negotiating a new charter that would equalize power and trade opportunities, but there are deep divisions over the formula for revenue sharing and a new trade regime.

Encompassing SACU, SADC's membership has grown since 1994 to fourteen states: Angola, Botswana, Congo, Lesotho, Malawi, Mauritius, Mozambique, Namibia, South Africa, the Seychelles, Swaziland, Tanzania, Zambia, and Zimbabwe. SADC's potential to foster economic prosperity through intraregional trade, investment, and infrastructural cooperation derives regional political stability from South Africa's leadership as the natural "growth pole." By the end of July 1998, SADC had 404 projects estimated at $8 billion under its Program of Action, concentrated primarily in the transportation and communications sectors.

SADC's major focus has, however, been trade liberalization and monetary integration, defined as the establishment of a customs union by 1996, a common market thereafter, and a common currency by the turn of the century, none of which has occurred. A trade protocol in 1996 then aimed at a free trade area by 2004. While the protocol takes effect when ten members ratify it, by the end of the decade only five had done so. Besides uneven progress toward trade liberalization, regional trade still reflects South Africa's industrial dominance; primary commodities enter South Africa and manufactured and semiprocessed goods flow out to the rest of SADC. Most SADC states, particularly Zimbabwe, have also complained about South Africa's protectionist policies and the difficulties of penetrating the fortress South African market, along with problems such as labor mobility, water resources, and security.

Institutional overlap and duplication of efforts with SADC are marked by the existence of SACU and COMESA, a larger grouping whose twenty-one members are SADC (minus Botswana, Lesotho, Mozambique, and South Africa) and IGAD, plus Burundi, Comoros, Egypt, Madagascar, and Rwanda.[81] With a population of more than 300 million people, COMESA seeks to create a free trade zone by 2000 (unachieved) and a common external tariff by 2004. By COMESA's third summit in Nairobi in May 1999, fourteen states had cut their tariffs by 60 percent, and intra-COMESA trade was estimated to be growing at the rate of 20 percent a year. Questions about whether COMESA would complement or compete with SADC arose in 1995 when South Africa declined COMESA membership and urged SADC members to reconsider their role in it; a joint SADC-COMESA ministerial committee recommended in August 1996 that both should exist independently rather than merging.

Singly or collectively, southern Africa's regional organizations seek to contribute to the phased continental economic integration, a goal advanced in the OAU's Lagos Plan of 1980 and reiterated in the Kampala Document.[82] The cooperation calabash, however, is contingent on significant progress on the other three calabashes since national security, stability, and development provide the fulcrum for sturdy states able to engage one another in collective schemes. The political and economic gains in southern Africa since the early 1990s are threatened by the persistence of internal conflicts, intolerant political practices, and fragile economies.

Conclusions

The experience of Africa's regions calls for a reconsideration of the central tenets of the Kampala Movement in regard to security, stability, development, and cooperation. Regionalism was to be a dominant feature of global politics in the post–cold war era, deriving increasing significance from the shift of responsibility for security to regional actors following the disappearance of superpower rivalry. The great powers are no longer interested in policing the world, and the more immediate threats to security just reviewed now derive from domestic weakness and regional dynamics, rather than the global conflicts that characterized the cold war. Together with economic interdependence under globalization, this enhances the role expected from regional bodies to legitimize humanitarian intervention and promote cooperative security arrangements based on mutual reassurance, rather than deterrence. Regionalism could also provide the framework for the emergence of new collective identities and more effective institutionalization of cooperation, besides reducing international problems to manageable proportions. Most significantly to developing countries, regionalism can mitigate ethnic and communal conflict by severing the historic link between sovereignty and self-determination through the creation of broader regional identities. This could lead to the unpacking of sovereignty and its distribution upward and downward, coupled with regional exigencies making regional acceptability conditional on democratization and respect for human rights.[83]

Weaknesses in security, stability, and development feed on one another and undermine cooperation in regional bodies such as ECOWAS, CEAO,

IGAD, SADC, and others, while elevating the need for it. Not only have regional institutions been bypassed by states pursuing their aims with military means, but also the international community, employing logic similar to that of the cold war, has often tolerated undemocratic, even antidemocratic, tendencies and policies. It is difficult, even with the benefit of hindsight, to see what could have been done to avert this fate. In the early 1990s, the leaders of each region appeared to be making all the right moves, spurred by the same awareness as the leaders of the Kampala Movement. They developed institutions of regional cooperation, tried to resolve conflicts collectively, and attempted to develop viable political structures internally. Most of the CSSDCA recommendations for security, stability, and cooperation were more or less followed. But insecurity, instability, underdevelopment, and conflict still persisted or erupted anew. What went wrong?

Some analysts tried to look for structural reasons for the endemic instability in Africa. The absence of a stabilizing influence of a regional hegemon in some regions (East and Central Africa) or the presence of the domineering interests of a regional hegemon in others (West and Southern Africa) is cited contradictorily as a factor, as well as traditional rivalries between old and new states. Some even see the character of the African state itself, and the role it plays in the zero-sum game conflict over resources, as the determining factor, suggesting perhaps that dissident groups should be "bought."[84] Part of the problem also lies in the excessive militarization of the region, which resulted from prolonged armed conflict.[85] Countries of various regions—Burundi, CAR, Chad, Congo-Brazzaville, Ethiopia, Liberia, Niger, Nigeria, Rwanda, Somalia, Sudan, Uganda, Upper Volta (Burkina Faso), and Zaire (Congo)—experienced significant militarization since the 1960s, the impact of which was felt on most aspects of life, including their economies. This militarization, which was the consequence of regional tensions and attempts to suppress actual or potential rebellions, was accelerated in the 1970s, just as economic growth rates were declining in these countries and population growth was accelerating.

However, it was not just the fact of militarization that is noteworthy. The new regimes in Burundi, Eritrea, Ethiopia, Rwanda, and Uganda (but unlike comparable experiences in Liberia, Chad, and Sierra Leone) represented a new and extremely interesting development in African politics. Prolonged insurgencies, during which relatively cohesive ethnic-ideological alliances were forged, culminated in the armed political party, turning the state's monopoly of legitimate force into the preserve of an ethnic ideological party-state. The same phenomenon materialized in Sudan, by a reversed process. There a civilian sectarian political party took over political power through a narrowly based military coup and proceeded to militarize itself and to monopolize state power. In all these cases, the state was being reconstructed from the perspective of the new militarized party, and the new dominant groups have been reluctant to effect a genuine power sharing. This reluctance was at the heart of the rising tension that continued to destabilize the region.

This would suggest the need to pay particular attention to the stability component of the Kampala program. African leaders have been arguing, not without some justification, that the experience of their countries with Western-style democracy has not been successful. Multiparty politics, they claimed, accelerated the fragmentation of African societies along ethnic and sectarian lines. However, historical evidence seems to indicate that it had been repressive governments resisting power sharing that were responsible for the accelerated fragmentation of societies. Ethiopia, for example, which had never tried multiparty politics before 1991, has experienced more fragmentation along ethnic lines than any of its neighbors. Nigeria, under military rule for most of its life, is experiencing destructive ethnic tensions at the same time as democracy returns. The dictatorships of Siad Barre in Somalia, Idi Amin in Uganda, Gaafar Nimeiri in Sudan, and Samuel Doe in Liberia have done more to highlight, exploit, and exacerbate ethnic and religious differences than would have been possible under the worst form of competitive democratic politics.

The only way to move forward is to recognize the reality of advanced ethnic fragmentation and try to deal with it. This advanced state of fragmentation in the polities of the region led to a phenomenon that is the reverse of what Wolfram Hanrieder called the "domestication of international politics."[86] In his analysis, increased state interdependence and increased state roles in domestic social and political welfare cause states to concentrate more on the "low politics" of economic and redistributive issues, as opposed to the "high politics" of power and security. As a result, international political processes come to resemble domestic politics more and more. A diametrically opposed phenomenon, the "internationalization of domestic politics," predominates in many regions. Political and ethnic groups not only claim autonomy from the state but also actually act in the way classical realist theory of international relations describes the conduct of states in an anarchical international system. Such groups do not recognize the authority of existing states and conduct themselves competitively vis-à-vis other groups, rather than cooperatively. They present themselves as independent actors in the international arena and enter into alliances and relations often directed against their supposed states or other groups within them. Morally and psychologically, they feel no affinity to the state to which they belong, and they even call for sanctions and war against it. And at home, they are caught in a security dilemma with other political and ethnic groups. This tends to place many African states in the category of those states described by some analysts as "weak states" whose internal affairs mirror "all the worst and none of the best features of anarchic structure at the international system level,"[87] or as "collapsed states," where legitimate authority, law, and order have vanished.[88] This makes it meaningless at times to speak of national security in such states.

Behind this development is a mistrust of existing states and pessimism about their amenability to reform. The first priority is therefore to restore confidence in the state and national politics. Some countries, such as Ethiopia, Nigeria, and South Africa, tried to face this problem head on, by enshrining and institutionalizing the reality of ethnicity into the constitution, recognizing the existence of a multination state, complete with the right of self-determination for its constituent "nations and nationalities," or through a federation with careful allocation of resource revenues and balancing of political coalitions. There is an urgent need to recapture the spirit of cooperation and political reform that has manifested itself briefly in various regions, starting with a firm commitment to reform and genuinely pluralist politics. Failure to recognize ethnic and political pluralism could not disguise differences and conflicts; quite the reverse, in fact, for it underlines a recognition of differences that could not be reconciled within the democratic process and thus have to be swept under the carpet. This is likely to allow tensions to persist and fester. And given the cross border linkages of ethnic groups, this situation threatens a wider regional conflict.

On the regional level, political security and economic cooperation need to be revived. Institutional cooperation and peacemaking are the key. The lack of progress in peacemaking efforts needs to be reversed, and the search for local solutions pursued with vigor and imagination. Success or failure on this front will have a profound impact for the whole continent and could easily determine the fate of its organization. On the theoretical level, a deeper understanding of the fundamental structural causes that appear to militate against sustained cooperation needs to be developed. Goodwill alone will not suffice. It is into this situation that the Kampala Movement was born.

3

Regimes in Other Regions

A t the same time as Africa has been struggling with instability, insecurity, stagnation, and conflict, other regions of the world have also tried to create regimes and enact frameworks for common progress. These efforts, generally more successful than those in Africa, can be a source of ideas and an object of comparison for Africa, as the continent strives to attain peace, stability, and economic development.

The post–World War II half-century has been marked by efforts to give an institutional framework and a normative content to the idea of regionalism. Generally this has meant the creation of a regional organization, equivalent to the Organization of African Unity (OAU) in Africa, which would give member states an opportunity to create norms governing their relations and to work for security and development within an organizational framework. One of the oldest such organization—dating from just after World War II—is the Organization of American States (OAS), which served as a model for the OAU as its African charter was being drawn up in 1963. Another regional organization, younger than the OAU, is the Association of South East Asian Nations (ASEAN). Both have combined organization and guidelines to form a regime of cooperation for security, stability, and development in their regions.

In other cases, the region proceeds directly to the elaboration of norms and behavioral guidelines for the region before moving on to the creation of a new, overarching organization. This apparent reversal of the usual process occurs, however, only when the region has already cooperated within an organizational framework of limited norms and then seeks to reach beyond that organization or introduce a radical change in norms. Such a change occurred in Europe, where a number of preexisting organizations established to meet the needs of cooperation in the cold war were bridged and eventually in part replaced by a new normative regime in the Conference on Security and Cooperation in Europe (CSCE), which two decades later, after the passing of the cold war, turned itself into an organization (OSCE). It was the CSCE that inspired Olusegun Obasanjo's efforts to create an African model, the Conference on Security, Development, and Cooperation in Africa (CSSDCA).

The two types of experience point to the need for some kind of "mechanism" for launching durable regional cooperation and for spurring reform and innovation. This typically depends on leadership that comes from a sponsoring country that plays a mediating role, a coalition of countries that builds momentum and consensus, or a grassroots movement that presses for normative and institutional change. The presence of a regional hegemon or dominant member allows for a sponsoring country to take the lead, such as the United States exerted over the creation and development of the Organization for American States and Indonesia played in ASEAN. The dominant position of Nigeria in Africa positions it for a similar role. In Europe, however, the United States took a back seat in the creation of the OSCE, thus opening the way for Western European countries along with the neutral and nonaligned states to take the lead in promoting multilateral approaches to rapprochement with the East. Africa has still to see a supportive coalition of diverse forces to provide a base for the Kampala Movement, either among OAU member states or within civil society.

ASEAN, the OAS, and the OSCE all emerged from previous limited or failed experiments in regional cooperation. They also underwent processes of regime evolution, leading to the enhancement of their normative scope and stringency, as well as the expansion of areas of cooperation. Each had experiences similar to the CSSDCA's relations with the OAU yet different in detail. Each regional organization has confronted challenges by developing mechanisms to ensure compliance and manage conflict, and each has pursued a course based on its own history and culture.

In all four continents, the end of the cold war brought new opportunities and difficulties, including the rise of transnational problems such as drug trafficking, narcoterrorism, transnational prostitution rings, population movements, and environmental dangers. At the same time, each region had to face ethnic conflict and internal war. Regional organizations are under increasing pressure to respond to these problems themselves, following principles of subsidiarity, rather than expecting the United Nations to come to the rescue. Each region has its version of "African solutions for African problems." This has turned the spotlight on the need for conflict prevention and early warning for security and for the promotion of democracy and human rights for stability. Yet each of the three regions has developed different kinds of policy tools and normative responses to the new conditions from which the African experience with the Kampala Movement can draw useful lessons and inspiration.

ASEAN and Asia Pacific

ASEAN is one of the most successful regional organizations and represents a significant achievement among developing countries since its founding in August 1967, four years after the OAU. Its membership comprises Brunei, Indonesia, Laos, Malaysia, Myanmar, the Philippines, Singapore, Thailand, and Vietnam, with Cambodia as the latest member since 1999.[1] ASEAN has helped maintain peace in a troubled region, while charting new areas of security, economic, and political cooperation in the post–cold war era. There is much discussion about the "ASEAN Way,"[2] a code of conduct governing interstate relations, based in principles well established in international law, and a particular decisionmaking process, steeped in regional traditions of consultation and consensus building. What sets ASEAN apart is the way common norms such as nonintervention, sovereignty, or peaceful settlement of disputes are put into effect. To arrive at consensus decisions, members insist on a style encompassing discreetness, informality, pragmatism, and expediency, elements that also correspond to African traditions of handling conflict.[3]

ASEAN members have insisted on avoiding heavy institutionalization in their approach to cooperation, keeping bureaucratization at a minimum, in contrast to the OAS, and to some extent more recently, the OSCE. Consultations are open-ended—not tied to timetables—and members are given time to adjust their positions to the momentum of ASEAN cooperation. Alongside annual meetings of foreign ministers, a formal summit of leaders every two years, and an informal summit in intervening years, the ASEAN process encompasses many forums for consultations on various issues by many different levels of officials, civil servants, and parliamentarians—with 200 to 300 meetings annually. This is a far more intense schedule of cooperation than exists on the continental level in Africa, where subregional cooperation—at least in the West and the South—is far more important than continental interaction. The work is handled by national ASEAN secretariats and the foreign ministries of each member and the host of the annual ministerial meeting.[4] ASEAN states have never considered the association an alliance or collective security arrangement, in contrast to the OAS or the OAU. There has been no consensual threat assessment and no joint commitment to come to one another's aid in the event of external attack.[5]

ASEAN's success is built on the foundations of earlier failed attempts at regional cooperation. Its predecessors include the Association of Southeast Asia (ASA), set up in 1961 by Malaysia, the Philippines, and Thailand, and MAPHILINDO, created in 1963 by Malaysia, the Philippines, and Indonesia. Both efforts were undermined by tensions and suspicions among the member states, but the experience contributed key norms and principles that ASEAN encompassed.[6] The idea of a more inclusive organization was put forward by Thailand's foreign minister during a reconciliation meeting with MAPHILINDO and pursued thereafter by Indonesia with the three ASA members plus Singapore.[7] The evolution was similar (and contemporaneous) to the OAU's creation out of the competition between the Casablanca and Monrovia Groups in 1963 through the efforts of Ethiopia.[8]

ASEAN Core Principles

The preservation of regional cohesion—unity and harmony—has been the key objective from the outset, even at the cost of dynamism or efficiency.[9] The core principles of ASEAN emanate from this focus and guide the decisionmaking and policy processes. First and fundamental is ASEAN's practice of consensual decisionmaking, which allows all members to have a veto, although it can impede decisive action.[10] D. F. Anwar argues that "given the early years of hostility and suspicion among the ASEAN members, it was felt that the most important task of ASEAN was to promote confidence building measures (CBMs) and build up trust. A consensual decision-making process helps to bind all the members to an agreement. All become stakeholders in outcomes."[11] To enable cooperation in the economic field, ASEAN later adopted a "6-x formula" (that is, less than unanimity required) and more recently "9-x", but preference is given to "deliberation" to reach consensus, rather than voting.[12] ASEAN consensus building avoids open and public disagreement and endeavors instead to allow members to save face, much as consensus is the norm in the OAU, even at the expense of action.

The decisionmaking approach is shaped by Indonesia's political culture of *musyawarah* and *mufakat* (deliberation and consensus), derived from the Arabic *shura* (consultation) and *wifaq* (agreement).[13] These processes are adopted from traditional village politics in parts of Indonesia and to some extent in Malaysia and the Philippines, and more broadly the Arab East and indigenous Africa. *Mufakat* and *musyawarah* involve a slow incremental process of unanimous decisionmaking also practiced in national policy making and conflict management.[14] Not unlike problem-solving approaches promoted by Western scholars, agreement comes through integrating ideas and a conceptual synthesis of the minority and majority points of view. If there are too many proposals or differences to forge a common approach, the decision may be postponed or the parties may agree to disagree. Cooperation for the sake of the common good is the goal.[15]

There is little emphasis on monitoring for compliance, lest intrusive instruments be seen as confrontational. Nor do ASEAN members engage in a diplomacy of public shaming as has been used often by the West, especially during the cold war years of the CSCE.[16] This practice would be antithetical culturally and also strategically, since ASEAN members use regional unity to overcome their individual weaknesses and gain in bargaining power with the rest of the international community. Such objectives require minimizing differences among themselves in handling the outside world.

Second, the process of regional cooperation is nearly as important as the outcome.[17] So even if ASEAN has acquired a reputation of engaging in little more than "shop talk," regular interaction and consultation is valued as a confidence building measure and an end in itself, as well as a means to promote unity and harmony. Members become well acquainted with one another and with their positions on different issues. This interaction helps promote learning and convergence and makes reaching consensus easier over time.[18]

Third, equality of the member countries is the overarching principle, despite their disparities in size (for example, Brunei's 296,000 people to Indonesia's 200 million, larger than Africa's span of 500,000 in Equatorial Guinea to 120 million in Nigeria). As a consequence, leadership in ASEAN— as in the OAU—has been more than simply a matter of regional hegemony, as has so often been the true in the experiences of the OSCE or the OAS. Instead, various members take the lead according to their interest. For example, Thailand began working for a settlement of the Cambodia conflict by 1987 under ASEAN auspices, eventually bringing in Indonesia.[19] Singapore has led the way in promoting ASEAN economic cooperation. Rather than acting as a hegemon, Indonesia exercises procedural leadership, much like the village chief who guides *musyawarah* and *mufakat*, seeing itself as first among equals and expecting advance consultations before new regional policies are launched. [20] Smaller ASEAN members have been willing to accept this role under Indonesian president Mohammed Suharto, as a welcome change from the earlier interventionist policies of President Ahmed Sukarno. In Africa, Ethiopia's position was similar, especially under the emperor, whereas Nigeria and South Africa more recently have assumed leadership positions.

Fourth, ASEAN members—like OAU members—have avoided conflicts by adhering strictly to the principles of respect for each other's sovereignty and territorial integrity, and noninterference in each other's internal affairs. These norms were borrowed from the Bandung Principles of Non-Alignment in 1955 and incorporated into the OAU Charter and the Bangkok Declaration that set up ASEAN. Noninterference is, in fact, the primordial principle and marks an important break with past practices of assisting antigovernment forces of fellow ASEAN and OAU members. This principle has been put to the test with tensions over East Timor, for example, leading Philippine officials to block foreign participants from attending conferences sponsored by nongovernmental organizations on East Timor so as not to antagonize the Indonesian government. Even so, by allowing the event to take place, Philippines president Fidel Ramos was considered ungrateful by Indonesia for Suharto's help in resolving the Moro conflict, since Indonesia had avoided criticizing Philippine policy toward the Muslims in the South or assisting the South despite local sympathy for the Moros.

In the aftermath of the violent withdrawal of Indonesia from East Timor in 1999, newly elected Indonesian president Abdurrahman Wahid's success in rallying ASEAN members (and also establishing closer ties with India, China, and Japan) can be attributed to the affront Indonesians felt at the hand of the Western-led coalition of countries forcing multinational military intervention in East Timor.[21] Similarly, ASEAN has pursued a policy of constructive engagement, not confrontation, with Myanmar (Burma). It has sought to encourage reform through commercial and political contacts, resisting Western pressure for sanctions.[22] Except for helping to obtain the release of opposition leader Aun San Suu Kyi, the policy has not yielded any national reconciliation or restoration of the democratic process. Cambodia is another example of ASEAN members putting aside their different views of the conflict and working together to develop a sense of community.[23]

Comprehensive Security

ASEAN has evolved within a conceptual framework of comprehensive security. For ASEAN governments, national security is an outwardly and inwardly oriented concept. During the cold war, concerns arose about superpower rivalry in the region, but regime survival has always been more important in the face of persistent dangers of insurgency, subversion, and political unrest. For Indonesians, national and regional resilience has been paramount. This means "a dynamic condition of will power, determination and firmness with the ability to develop national strength to face and overcome all manner of threat internal and external, direct or indirect" that might threaten their way of life.[24] Malaysia sees national security as "inseparable from political stability, economic success and social harmony," and comprehensive security as essential for regional stability.[25]

Although ASEAN members have taken bilateral, not regional, approaches to the resolution of bilateral disputes,[26] these initiatives are generally embedded in a regional normative framework, including such principles as respect for sovereignty, territorial integrity, and peaceful settlement of disputes, described as "thinking multilaterally but acting bilaterally." [27] By keeping disputes bilateral, other members have been saved from having to choose sides, which could disrupt ASEAN relations as a whole. ASEAN members have also been actively mediating in bilateral disputes, but typically this work is done behind closed doors.

Another implication of thinking multilaterally and acting bilaterally has played itself out in intra-ASEAN defense cooperation, a legacy in part of the ASEAN states' rejection of multilateral defense cooperation during the cold war to avoid provoking Indochinese adversaries. Indonesia carries out bilateral military exercises with every other ASEAN member and, under the Treaty of Amity and Cooperation signed in Bali in 1976, ASEAN members have also renounced the use or threat of force to settle disputes. With the use of force essentially outlawed, ASEAN is moving in the direction of becoming a security community. In this development, it is far ahead of Africa.

Mechanisms for Conflict Management

ASEAN developed a regional security mechanism with the Declaration of the Zone of Peace, Freedom and Neutrality (ZOPFAN) adopted in Kuala Lumpur in November 1971 to insulate the region from great power politics and achieve autonomous regional collective defense.[28] ZOPFAN also provided a military code of conduct based on a commitment to neutrality drawn from the founding Bangkok Declaration, which calls for freedom from external interference without imposing legal obligations on the signatories. So neutrality here means "nonparticipation and impartiality of Southeast Asian states in conflict between other, especially extra-regional states" and also "non-interference of external powers in the domestic and regional affairs of the neutral states."[29] Once again the norm of noninterference, critical in defining ASEAN's efforts to retain regional unity and autonomy in the context of the cold war, appears paramount. These concerns also resonated in the historical development of hemispheric cooperation in the Americas and have also been dominant in Africa.

The 1976 Treaty of Amity and Cooperation (article 15) empowers the ministerial High Council to "recommend to the parties in dispute appropriate means of settlement such as good offices, mediation, inquiry or conciliation." As with the OAU, a committee established for mediation, inquiry, or conciliation has not been used. Parties to a dispute are not bound to accept the mediation of the High Council, which also has no authority to take initiatives in dispute settlement, and there are no means of imposing sanctions on the parties.[30] Informal methods prevail, with states preferring to work out differences bilaterally, while sometimes calling on other ASEAN members for mediation to this end. The key principle again is keeping away outside interference and insisting on Asian solutions to Asian problems.

End of the Cold War

At the same time as it was throwing new challenges at Africa and setting the stage for the Kampala Movement, the changing international context after the cold war was posing renewed challenges for ASEAN. The West's growing interest in human rights and democracy shone the spotlight on many regions of the world.[31] The ASEAN–European Community foreign ministers' meeting in 1991 linked human rights to any new economic cooperation agreement. In 1992 the Dutch minister chairing the Inter-Governmental Group on Indonesia called on ASEAN to take up the East Timor question. In the ASEAN region, as in Africa and Latin America, states saw in such initiatives an effort to punish them and push them into a hidden agenda. While such pressure has led ASEAN states to close ranks in the past, there are concerns that this response will become more difficult in the future if conditionality is imposed by more powerful forces, like Japan or the World Bank. In the 1990s, ASEAN turned toward the development of a free trade area as a means to promote unity, but the 1997–98 economic crisis has threatened to increase competition among ASEAN members for markets, trade, and capital and has led to policies to push out "foreign workers," even when this action was directed at workers from neighboring ASEAN states. African states have felt the same pressures, and both regions have suffered from xenophobia and ethnic conflict as a result.

The fading of the cold war has also turned the spotlight on many different regional security issues, energy needs, overlapping maritime claims, and human security concerns, such as human rights violations, environmental degradation, transnational crime, ethnic conflict, involuntary migration, or the drug trafficking and cross-border smuggling of the infamous Golden Triangle region that makes up Myanmar's border with China, Thailand, and Laos, and the ensuing dangers of a regional arms race and the outbreak of conflict.[32]

International changes have also brought positive pressures for regional ties within Pacific Asia. There has already been greater integration of Chinese and Vietnamese economies into regional trading networks. The United

States has reduced its presence in the region, letting major nearby states such as China and Japan emerge as leaders.[33] In response, the newly established ASEAN Regional Forum (ARF) and ASEAN's strategic position in APEC (Asia-Pacific Economic Cooperation) have enhanced the region's economic bargaining position. Despite appeals from Western leaders, a fast track approach to launching a CSCE-type endeavor was explicitly rejected.[34]

The ARF approach is a kind of "soft regionalism," shaped by the variety of ongoing political, strategic, and economic constraints on the development of deeper regional ties. The ARF has its origins in a 1992 summit in Singapore and gained the support of Japan, the United States, South Korea, and China within a year. Signaling an important shift in U.S. foreign policy, the Clinton administration saw the ARF as "ASEAN's contribution to a process that could encourage the sharing of information, the easing of tensions, the resolution of disputes, and the fostering of confidence."[35] For Japan, the ARF provided an opportunity to legitimize its voice in regional security affairs independent of the United States, while also enabling a South Korean–Japanese security dialogue to unfold in the same context as the United States and China. For China, ASEAN leadership of ARF meant the United States and Japan would not dominate, making the forum more acceptable. In any event, China could hardly afford to remain isolated from such regional security matters.

In July 1994, the original six ASEAN members held the first meeting of the ASEAN Regional Forum, with seven dialogue partners, plus China and Russia, and three observers—Vietnam, Laos, and Papua New Guinea. The idea of the ARF was essentially to extend the commitment of the Treaty of Amity and Cooperation to resolve disputes peacefully to other key states— "a kind of minimal diffuse reciprocity."[36] China is the unstated object of concern. The aim is "to encourage China to explain and clarify its security policy and planning." Other ASEAN members would reciprocate the greater transparency, but for China, the chief payoff would be improved access to U.S. and Japanese defense planning.

The ARF has developed into a comprehensive security forum, boasting twenty-one members, including ASEAN states and observers, and their dialogue partners (Australia, the European Union, China, Russia, and India). By 1997 the ARF had also set up three working groups, dealing with confidence building, peacekeeping operations, and maritime search and rescue. At

Thailand's initiative, and with UN support, three ASEAN-UN preventive diplomacy workshops were also held, and the possibility of setting up a peacekeeping training center was discussed. But neither ASEAN nor the ARF has yet dealt with key problems—like bilateral border and territorial disputes, ethnic tensions, smuggling, piracy, and illegal movement across borders.

ASEAN countries have introduced proposals and convened workshops to consider other confidence building measures, such as an ASEAN Arms Transfer Register proposed by Malaysia, advance notification of military exercises, a hot line, and other things. But the division within the ARF on these proposals mirrors differences in APEC on economic matters, with ASEAN and China preferring to keep discussion general to avoid disagreements, and the United States, Australia, Canada, and Japan looking for practical measures for immediate implementation. Like Latin Americans, ASEAN members and China tend to see confidence building measures as challenging the traditional ways of doing business. The vocabulary of nuclear deterrence, arms control, disarmament, and confidence building measures, as well as transparency and verification, comes across as Western constructs, embedded in Western cultural and political customs. However, ASEAN leaders are adverse to transparency because they fear it could undermine national military readiness and deterrence. Even the most flexible ASEAN government would accept only voluntary, nonbinding commitments. For example, Malaysia distinguishes between voluntary public announcements about arms acquisitions and the opening of installations for inspections, which is unacceptable because it "goes against the grain of military culture."[37] Even so, the Southeast Asian Nuclear Weapon Free Zone, signed by ASEAN member states as well as some other countries, and which came into effect in 1997, incorporated the first multilateral constraining measures. Although not binding under international law, it nonetheless contains elaborate procedures for monitoring compliance and verification, including an implementation commission.[38]

An important new feature of ASEAN cooperation involves participation by civil society, which may become a source of innovation for the association, much as the Kampala Movement has tried to be for the OAU. ASEAN's civil society involvement, however, is much more structured than Africa's. The key players are the National Institutes for Strategic and International Studies

(ASEAN-ISIS), made up of academic and nongovernmental specialists in the member states, which influenced ASEAN to institute a dialogue about security in the early 1990s. In 1993 the National Institutes for Strategic and International Studies were incorporated into the Council on Security Cooperation in the Asia-Pacific (CSCAP), a new informal diplomatic organization with other nongovernmental membership paralleling the ARF's official representation and modeled after the Pacific Economic Cooperation Council dialogues of business people and academic economists dating back to the 1970s. The CSCAP supports official forums, with national committees and working groups headed by a council with ten leading research institutes from ASEAN, Australia, Canada, South Korea, Japan, the United States, and subsequently China. The CSCAP has working groups on maritime cooperation, security cooperation in the North Pacific, confidence building measures and transparency, and cooperative and comprehensive security.[39] There has even been an effort to promote and sustain people-to-people contacts. Since the early 1990s, each year has been promoted as a "visit ASEAN year," singling out an ASEAN country for intra-ASEAN tourism.

Nevertheless, ASEAN is as far as the OAU is from resolving outstanding disputes among its members. The crises in Indonesia, including the violent secession of East Timor and demands for independence in the rebellious province of Aceh, pose serious challenges to ASEAN, which has been practically at a standstill at the turn of the millennium as a result of political instability in Indonesia.[40] ASEAN members have appealed for a more proactive stance on internal crises. The former deputy prime minister of Malaysia called on ASEAN to develop a policy of "constructive intervention" before crises such as the 1997 coup in Cambodia erupt full blown. He argued that "ASEAN's direct involvement in the affairs of its members is but the application of an ASEAN solution to an ASEAN problem. Given the nature of the problems we may face in the region, where the threat of spillover of domestic economic, social and political upheavals can seriously undermine the stability of the entire region, we should reach a consensus to adopt this approach."[41] Like Africa, Southeast Asia is reaching out from its organizational base—ASEAN in Asia, the OAU in Africa—to seek new ways of meeting endemic challenges. ASEAN broadens its geographic and functional scope from within, without the counterproject that the CSSDCA represents for the OAU.

The Americas and the OAS

The Organization of American States has enjoyed an extraordinary revival in the 1990s, owing to its shift from a declaratory position in support of democracy to enforcement of this norm through many innovative instruments and approaches, a shift that the OAU follows at a considerable distance. The OAS commitment to protect and restore democracy has put it at the forefront of regional organizations around the world and of international law as well. These are significant departures from the traditional purposes of the OAS, which have focused on collective defense from external threats and institutional containment of U.S. hegemonic influence over the region. The OAS norms, like those of the OAU, have long centered on the protection of sovereignty and noninterference in internal affairs. Consequently, the institutionalization of a "right to democracy" norm in the OAS has not come without arousing old concerns about the political motivations and purposes of the region's hegemon. For OAS member states, the challenge of the new millennium is to further develop the organization's institutional capacity not only to respond to democratizing crises but to prevent their unfolding. This means giving more attention to the root causes of violence and conflict that still undermine security and stability throughout Latin America, and to this end, creating effective institutional machinery for purposes such as conflict prevention and peacekeeping, and thus requiring concerted multilateral approaches.[42]

Origins of the OAS

The OAS is the culmination of various stages of Western hemispheric initiatives in institution building, from the early 1800s to the First International Conference of American States held in Washington in 1889–1890.[43] However, at its founding in 1948, the OAS was designed as part of a broader post–World War II effort to forge a new world order.[44] More than ASEAN and the OAU, the OAS has its dominant member, in the United States, and vast differences in size, population, and power among its Latin and English-speaking members, with attendant differences in priorities for OAS action. But since 1990 Canada has helped bridge the traditional divide between English-speaking and Ibero-American states, and as a power in its own right, it helps to diffuse the polarization between the United States and the rest of the OAS membership.[45]

Today, member states typically consult and coordinate with one another, forming ad hoc "steering caucuses" whose composition differs depending on the subject at hand. This approach requires multilateral diplomacy and consensus building based on the juridical equality of states. Consensus building is consistent with Latin American cultural tendencies, which emphasize building close ties and avoiding confrontation among equal partners. The preference is to reach decisions without damaging other states' status, or to at least give the impression of consensus even if it is really imposed. Hence style is important, and as in ASEAN and Africa, a chief concern is to help others avoid loss of face.[46]

The OAS structure has also undergone important changes since its inception. Most notable are the 1967 amendments to the 1948 Charter of Bogotá, which replaced the practically defunct Inter-American Conference with a newly created annual General Assembly, the principal OAS organ. A Permanent Council, meeting in continuous session, serves as the preparatory committee of the General Assembly and is responsible for policies and relations among the member states. Meetings of the foreign ministers take up matters of urgency, but it is the Permanent Council, deciding by an absolute majority vote, that acts until the foreign ministers are able to convene. A General Secretariat under the direction of the secretary general carries out the programs decided by the General Assembly. Other key organs of the OAS focus on development cooperation and technical assistance, while legal matters are handled by the Inter-American Juridical Committee, as well as an Inter-American Commission and an Inter-American Court on Human Rights.[47] Many of the institutions of the OAS find a parallel in the OAU, which was modeled on the pre-1967 OAS in its foundation in 1963.

The OAS Charter codified hemispheric cooperation, dispute settlement, and collective security mechanisms already adopted in the Americas before and after World War II.[48] But as a cold war instrument, the OAS Charter contained an implicit bargain: "In return for U.S. nonintervention in their internal affairs, the Latin American countries would support the U.S. internationally, and accept collective responsibility for security in the hemisphere."[49] The OAS's early record of accomplishment focuses on its role as an instrument of dispute settlement: from 1948 to the 1960s, it resolved as many as forty disputes. Over the same period its focus expanded with the establishment of the Inter-American Bank and OAS technical assistance programs to include economic and social development. President John F. Kennedy's initiative that led to the 1961 Alliance for Progress gave impetus to expanding OAS technical assistance. This period also saw important developments in human rights through the Inter-American Commission on Human Rights created in 1959, the American Convention on Human Rights signed in 1969, and the Inter-American Court on Human Rights inaugurated in 1979, though its jurisdiction has been limited because many member states have not acceded to it, including the United States.[50]

Yet the OAS cooperation system and normative regime were undermined repeatedly throughout the first decades of existence, in ways that exceeded the African disruptions during the same period. On the one hand, as in Africa, the emergence of dictatorships put the further development of representative democracy on ice; the draft convention on Effective Exercise of Representative Democracy, for example, was simply too controversial for adoption.[51] On the other hand, U.S. interventions in Guatemala in 1954, the Dominican Republic in 1965, Grenada in 1983, and Panama in 1989 instilled deep distrust of the United States and suspicions about its hegemonic designs over the hemisphere. President Richard Nixon not only allowed the Alliance for Progress program to die out but emphasized bilateral over multilateral diplomacy. Despite meetings by the Permanent Council in 1962 to reaffirm democratic solidarity and adopt stiff attitudes toward coups, the United States also resisted encouraging democracy within the OAS for fear of undermining the regional coalition of anticommunist governments.[52] And in the same year, the OAS excluded Cuba from further participation in the OAS and other agencies and conferences of the Inter-American system and imposed limited economic sanctions. Its Marxist-Leninist government was considered "incompatible with the principles and objectives of the inter-american system."[53] Africa never underwent such disruptions at the hands of a dominant member, nor did it ever exclude a member.

Yet out of this situation, several factors conspired to encourage greater subregional cooperation, in reaction to the current developments. Although a similar evolution occurred in Africa, notable in the form of the Kampala Movement, it did not take the same forms as in Latin America. However, the Latin American events highlight potential areas of activity that Africa can well emulate.[54] Opposition to U.S. unilateral actions in Central America also prompted Latin American states to seek closer cooperation among themselves. The systematic and widespread human rights abuses of the Somoza regime in Nicaragua coincided with the dramatic shift of the new U.S. president, Jimmy Carter, to make human rights a centerpiece of attention.

Concern in the 1980s with conflicts in Central America led to the formation of the Rio Group and the Central American Esquipulas and then Contadora Groups. All Latin American states now participate in the annual summit meetings of the Rio Group, as well as its frequent foreign ministers' meetings and caucuses in the United Nations. The Esquipulas Group also meets as a consultative mechanism for Central American states. In turn, the English-speaking Caribbean states established their own institution, the Organization of Eastern Caribbean States.

These renewed efforts at cooperation produced a series of watershed developments at the start of the 1990s. First, the OAS broke new ground in collective defense of democracy by monitoring the 1990 Nicaraguan general election and the Contra settlement. Second, in response to a Mexican proposal for free trade, U.S. president George Bush launched the Enterprise for the Americas. With provisions for debt relief, increased foreign investment, and a free trade area spanning Alaska to Patagonia, the initiative was seen as a sign of a new approach from Washington based more on partnership than imposition. These developments created a new sense of momentum that was seized at the 1991 summit in Santiago, Chile, where a landmark document—"The Santiago Commitment to Democracy and the Renewal of the Inter-American System"—revitalized the OAS. The momentum culminated in the 1994 Summit of the Americas at Miami, which revamped the framework of hemispheric cooperation. The convergence of interests between Washington and Latin America that took shape with the end of the cold war made the breakthrough possible.[55] In the absence of competition between the superpowers, and in the face of growing globalization, Latin American states were prepared to use the OAS as a means to promote a cooperative rather than a balancing relationship with the United States. Neither the commitment to action nor the internal structural dynamic are replicated in Africa within the OAU.

In the 1990s, a "three-leg hemispheric system" took shape, consisting of the regional institutions (the OAS, the Inter-American Development Bank, the UN Economic Commission for Latin America and the Caribbean

[ECLAC]), the ministerial meetings and working groups set in motion by the Miami summit, and the growing array of partnerships between public sector agencies and civil society organizations to implement the Miami decisions.[56] Where the OAS had once claimed exclusive preserve over Latin America, new "opportunities emerged for OAS-UN cooperation in conflict resolution, peacekeeping, and the promotion of human rights and democracy. While the United Nations has taken the lead (for example, El Salvador) in some instances, there has also been an effective division of labor between the two organizations (for example, Nicaragua, with the OAS monitoring elections in the context of the UN Observer Mission and disarming and reintegrating the Contras in the framework of the Commission for International Support and Verification, and Haiti, with the OAS mission and then a UN peace enforcement and peacekeeping operation).[57] In other cases, the OAS retained its leading role (for example, Panama, in negotiations to end Manuel Noriega's dictatorship, and with Peru and Ecuador, to end the border dispute). The OAS was the first regional body that could suspend a member state if its democratic government is overthrown, an initiative followed in the Kampala Principles in 1991 and in the OAU in 1999 to be used against Ivory Coast the following year. Thus the Inter-American regime of cooperation—though not without limitations—has already taken significant steps toward collective action to respond to intrastate violence and instability, whereas ASEAN and Africa are still mostly at the dialogue stage of dealing with such problems.[58]

Evolution of OAS Norms and Collective Security

The OAS has a long history of articulating and implementing regional norms. A key aspect of the OAS's evolution has been the shift from declarations to the development of collective means to enforce compliance. An emerging consensus favors problem-solving approaches over legal safeguards, which had been a pervasive cultural preference among many Latin American states. They still express concern that the push to legitimize intervention will serve to justify the imposition of political interests, but the traditional emphasis on sovereignty and nonintervention as the bedrock of OAS cooperation protects against these dangers.[59] Squaring the needs of normative compliance and of sovereignty continues to be a challenge to the OAS, as it is in the Kampala Document, but has not yet come to be in the OAU.

The OAS has interpreted the principle of nonintervention as "excluding only forcible unilateral intervention, and not as an obstacle for collective action by the organization in matters concerning the survival of a democratic government."[60] In effect, sovereignty is only honored in countries with democratically elected governments. This basis for intervention contrasts with international law, which has moved toward intervention on humanitarian grounds.[61] So, for the OAS, *peaceful* collective action and protection of democracy are the pillars of a new doctrine. This still means that no unilateral intervention is acceptable.

COLLECTIVE DEFENSE AND PEACEFUL SETTLEMENT. Collective defense and collective security have been the basis of cooperation in the OAS, though a main impediment has always been a "strong bias against foreign invaders so that no collective initiative was conceived of to defend one member from another."[62] The Inter-American System for Latin American States was a means not to legitimate but to contain American power. So the central norm was nonintervention, as found in article 18 of the OAS Charter. Until 1970 the focus was on the peaceful settlement of disputes and diplomatic means; more than twelve bilateral and two hemispheric treaties on arbitration, mediation, and conciliation of disputes were signed between 1920 and 1970 but rarely applied. The formalistic nature of the instruments, with the lack of an enforcement mechanism, reflects the members' reluctance to use them, problems not unlike those found in ASEAN with the creation of the High Council and in the OAU with its stillborn Commission on Mediation, Arbitration, and Conciliation.

The OAS members have also had recourse to the Inter-American Treaty of Reciprocal Assistance signed in Rio de Janeiro in 1947, which has been more frequently invoked. Providing for collective defense against outsiders, as well as collective security for member states against one another, the Rio Treaty and its peaceful dispute settlement mechanisms have been applied to the 1949 and 1955 Nicaragua–Costa Rica disputes, the 1957 Honduras–Nicaragua conflict, and the 1969 El Salvador–Honduras Soccer War.[63] Nevertheless, they were not used during the Falklands War, nor did they deal with the Nicaraguan conflict during the 1980s, thus damaging their normative development.[64]

Many Latin American peacekeeping interventions have relied not on the traditional model of the impartial outsider expert but rather on a partial insider mediator. Central Americans—like Africans—typically look for "confianza," or trust, rather than neutrality in a third party. Unlike neutral outsiders chosen for their lack of ties with disputants, partial insiders are selected precisely for their close relations, positive connections, and personal attributes. "This *confianza* ensures sincerity, openness, and revelation and is a channel through which negotiation is initiated and pursued." [65] The combination of partial insiders and neutral outsiders played an important role in the peace process in Central America, as it also did in the Equipulas Group led by Costa Rican president Oscar Arias. These partial insiders laid the groundwork for the end to the fighting in El Salvador in 1988 and negotiations with the Sandinistas, and an agreement for Nicaraguan elections and Contra demobilization and repatriation, as well as other accords that set in motion the regionwide peace process.[66] The United Nations, as a neutral outsider, brought much-needed resources to provide the security and vast social, financial, and political assistance needed. It also built on U.S.-Soviet interests in defusing regional conflicts.[67]

Latin America and Africa share a major success in nuclear nonproliferation. The Treaty of Tlatelolco—like the Pelindaba Treaty in Africa—is a landmark achievement.[68] The Argentinean and Brazilian about-face on nuclear competition turned a rivalry into a partnership, with the establishment of unprecedented mechanisms of mutual confidence and transparency, and, with Chile, a ban on chemical and bacteriological weapons.[69] But the proliferation of small arms and mines and the rapid rise in violent crime remain major concerns.[70]

PROMOTION OF DEMOCRACY. As the cold war ended, the promotion of democracy acquired new life as a norm of the OAS, although it had been part of the organization's traditional discourse. The principle of democratic governance was formalized already in the Conference of Washington of 1907 for the Central American region, in the 1936 Declaration of the Principles of Inter-American Solidarity and Cooperation of the Inter-American Conference on the Consolidation of Peace, and in chapter 2 of the Bogota Charter, which called for effective exercise of representative democracy. But the post–cold war era is different: "The current promotion of formal democracy is not necessarily a product of Washington's hegemonic interest. The democracy rule rather seems to resemble a unanimous distaste for power concentration in the hands of a few and a rejection of the corrupt practices and repressive methods of military dictatorships."[71] Now the pursuit of democracy is driving cooperation in the OAS and has put the OAS in the lead in the shaping of international law.

The elevation of the protection of democracy to a "regional entitlement" has been accompanied by the weakening of sovereignty and nonintervention principles on the one hand, and the emergence of a human rights regime on the other (developments that opened the door to UN-OAS task-sharing in Latin America). The origins of the new attention to the right to democracy lie in a resolution the OAS passed in 1979 calling for the replacement of the Nicaraguan dictator Somoza and installation of democracy and a multiparty government, legitimizing among others the Sandinista revolutionary movement. By the early 1990s, the OAS had passed resolutions also condemning dictatorial regimes in Panama, Peru, Guatemala, and Haiti and became involved in the 1989–90 electoral observation mission to Nicaragua, thus awakening from nearly a decade of inaction. The OAS members, unlike the OAU members, have not hesitated to pronounce and even act on the governance systems of their neighbors.

Several documents are key to the elaboration of the right to democracy. First, the Special General Assembly of the OAS held in Cartagena, Colombia, in 1985 produced the Protocol Amendment to the OAS Charter, to state that "representative democracy is an indispensable condition for the stability, peace and development of the region."[72] Chapter 1 of the charter was also amended to read that an essential purpose of the OAS was the promotion and consolidation of representative democracy with due respect for the principle of nonintervention. These normative changes provided a basis for more than twenty electoral missions organized by the OAS since 1989,[73] despite some failures, such as the inability to bring about changes in Panama with Gen. Manuel Noriega or in Haiti with Gen. Raoul Cedras.

The groundwork for implementation was laid in May 1991 by a declaration by the Presidential Council of the Andean Group, calling for an amendment to the OAS Charter to provide for immediate collective suspension of diplomatic relations with any member of the organization in the event of an illegal interruption of the constitutional system. In response, the General Assembly in Santiago in 1991 adopted the Santiago Commitment to Democracy and the Renewal of the Inter-American System, and also the related OAS General Assembly Resolution 1080 on Representative Democracy.

The approach is largely political, and as critics point out, the mechanism lacks teeth. Whenever there is a threat to democratic political processes, the secretary general of the OAS activates a response by convening the Permanent Council to make recommendations for individual member states to take action. This move has allowed the OAS to respond in the Haitian, Peruvian, and Guatemalan crises to defend democracy, and gives the OAS a normative basis to legitimize UN intervention, as was necessary in the Haitian case to give teeth to the OAS embargo.[74] The OAU adopted a similar commitment in July 1999 in Algiers, to be used in 2000, to refuse a seat to the Ivory Coast junta, but further tests are yet to come. The African body is hampered by the fact that it is peopled with nondemocratically elected heads of state. It must first change its membership, so that a pro-democracy regime can protect, not threaten, its members.

HUMAN RIGHTS. The OAS is also developing a human rights regime, whose roots run deep. Seven months before the Universal Declaration on Human Rights in 1948, the American states had adopted an American Declaration on Human Rights. The Charter of Bogotá is also explicit on human rights and democracy: its preamble states "the true significance of American solidarity and good neighborliness can only mean the consolidation on this continent, within the framework of democratic institutions, of a system of individual liberty and social justice based on respect for the essential rights of man."[75] Brazil even wanted to make the entry of member states into the OAS contingent on adoption of a democratic form of government and the guarantee of fundamental human rights.[76] The legal character of human rights protection has been further developed through other inter-American instruments, including the 1969 American Convention on Human Rights, the Inter-American Convention to Prevent and Punish Torture, the Inter-American Convention on the Forced Disappearance of Persons, among others.

The supervisory role in human rights rests with the Inter-American Commission on Human Rights (IACHR) and the Inter-American Court on Human Rights, which has been instrumental in improving member governments' observance of basic rights through persuasion and publication.[77] Its annual reports include sections on individual countries and cases, and its special reports have effectively challenged dictatorial abuses and helped transitional processes in Argentina, Nicaragua, and El Salvador. The IACHR can launch inquiries without the approval of the General Assembly or the secretary general. However, the work of the court has become more complicated and sensitive now that it is dealing with democratic societies, and with terrorism, narcotics trade, and violent crimes. There is also an influential network of human rights nongovernmental organizations that have worked with the Inter-American Commission on Human Rights and have helped to prosecute cases.[78] Africa voted its Charter of Individual and Group Rights only two decades after the founding of the OAU, and its exercise has been thin as yet, a gap the Kampala Movement seeks to fill.

INTERNAL SECURITY. The real source of conflict in the 1990s is not interstate but intrastate, stemming from many social and economic forces: challenges of the second-generation economic reforms, fragile democracies, poverty, corruption, terrorism, drugs, migration, and so on. In response to these problems, the OAS began a series of initiatives in the early 1990s leading to the development of a framework agreement, Cooperation for Security and Development in the Hemisphere: Regional Contributions to Global Security. The document covers socioeconomic conditions in relation to security, and specific goals and objectives on arms control, transparency in arms acquisition, and reporting of UN and global efforts.

Latin America, especially at the bilateral level, had a history of engaging in confidence building measures long before these ideas became the focus of attention in Europe in the CSCE negotiations.[79] These are significant achievements in any conflict, but perhaps more so in Latin America where such measures challenge the traditional primacy of the military in military-political relations and are often seen by the military as a means of reducing their numbers, budgets, and influence, and of conducting spying (a view that reinforced the military's assumptions of the United Nations acting as a front for leftists forces in the world). At the same time, civilians in Latin America are not accustomed to discussing security affairs.[80] Other challenges remain, especially in promoting confidence building measures to deal with internal problems, such as ideological conflicts between the military and political leadership, as in Guatemala, or transnational threats, such as terrorism and drug trafficking, or inadequate funding of postconflict peace building, as in Nicaragua and in El Salvador.

The generals of Latin America will not easily give away their privileges, but there has been some pressure for change. For example, some generals in

Argentina responsible for the "dirty wars" of 1976–82 were brought to trial, thus improving transparency in civil-military relations and helping to dismantle the authoritarian state. Similar developments have also transpired in Brazil. But the situation in Chile is still clouded by General Pinochet's involvement in the political process. In other countries such as Peru and Colombia, guerilla insurgencies complicate the process of creating more open civilian-military relations.

In general, the OAS and its members are far ahead of Africa in establishing regimes for security and stability. Part of the reason for this advance lies in the longer history and experience in institutionalized relations in a continent that achieved independence nearly a century and a half before Africa did. But part comes from the internal developments in Latin American states, where democratic regimes found it in their interest to promote democracy, human rights, and collective security. On this model, new regimes in Africa depend on new regimes in African countries, and in turn on the development of civil society to press for reforms and hold their governments accountable.

Europe, North America, and the OSCE

The OSCE is the institutionalized regime closest to—and indeed the model for—the Conference on Security, Development, and Cooperation in Africa (CSSDCA). An initial glance shows that the OSCE arose, however, from a very different context than did the CSSDCA. The European organization evolved from an effort in the midst of a delicately controlled local conflict to contain the conflict's effects and restrain its participants. It was built on existing international organizations, provided an overarching framework for them, and filled gaps in their operations. In these characteristics, it bears some resemblance to the CSSDCA. Like the CSSDCA, the OSCE was supported from the beginning by a vigorous net of organizations and activities in civil society, which continue and are crucial to its existence, a fact that may instruct the Kampala Movement.

The OSCE has been central in overcoming the structures of cold war confrontation and promoting democratization, conflict prevention, and postconflict rehabilitation in the post–cold war period. The OSCE stems from the 1975 Helsinki Final Act, the keystone document signed by the original thirty-five participating states from Eastern and Western Europe and North America. The 1990s have seen the transformation of the OSCE from a cold war multilateral conference process (known as the Conference on Security and Cooperation in Europe, or CSCE) into an international organization and regime. With these institutional changes, the OSCE has placed greater emphasis on implementation and action, which is reflected in its increasing number of field operations. By 1999 nineteen missions were deployed throughout Europe and parts of the former Soviet Union. The Verification Mission deployed to Kosovo in October 1998 is the largest and most complex operation to date, with up to 2,000 verifiers.

Since its inception, the CSCE's main contribution has been in soft security. During the cold war, it helped to promote the idea of the indivisibility of security across a divided Europe and the close relationship between individual security and security between states. To these ends, the CSCE developed numerous human rights standards and measures for building confidence and security. The end of the cold war substantially altered the nature of the security threats facing Europe, forcing the OSCE like ASEAN, and the OAS, and presumably the OAU—to retool and adapt institutional structures and goals. As in other regions, including Africa, intrastate conflict and democratization are among the most pressing challenges, and for this reason the OSCE remains the pacesetter, as well as original model, for the CSSDCA.

The OSCE had its origins in a 1954 Soviet proposal to convene an all-European security conference. This meeting would have excluded North American participation, so it was rejected by the West. Other Soviet bloc proposals followed but failed for similar reasons. What finally succeeded was an initiative launched by Finland to convene a security conference that would involve all concerned states, including the United States and Canada, as well as the neutral and nonaligned countries. Finland carried out the critical third-party role necessary for facilitating prenegotiation and agenda building and engendering the commitment of potential participants to commence multilateral preparatory talks outside Helsinki in November 1972. The same role is played in Africa by Nigeria, although not as a small-state mediator but as a large principal state.

Two main concerns formed the basis of the initial bargain that established the regime: the Soviets' insistence on recognition of the "immutability of

European frontiers" and the West's insistence on a human rights agenda, which it sought to include partly to assure both Eastern governments and its own domestic audience that "security and status quo are not entirely synonymous."[81] The effect of the West's emphasis on freer movement initiatives (for example, individuals, information, cultural exchanges, emigration) as its sine qua non for convening the CSCE was to polarize the negotiating dynamics. The bargaining thus involved trading off recognition of frontiers in exchange for the right of free movement of people and the guarantee of human rights. Balancing progress in security with improvements in human rights became the primary engine behind the development of the CSCE process during the cold war. While such values, and others, are present in the Kampala Document, they do not provide the elements for internal bloc cohesion or for a founding trade-off.

Three coalitions from the outset wielded power over the CSCE's emergence. The NATO allies, in Europe and North America, made up the Western bloc. They did not always act with one voice, as European Community members sometimes presented their own proposals and often adopted an independent position as a means to promote European political cooperation.[82] However, to coordinate the Western position in CSCE negotiations, EC states caucused first, then NATO. The Nixon-Kissinger administration saw the CSCE as a regional enterprise that could jeopardize bilateral U.S.-Soviet accommodation on strategic nuclear issues, Vietnam, and other regional security issues. While the EC emphasized human rights, the U.S. demands were limited to obtaining agreement based on mutual respect for different systems of government and nonintervention in internal affairs.[83] The second major coalition consisted of the Warsaw Pact states of the Eastern bloc.

By default more than design, the third principal grouping consisted of the neutral and nonaligned (N+N) countries in Europe: Finland, Austria, Sweden, Switzerland, and Yugoslavia, along with such microstates as Cyprus, the Holy See, Liechtenstein, Malta, Monaco, and San Marino. Finland's early role as "conductor" in orchestrating the Dipoli Consultations may also have contributed to expectations that the N+N should perform intermediary services to overcome the polarized atmosphere of the talks. The third-party role was also necessitated by the rule of consensus, as much as the complex nature of multilateral negotiations among thirty-five participating states dealing with a multi-issue agenda. Thus the N+N was indispensable in engendering commitments between East and West through the use of compromise language carefully vetted across the bloc lines. In so doing, they often kept the CSCE negotiations alive. Such coalition dynamics are not as well developed in Africa. A similarly sized multilateral negotiation of some fifty states does not rest on a similar structure. All states fear parts of the Kampala regime to some extent, and none has specific demands to trade off in a creative bargain. Yet, at the same time, all states to some extent feel a need to remedy the problems that the Kampala Movement targets. If the OSCE (like the OAS and ASEAN) was created through coalition efforts, the CSSDCA depends on effort of accretion, a gradual gathering of support for the entire program rather than exchanges of concession among blocs.

OSCE Norms and Principles

According to the rules of procedures, all states were to participate in the CSCE as sovereign equals in a decisionmaking process guided by the rule of consensus. Defined as the absence of any objections to the decision in question, the consensus rule meant that final agreements would either be reduced to the least common denominator, or they would depend on some element of integration as well as trade-offs and package deals.

The Helsinki Final Act is a wide-ranging framework agreement. Politically but not legally binding, it encompasses four "baskets," a reference to the four main subjects of negotiation: security in basket 1, cooperation in basket 2, human rights (related to Kampala's stability calabash) in basket 3, and implementation in basket 4, one short of the development component of the CSSDCA.

The Final Act sets out standards and principles of security for states among states, norms for a nation's treatment of its own people, and guidelines for international cooperation involving people-to-people contacts. Security of the individual, based on respect for human rights, is set out as a fundamental aspect of interstate security. The multidimensionality of the CSCE concept of security empowers people to demand of their own state the fulfillment of its international obligations and to pressure their governments to hold other states accountable for violations. Cooperation in the CSCE is not seen as an end in itself but as directly related to improving mutual understanding, confidence, friendly and good-neighborly relations, international peace and justice.

The Final Act is a result of compromises between the socialist camp's insistence on the primacy of nonintervention in internal affairs (principle 6) and the West's emphasis on human rights and international cooperation. Thus the West relied on the human rights provisions included in basket 3 and principle 7 on Respect for Human Rights and Fundamental Freedoms to challenge the Soviet attempts to limit the Final Act's scope based on principle 6. The West sought to balance principle 6 with principle 10, fulfillment in good faith of obligations under international law. The West joined the N+N in seeking to delimit the East's recourse to nonintervention in internal affairs as a defense against noncompliance on such matters as human rights.

The CSCE's effectiveness resided partly in the "interdependence which unites rigorously all its components . . . [and] forms an indivisible whole that requires parallel and even progress" across all of its substantive areas.[84] This principle of interdependence lent itself to greater rigor in the follow-up processes, providing a justification for the West to return to a review of implementation of CSCE principles and commitments (as new Eastern bloc human rights violations came to light), even when the negotiators had already finished the review of implementation to consider other matters, such as new commitments. If the baskets—"calabashes" in African parlance—in the Kampala Document found their inspiration in the Helsinki Final Act, the Kampala Movement did not rest on any trade-off similar to Helsinki's that engaged the opposition in the negotiations and locked it into support of the documents' principles.

The Final Act broke new ground in two areas—multilateral approaches to confidence and security building measures in Europe (admittedly modest efforts at first) and human rights. But the latter had a penetrating character from the outset that extended beyond traditional human rights instruments. The CSCE commitments entered into matters traditionally left to the discretion of the states concerned, which, by the 1990s, came to include the structure of government, rule of law, and democratic pluralism. As Arie Bloed notes, "The myth that the political system of a state is irrelevant for adequate protection of human rights has been definitively discarded."[85]

How to proceed beyond the signing of the Helsinki Final Act was a sticking point in the initial negotiations. The Soviet Union's early enthusiasm for promoting the CSCE's institutionalization gave way to restraint as the political nature of the bargain became clear. Instead, the Soviet Union sought a speedy closure on the negotiations and a final agreement based on vague recommendations for further cooperation. Because of the consensus rule, the possibilities for institutionalizing the CSCE from the outset were circumscribed, despite support from some Western countries and many neutral and nonaligned states. The Final Act limited the continuation of the CSCE to a vaguely conceived follow-up meeting to be held in Belgrade in 1977, and participating states were charged to pay due regard to and implement the provisions of the Final Act unilaterally, bilaterally, and multilaterally; proceed to a thorough exchange of views on the implementation of the provisions of the Final Act and, in this context, to deepen their mutual relations; and continue the multilateral process. This meant that from the outset, the CSCE's capacities to monitor compliance to the Final Act, take enforcement action, or set news standards and promote regime governance were minimal.

Ultimately, though, implementation has not been a rote process but rather a creative and inventive one that extends into the postagreement phase of negotiations: new normative commitments to extend or delimit the scope of the Final Act and procedures to institutionalize the CSCE. These challenges were faced in the first of three follow-up conferences held in Belgrade (1977–78), Madrid (1980–83), and Vienna (1986–89), as well as numerous intersessional meetings of experts. The November 1990 summit meeting of the CSCE was the culminating event that led to the adoption of the Charter of Paris. This manifesto marked a watershed in East-West relations and the metamorphosis of the conference into an organization. Since then, follow-up meetings have taken place in Helsinki (1992), Budapest (1994), Lisbon (1996), and Istanbul (1999), and intersessional meetings have also been held. However, these postagreement negotiations became somewhat less important as the OSCE developed during the interim into a formal international organization.

Managing East-West Conflict

That the CSCE started out as a political, not legal, agreement enabled participating states to adjust their negotiating positions rapidly to changing conditions on the ground in Eastern Europe.[86] Like traditional human rights instruments, which often start with general principles, a few specific rules, and some exceptions, the CSCE began with a general statement on human rights, to which each succeeding CSCE agreement added commitments, better-defined rules, and clarifications of their scope. As Thomas Burgenthal notes, "This type of interpretive rule-making takes the place of judicial interpretation. While not adjudicatory in character, it serves to anticipate and resolve disputes about the specific meaning of CSCE commitments. It also promotes compliance by eliminating or weakening legal arguments advanced to excuse nonperformance."[87] Through a diplomacy of public shaming, the West sought to plug the loopholes and eliminate the ambiguities planted by the East to avoid compliance. For example, the CSCE was able to introduce new human contacts provisions in Madrid to counter the imposition of martial law in Poland and score pioneering breakthroughs on human dimension commitments (for example, national minority rights in Copenhagen in 1990) even as the East-West system was changing underfoot.

These products of postagreement negotiations may be viewed as authentic interpretations of the Final Act. Some subsequent provisions encompass recommendations within the domain of the Final Act, but which the Final Act had not dealt with in concrete terms or only developed in limited fashion (for example, disarmament, minority rights), whereas others modify the substance of the previous recommendations (for example, confidence and security building measures, human rights). The Belgrade negotiations and the Madrid follow-up opened an important debate on expanding the military-security dimension of the Helsinki Final Act and agreed on an improved regime on confidence building measures—renamed confidence and security building measures (CSBMs)—negotiated at the 1986 Stockholm Conference on Disarmament in Europe.[88] These provisions marked a breakthrough in East-West security negotiations in the post–World War II era and prepared the way for on-site inspection in the U.S.-Soviet Intermediate Nuclear Forces agreement of 1987 as a means to verify the dismantling of intermediate-range nuclear weapons.

The CSCE on-site inspection provisions also set precedents for more intrusive mechanisms for human rights. The first nonvoluntary CSCE human rights mechanism was agreed at the Vienna follow-up meeting (1986–89).[89] Approximating an interstate complaints procedure, the Vienna Mechanism (used extensively during the transition period to the post–cold war era, and at least seventy times during 1989) allows for a system of supervision that can function permanently whenever any state wishes to apply the mechanism to obtain information from another state on possible violations. This provision includes a binding commitment to hold bilateral meetings with other participating states to examine the situation and provide notification about the situation to all CSCE states. To the previously limited intergovernmental procedures, the Moscow Mechanism in September 1991 added a system of missions of independent experts, or rapporteurs, who can be sent to a state against the state's will, as long as the initiating state has the support of at least five other CSCE states.

The Vienna meeting of the CSCE was also a turning point in the development of consensual understanding on human rights and on the formal observance and domestication of the CSCE principles in the legislative practices, foreign policy initiatives, and treaties of participating states. By the conclusion of the Vienna meeting, the idea of human rights was taking shape as one of the elements uniting Europe, to redress an overemphasis, as perceived in the West, on the military dimension since the Madrid follow-up meeting and the 1984 Stockholm Conference on Disarmament in Europe (CDE).[90]

The OSCE's Post–Cold War Mission

The CSCE was not the only East-West institution that, having fulfilled its basic purpose, had to find a new reason to exist after the revolutions in eastern Europe in 1989 and 1990. NATO and the Warsaw Pact faced similar challenges in the changed political landscape. At the same time, the OAS and ASEAN lost their roles as participant and nonaligned coalitions in the cold war, respectively, and the OAU lost its collective defense mission as a national liberation coalition. Power differentials among the CSCE participating states became more salient in the redefinition of its purposes than they had been during the previous regime-building processes, producing the type of "new CSCE" that emerged during the first few years following the end of the cold war. The powerful states became more active; the regime was established, and it was now able to limit the efforts of new power contenders (especially Germany) and smaller aligned, neutral, and nonaligned states to make the CSCE into a regional security organization with "teeth."

Of particular significance was the failure in Paris to create a stronger Conflict Prevention Center (CPC) as part of the new institutional structure. The initial German proposals, and those of smaller countries like

Czechoslovakia, had called for the CPC to be at the origins of a European collective security system, which would replace the two alliances. Despite initial support from the Soviet Union and the Eastern bloc, as well as the appearance of a similar Canadian proposal, the project for developing a strong CPC was met with resistance by the United States, France, and the United Kingdom, who presented alternative proposals.[91] The United States pushed for the primacy of NATO, whereas the French-British proposal limited the CPC to support for the implementation of CSBMs and to a procedure for the conciliation of disputes. Motivated by fear of precedents that might be established for actions elsewhere, the Soviets took the lead in preventing the CSCE from intervening in Yugoslavia, arguing that the CSCE should prevent only conflicts between countries and not interfere in disputes within states. U.S. reservations, the lack of Soviet influence, German unification, and continued adherence to NATO produced a post–cold war OSCE based on a minimal organizational structure and a mixture of old and new practices for follow-up and expert meetings and substance. [92]

The OSCE decisionmaking process still includes summits, but the central responsibilities rest with the Ministerial Council and Permanent Council. Decisions are still adopted according to the consensus principle, although in January 1992 it was decided that in cases of clear, gross, and uncorrected violation of OSCE commitments, action could be taken without the consent of the state concerned. This option was exercised first regarding the conflict in the former Yugoslavia (Serbia and Montenegro) in 1992, leading to Yugoslavia's suspension. There is also a provision for consensus-minus-two, by which the OSCE can call on two participating states in dispute to seek conciliation, but this measure has not been invoked. The secretary general's office also assumed some of the responsibilities of the Vienna Conflict Prevention Center, which was transferred and made subordinate to it by decision of the December 1993 Rome Council. The Office on Democratic Institutions and Human Rights (ODIHR) has assumed certain supervisory functions in the human dimension, including in relation to the Moscow Mechanism, and established guidelines and procedures for creating democratic electoral systems.[93] At the 1994 Budapest summit, the OSCE also adopted the Code of Conduct, a landmark development in security cooperation that breaks new ground with new norms regulating military-civilian relations in democratic societies. The Economic Forum (strongly advocated by the United States as a means of averting the rise of pan-European economic cooperation through the European Union) oversees monitoring of economic and environmental developments, with an eye to alerting OSCE states of any threat of conflict, as well as facilitating economic and environmental policies of participating states with transitional economies.

The OSCE parliamentary body provides another avenue for political dialogue, although it is only advisory and has no enforcement powers. The parliament has favored enhancing the OSCE's collective security functions and creating its own third-party missions. It has presented extensive recommendations for improving the overall capabilities of the OSCE and has helped promote consensus on new norms and cooperation leading up to the 1999 Istanbul summit meeting.[94]

As the ethnic conflict escalated in Yugoslavia and elsewhere in the former communist states, UN Secretary General Boutros Boutros Ghali called on the CSCE to respond more effectively. This required new definitions of the "problem" to be dealt with among CSCE participating states, to include intrastate conflict, national minorities, policy guidelines, agreed measures for a situation in which violations of national minority rights called for CSCE action, and appropriate instruments.

Subsequently, national minority rights have been treated in several CSCE documents, although the Copenhagen Report of the Conference on the Human Dimension of the CSCE (1990), and to a lesser extent the Report of the Geneva Meeting of Experts on National Minorities of July 1991, embodied the major achievements within the CSCE and also constituted progress on the international level.[95]

Additional provisions for national minority rights were not reached without causing concern among participating states that the privileged treatment of national minorities could compromise the territorial integrity of the national state, a concern clearly expressed in paragraph 37 of the Copenhagen Report. While the CSCE championed the right of self-determination of peoples, it did not refer to a right to secession as a principle of international law. The right of self-determination was rather viewed in the context of the standards for state behavior in cultural expression, religion, language, human contacts, democracy, education, science and commerce, and political expression, including the possibility for autonomous administration.

The OSCE institutional response to the challenges of national minorities has its most innovative tool in the office of the High Commissioner on National Minorities (HCNM), which can gather information, carry out visits, and promote dialogue on situations that could develop into conflicts. The goal of the office of the High Commissioner is to de-escalate tensions, improve relations, and facilitate recourse to nonviolent methods to solve problems. If dissatisfied with the results, the office of the High Commissioner may issue an "early warning," calling for further action by the Permanent Council and member states. Former Dutch foreign minister Max van der Stoel, who served as high commissioner since the creation of the post, has received high marks for his efforts involving minorities in numerous OSCE states, including Albania, Croatia, Estonia, the former Yugoslav Republic of Macedonia, Hungary, Kazakhstan, Kyrgyzstan, Latvia, Romania, Slovakia, and the Ukraine.

As the example of the High Commissioner on National Minorities illustrates, mechanisms for conflict prevention and management, which are the most flexible politically, have proved to be of most use. The OSCE has made its greatest impact through the use of a variety of "missions." Numbering nearly two dozen, they include an OSCE presence in Bosnia, Chechnya, Nagorno-Karabakh, Moldova, Belarus, Tajikistan, as well as many of the places where the HCNM has been active. Further, recognition is growing that efforts to apply these third-party tools must be coupled with the promotion of democratization, economic development, consistency in human rights monitoring, and postconflict peace building to ensure a comprehensive approach to the construction of a peaceful civil society and unity across Europe. Thus the organization is an exemplary flexible political regime that has emerged pragmatically. Its norms and institutional structure are evolving, epitomizing a process to which the Kampala Movement aspires.

Conclusions

Much of the literature on regional regimes suggests the possibility of the Kampala Movement looking to the OSCE, the OAS, or ASEAN as models. If the Kampala Movement in Africa draws its inspiration from Helsinki and the OSCE, the OAU was modeled on the OAS and is similar to ASEAN. At the same time, each of these institutions has drawn from deeply rooted regional traditions to promote security, development, and cooperation. However, certain overarching factors seem important for the emergence and development of cooperation. Appropriate leadership is one such component, which may come in the form of a regional hegemon or from a driving coalition mediating between blocs. The end of the cold war has also underscored the way the structure of the international system creates incentives and challenges for regional regimes, not only at the infrequent times of sea change but also in the long stretch. As illustrated by the efforts of ASEAN, the OAS, and the OSCE to retool themselves to deal with transnational problems, democratization, and intrastate conflicts, an important ingredient of regional cooperation is the learning curve that attends institutional change and innovation.

ASEAN does not fit typical neoliberal theories in its development, which assume the emergence of an issue-oriented regime and elaboration through spillover effects.[96] It has prospered by avoiding clearly defined institutional structures and legalistic commitments and, like the OSCE, has also shown that slow, gradual regional political cooperation can be a powerful strategy for regional peace. Several factors have been key to its resilience: the determination of members, its own momentum, and the establishment of clear rules of conduct for all to follow. Yet these factors have related to internal relations among members, not to some galvanizing external threat (as happened with the OAU) or even internal containment (as with the OAS). Indonesia's abandonment of its confrontational foreign policy and commitment to regional harmony—much like the Soviet Union's policy shift in the OSCE and South Africa—were key in launching and building ASEAN. For Indonesia, ASEAN has served as a "golden cage" that allowed the New Order government under President Suharto, who took over from President Sukarno in 1966, to stress political stability and economic development by pursuing regional harmony. For other ASEAN states, similar incentives were at work, including the attraction of foreign investment and development assistance.

Membership in ASEAN was also seen as a "bulwark" against communism during the cold war, which helped it obtain assistance from major donor countries and financial institutions. It was also a community of interest that could help to deal with Japan and China, much as the OAU was seen as a common protection against colonialism. The ASEAN ring of friendship provided a security buffer. Indonesia also believed that ASEAN enhanced its international status and afforded it some protection from international pressures, especially regarding East Timor. But ASEAN could protect Indonesia more efficiently during the cold war than after, when superpower competition no longer shaped the rules of the game and, instead, the West emphasized human rights and democracy. It was of no help in the East Timor crisis of 1999 or the subsequent internal threats to Indonesian national unity, just as the OAU faded into insignificance before the African crises in the central reform, including the Rwandan Genocide and the ongoing War of the Zairean Succession.

ASEAN members expected their association to help promote regional autonomy, based on the members' national and regional resilience. Good relations would reduce insecurity among smaller members and obviate the need for reliance on outside military protection. The Bangkok Declaration stated that foreign military bases in the region were temporary and should not be used against neighboring states. ASEAN has allowed member countries to carry out intensive and extensive military cooperation without need for a formal military alliance, which Indonesia has historically opposed. Yet despite calls to create a common security regime in Asia much like that which emerged in Europe, ASEAN members have resisted formalization and supranational arrangements. They are instead committed to a more flexible political approach and consultation to promote regional cooperation and security. African states within the OAU are not even close to forming a common security regime, which only underscores their need for a new set of norms.

The ASEAN experience is similar in many ways to Africa's experience with the OAU, but it does not give much insight into the prospects for OAU reform through a CSSDCA. ASEAN has not had its "reform," as the CSSDCA challenges the OAU to carry out. ASEAN structures and practices have been culturally grounded—like those of the OAU—and generally adequate to ASEAN's challenges and problems—unlike the experience of the OAU— even if ASEAN still faces considerable hurdles to becoming a truly effective regional tool for the promotion of peace and comprehensive security.

The OAS institutional machinery was built under U.S. leadership to deter the Soviet threat. The Rio Pact and the OAS were classic collective defense arrangements with some reference to collective security. But integration is proceeding across Latin America and throughout the hemisphere, opening up new opportunities and relationships. A principal feature of inter-American —like inter-African—cooperation is the emergence of subregional group-ings in the 1980s and 1990s; in Latin America, these groups were originally security oriented, but they took on economic goals, the reverse of the African pattern. For example, the Esquipulas plan, which provided a framework for peace in Central America, restarted the Central American Common Market and the Alliance for Sustainable Development. By the mid-1990s, trade was growing in the region at nearly 25 percent a year. In South America, the Rio Group, originally formed to guide the Central American peace process, has continued to meet and coordinate foreign policy. Mercosur, the subregional free trade pact established in 1991 among Argentina, Brazil, Paraguay, and Uruguay (with Chile and Bolivia and associate members) has exceeded expectations, while traditional sources of border tensions in the Southern Cone have subsided. These developments point the way for Africa's sub-regional groupings, which still lag behind the Western Hemisphere's exam-ple in trade, integration, and development.

But the chief issues before Latin America today are transnational and will require new, more hemispheric solutions. On security matters and other issues like trade, human rights, environmental dangers, and narcotics, a pressing need for multilateral responses remains.[97] Subregional groupings lack resources to deal with complex transnational dilemmas. National mil-itaries have substantial economic and business interests at stake in the drug trade. The antinarcotics programs of the governments, especially Andean, have led to the remilitarization of the region, and U.S. support to Colombia will include considerable military aid to fight the war against drugs.

The OAS experience, like ASEAN, remains much more relevant to the OAU than to the CSSDCA. However, with the passing of the cold war, the OAS has sought to activate some of the values that the CSSDCA tries to instill in the OAU, especially regarding sovereignty and democratization. Both ASEAN and the OAS are turning to civil society to promote their goals and activities, whereas the Kampala Movement started from civil society.

The OSCE has also witnessed a thorough transformation since the end of the cold war from a diplomatic process of multilateral negotiations into a lightly bureaucratized international organization. It has taken the lead among regional organizations in developing innovative institutional approaches to prevent and manage conflict. In the OSCE, new norms and approaches are evolving, as illustrated by the new initiatives adopted at the 1999 Istanbul summit on ending trafficking in human beings, especially women and children, promoting children's rights, especially in war fighting zones, overcoming corruption, protecting minorities such as the Roma, establishing REACT missions (Rapid Expert Assistance and Cooperation Teams), and police-related activities as part of postconflict rehabilitation efforts. However, great power interests often pose barriers to effective and early intervention to prevent conflict, as the violence in Kosovo and Chechnya illustrate. Europe probably has the richest set of institutional resources, but overlapping mandates and bureaucratic interests also create competition in the field and the danger of competing goals. These problems also underscore the need for more effective division of labor and use of resources among international organizations, which figured into the 1999 OSCE Charter for European Security under its Platform for Security. Indeed, in Europe, Latin America, and Africa, creative task-sharing between international and regional organizations is likely to be a major challenge for regional organizations around the world well into the new millennium.

The OSCE is the model for the CSSDCA, but its conditions of formation and operation differ greatly from the African setting. The CSCE had no OAU to reform, and the CSSDCA has no cold war divide to overcome but also to exploit in crafting a basic bargain. Like the other two organizations, CSCE/OSCE invigorated a public policy network in civil society to support its work rather than growing out of civil society itself. All these differences suggest innovations that the Kampala Movement must invent on its own, in the absence of direct parallels to adopt, if it is to emulate even the partial success of its peers.

In conclusion, ASEAN, the OAS, and the OSCE succeeded where earlier initiatives to launch regional cooperation stalled or failed. They have built on their early success to enhance normative commitments and areas of cooperation. For ASEAN, this success has more recently meant launching discussions on early warning and conflict prevention and promoting grassroots cooperation. For the OAS, the 1990s marked a shift from a declaratory practice of supporting democracy to developing mechanisms for its protection. In the OSCE, there is still a large gulf between the availability of mechanisms for conflict early warning and prevention, and their effective deployment, as the recent tragedies of Kosovo and Chechnya illustrate. Each of these regional experiments offers many lessons in the possibilities and requirements for enhancing security, development, and cooperation. But perhaps the most important lesson is that each region found its own path for building greater communication, understanding, transparency, trust, and respect. In each case, this triumph was achieved only by means of concerted leadership efforts, persistence, and innovation, all of which formed part of an ongoing institutional learning process. These regional experiences serve as an inspiration to Africa. Nonetheless, these groups followed their own paths, and Africa must find its own way too.

4

An Evolving Framework

In May 1991, five hundred people from civil society organizations and governments, including a number of current and former African heads of state, gathered in Kampala, Uganda, to discuss security and stability in Africa. The result was a proposal to launch the Conference on Security, Stability, Development, and Cooperation in Africa (CSSDCA). This proposal, known as the Kampala Document, was the result of a civil society movement that had been gathering steam during the two years prior to the meeting. The document was submitted to the summit of the Organization of African Unity (OAU) in Abuja, Nigeria, in early June but was not adopted. What could have marked the beginning of a far-reaching and ambitious process of restructuring the political framework, in which the OAU had operated for almost thirty years, was stalled at the level of heads of state. In July 2001, the same proposal, now endorsed by the heads of state, was bypassed at the last OAU summit in Lusaka as the organization prepared to turn into an African union. This chapter analyzes the CSSDCA proposal process, including the conception of the idea, the development of the process, and the nature of the movement from civil society to the state level. Now, participants hope that civil society will again embrace the movement.

The Roots of the CSSDCA Proposal

The CSSDCA is the brainchild of Gen. Olusegun Obasanjo, the former Nigerian military leader who left the presidential office voluntarily in 1979 in favor of an elected government. He returned as the duly elected president of the country twenty years later, having served a prison term for trumped-up charges of involvement in a coup plot against the military dictatorship of Gen. Sami Abacha. In the interim, in 1988 Obasanjo established the Africa Leadership Forum (ALF), a nongovernmental organization which by 1991 had a mailing list of more than 3,000 people from all walks of life in all African countries and abroad.[1] The stated purpose of the ALF is to encourage "diagnosis, understanding, and an informed search for solutions to local, regional and global problems."[2] It aims at generating greater understanding of developmental and social problems by organizing and supporting programs for the training of young and promising Africans with leadership potential.

In a speech given shortly before he established the ALF, Obasanjo argued that Africa could no longer continue "its tendency to always find ready-made scapegoats for our problems."[3] While recognizing the damage that colonial rulers had done to the African people, Obasanjo rejected the tendency "indefinitely to blame the past for our present."[4] A central issue at the first meeting of the ALF was a call for "a systematical examination of the failures of past and current African leadership in the development process."[5] Besides a series of development seminars held on Obasanjo's farm in Nigeria, the ALF organized several international conferences addressing problems facing Africa. The idea of initiating a Conference on Security, Stability, Development, and Cooperation in Africa was first introduced at one of these conferences, in order to address the problems that had led to the establishment of the Africa Leadership Forum in the first place.

Africa's Internal Crisis

The decision to establish the ALF arose from the state of affairs on the African continent: "After a generation of independence, it had become clear that most of the hopes and aspirations which had provided the spur for our independence struggle had not been realized."[6] Three decades of economic decline led the continent into a deep crisis. Between 1960 and 1989, Africa's share of the world national product dropped from 1.9 to 1.2 percent.[7] At the end of the 1980s, Africa's debt was the equivalent of 350 percent of exports or more than 80 percent of total gross domestic product.[8] Food production had decreased by 20 percent since 1970, while the size of the population doubled.[9] Per capita income, already at its lowest for two decades, had fallen by a further 4.2 percent since 1986.[10] Numbers like these led scholars and politicians to refer to the 1980s as Africa's "lost decade" and to Africa as "the economic crisis of our planet."[11]

In his ALF inauguration speech, Obasanjo argued that the main causes of Africa's economic and other problems were political and stemmed from a failure to establish democratic practices in African countries. The lack of democratic institutions led to a failure to "stimulate the spring sources of creativity in our people."[12] Oppressive regimes led to uproar and internal crisis. Between the beginning of the 1960s and the end of the 1980s, Africa experienced some sixty coups d'état and countless other coup attempts.[13] Internal conflicts displaced masses of people, both within their countries of origin and across international borders. The outflow of refugees often resulted in the destabilization of neighboring countries and even of entire regions.

Besides creating difficult conditions for its people, Africa's political instability discouraged desperately needed foreign investment: "There is hardly an African country that has no border dispute with its neighbor. Military coups continue to raise and pull down governments and in some cases wars, civil or otherwise, continue to rage—some running for over twenty years now. In the face of this evidence, is there any wonder that foreign investors are reluctant to invest in Sub-Saharan Africa?"[14] This lack of investment was one of the main reasons behind the poor economic performance of Africa compared with other developing regions of the world.[15]

By the early 1990s, the Organization of African Unity (OAU) had proved ineffective in addressing the political crises of the continent. When the OAU was founded in 1963, it established a mechanism for resolution of conflicts between member states—the Commission for Mediation, Arbitration and Conciliation. The organization's emphasis on the principles of sovereignty and noninterference, however, prevented member states from ever using the body. Although the OAU did set up ad hoc committees to deal with certain disputes, these were also of limited success in resolving the region's bloodiest conflicts. Again, in the climate of nationalism and fragile independence of the postcolonial era, the norms that restrained external intervention worked against the effective management of internal conflicts and sheltered some of the most irresponsible leaders.[16]

Member states' opposition to any infringement of national sovereignty also prevented the creation of a political decisionmaking body with executive or advisory powers. The OAU therefore remained an organization without any authority to make and enforce decisions on member states.[17] According to a former secretary general of the OAU, William Eteki, the basic problem was that "the OAU, even in its Charter, is not a supranational body. It is a sort of institution that cannot impose any solution, and consequently is sometimes unable to implement its own resolutions."[18] In this, the OAU was like any other regional organization—or even global security organization like the United Nations—but the absence of both consensual norms and an effective institution was particularly hard felt in Africa.

The deteriorating economic and political crisis of the continent and the fact that the existing national and regional political structures proved inefficient in solving them were major factors of motivation behind the establishment of the ALF and the CSSDCA initiative. "Something had to be done," explained General Obasanjo, commenting on the establishment of the ALF in 1989.[19] The global context added possibility to urgency. The end of the cold war and the emergence of a new international system gave Africans hope that it would be possible to "do something," while at the same time strengthening the view that change was necessary.

Impact of the End of the Cold War

The most direct effect of the end of the cold war in Africa was the end of extensive superpower interference on the continent. Africa had been an object of ideological rivalry between the Soviet Union and the United States for decades, from Mozambique and Angola in the South to Ethiopia and Somalia in the Horn. But with the fall of the Berlin Wall, that situation changed. Suddenly, expectations about greater autonomy and self-determination created optimism about the future of the continent. There was a perception that the end of the cold war would make it possible to see regional and national problems in their proper context instead of as episodes in the proxy confrontation of the superpowers. Scholars and politicians talked about "a window of opportunity" and claimed that the stage was now set for the formulation of "African solutions to African problems."[20] Another course change gave Africans hope in their ability to prevail in handling their problems—the change of regime in South Africa. Apartheid had been a cancer in the African body, seemingly impervious to winds of change on the continent and to ostracism by the outside world. Yet without significant foreign mediation or intervention, and without war or revolution, Africans themselves overthrew apartheid, completing their self-determination, achieving peaceful settlement of internal conflict, and introducing democracy. The collapse of the Soviet Union also strengthened the democratic movement in Africa. "Events in Eastern and Central Europe and the Soviet Union demonstrated graphically the vulnerabilities of illegitimate regimes."[21] A combination of pressures from within and the demands of the post–cold war international climate led to political reforms in many African countries. In 1990 alone, fourteen African countries experienced popular movements in support of liberalization and democracy, and more countries introduced multiparty politics than in all of the previous twenty-five years.[22] There was talk of a "second independence" in Africa.

The initial optimism was soon replaced, however, by a concern about the role of Africa in the new international system—a system in which economics, and not ideology, was at the center stage. Considering Africa's depressing economic performance throughout the 1980s, Africans started to fear that their continent would become marginalized in the global economy and politics. At the inauguration of the ALF, Obasanjo expressed deep concern, not only about the economic crisis of the continent but about its relative decline in the world economic system, "We are moving backwards as the rest of the world is forging ahead."[23] This concern was rooted in a realization that Africa's economic performance increasingly depended on the policies of other countries. With enormous debt, dependence on foreign aid, and desperate need for foreign investment, Africa became especially vulnerable to other countries' policies. To remain a player on the international stage was therefore seen as the most efficient, if not the only, way to exercise some kind of political autonomy. As Obasanjo stated, "Those whose actions impinge on Africa for good or for ill must remain engaged with Africa in the demanding task of seeking workable solution to the problems of Africa."[24]

During the cold war, the ideological rivalry between the superpowers had provided African countries with some geopolitical and strategic relevance, and for decades Africa counted on the cold war as an economic resource. Once this rivalry no longer provided the context for international politics, Africa was less sure of economic support. The loss of economic support and political attention that came with great power involvement had great influence on the debate about Africa's relationship to other states:

> Debates about Africa used to pit internationalists concerned about big power rivalry against regionalists concerned with African issues. Ironically, the internationalists have now voluntarily ceded the field to the regionalists. The latter used to call for the major powers not to turn Africa into an international battlefield but rather to let Africans solve their own problems. Now that the internationalists have declared the game over, the regionalists are desperately searching for a rationale to keep external interest and resources focused on Africa.[25]

The end of the cold war thus had two general effects on the political climate in Africa. On the one hand, the withdrawal of the superpowers from the continent and the democratic movement sweeping the region created strong optimism about Africans' opportunity to solve their own problems. On the other hand, and perhaps paradoxically, the emergence of a new international system made Africans fear the consequences of the superpowers' abandonment and their increasing marginalization. The CSSDCA process was strongly shaped by both of these effects.

Visions of a Solution

At a conference in 1989, Obasanjo argued that greater economic cooperation and integration were needed to solve the problems that the African states were facing. "No African country on its own unaided efforts can pull itself up by its own bootstraps."[26] The urgency of regional and ultimately continental unification had repeatedly been endorsed by African leaders, including in the 1980 Lagos Plan of Action, but the goal of effective integration remained elusive. After thirty years of independence and collective commitment to achieving economic integration, inter-African trade still accounted for only 5 percent of the continent's trade flows. The dominant outward links of the African economies, the strong sense of affiliation to different monies and monetary zones, and unwillingness to relinquish national sovereignty over economic and social matters were factors that hindered economic integration.[27]

When the ALF was established in 1988, Obasanjo claimed that what was needed was political cooperation along with economic integration.[28] This view was shared by a number of African and non-African politicians and scholars, among them the French minister of cooperation and development, Jacques Pelletier. At a conference in the Ivory Coast in 1989, he urged Africa to establish regional markets along the lines planned in Europe, saying, "The changes in Europe are, to my mind, a model. Without a regional market, sub-Saharan Africa will not be organized on a sufficient scale to become an area of economic growth. Without political coordination in all areas—fiscal, social and legal—it will remain too weak in the face of the large groupings which are being established everywhere in the world."[29] Similarly, Sadig Rasheed argues that "in a world where trade blocks and barriers are increasingly being erected and fortified, Africa has little chance of survival outside an integration framework of its own."[30]

In the early 1990s, Africans were gravely concerned about developments in Europe, Africa's biggest trade partner. Not only would the establishment of the European Union in 1992 tighten economic cooperation among the western European countries, but the opening of eastern Europe at the end of the cold war had created a new region that was competing with Africa for access to investment capital and aid resources. With their more educated work force and relatively cheap wages, eastern European countries were often more appealing to investors. Former permanent secretary in the Kenyan Foreign Ministry B. A. Kiplagat explained, "Eastern Europe is the most sexy beautiful girl, and we are the old tattered lady. People are tired of Africa. So many countries, so many wars."[31] African leaders also felt that European Community officials had lost interest in the Lomé Convention, which was a key achievement in European negotiations and cooperation with African, Caribbean, and Pacific countries.[32] The much awaited "peace dividend" freed by the end of the cold war arms race was flowing not to the world's poorest countries, but back toward eastern Europe, to the extent that it was flowing at all and not simply staying home.

In April 1990, the ALF organized a conference in Paris on the consequences for African countries of the diversion of aid and capital flows to eastern Europe and the lessons for Africans from the process of development in eastern Europe.[33] The conclusion of the meeting was that Africa would continue to be marginalized in the world economy and in the international system unless a composite and pervasive solution was found to Africa's interconnected problems. Participants agreed that Africa's predicament derived as much from the perpetual state of insecurity and instability as from economic circumstances linked to its history. They concluded that the continent collectively should create stable conditions for development, which would also make it a more viable partner with the rest of the world.[34] The meeting produced detailed recommendations for African countries and organizations, including the convening of a Conference on Security, Stability, and Cooperation to establish a new regime of norms and practices.

Evolution of the CSSDCA

In the year after the CSSDCA was conceived, and before the proposal was put forward at the OAU, the ALF sought to raise awareness and support for the project. Members of the organization first needed to gauge the viability of the proposal. They established contacts with heads of regional organizations and eminent African personalities "in an effort to devise ways and means of advancing the CSSDCA initiative."[35] Talks were also held with non-African actors who were potential partners or could share lessons from the European experience. After five months, the ALF gained enough support and attention to convene a series of four conferences to discuss the CSSDCA proposal. The composition of participants in these conferences, held between November 1990 and May 1991, reflected some of the main ideas behind the initiative.

Brainstorming in Addis Ababa, November 1990

The first brainstorming meeting on the CSSDCA proposal reflected the core principle that African problems should be solved by Africans. Some thirty African politicians and scholars participated in their individual capacities at the meeting in Ethiopia, which was coconvened by ALF's chairman Olusegun Obasanjo, OAU secretary general Salim Ahmed Salim, and executive secretary of the United Nation's Economic Commission on Africa (ECA) Adebayo Adedeji. The purpose of this meeting was to examine the applicability of the European experience of constructing the Conference on Security and Cooperation in Europe (CSCE) to African issues.

In his opening statement, General Obasanjo called for a "New Deal" for Africa.[36] He argued that the African transformation would have to be based on two fundamental principles: first, "a recognition that a sound national economy is the only durable foundation for national security and political stability;" second, "a realization that . . . tolerance for opposing political systems is a necessary prerequisite for economic development." Obasanjo envisioned a triad built on security, pluralism, and economic cooperation as the foundation for a new normative framework for the continent. Participating nations would participate as sovereign states, but because of the nature of interdependence, the notion of sovereignty would be "tempered by endeavors allowing areas for a community of interest to deal with common problems."

Within each of the components of the triad, Obasanjo proposed several basic principles. Under the political component, the key principles named were adherence to the rule of law, respect for human rights, free and fair elections, independent judiciaries, and the introduction of limited terms of political mandate. The security component was to be defined not only in military terms but also in economic and social terms. Obasanjo called for a revived OAU Commission for Mediation, Conciliation and Arbitration to be responsible for conflict resolution and prevention, nonaggression pacts, and the mobilization of military resources to intervene in domestic conflicts. The main principles under the third component of the triad, economic development, were an acceleration of the implementation process of the African Economic Community, independent central banks, and independent civil services.

In their respective opening statements at the Addis Ababa meeting, the secretary general of the OAU and the executive secretary of the ECA repeated Obasanjo's call for a new African order. Even so, Salim questioned whether it would be necessary and practical to pattern the African security plan strictly along the lines of the Helsinki system. He also reminded participants that Africa already had an all-embracing framework for cooperation: the OAU. Although the organization suffered from institutional weaknesses, Salim argued that it was better to make use of existing structures rather than to use scarce resources to create a parallel institution with the same objectives. In contrast, Adedeji emphasized the need for new political structures. He also praised the effort to move beyond a narrow economic focus to explore instead the essentially political nature of the African crisis.

Participants at the brainstorming meeting embraced the idea of a CSSDCA. In their final report, they expanded on the three dimensions initially highlighted by Obasanjo, renaming them "security," "governance," and "economic cooperation." Security was defined as "an all-encompassing concept that enables the people of Africa to live in peace and harmony and to have equal access both to the resources and to participate fully in the process of their governance." Participants distinguished between internal security, which includes the security of the people and of the state or government, and external security. They recommended the establishment of organs modeled after the UN Secretariat and Security Council, and of a Pan-African military force and a disarmament process.

Besides the minimum principles proposed by Obasanjo, participants added items to the governance component: political accountability, promotion of literacy, provisions for constraining human rights violations of national governments, and recognition of the dangers of religious fundamentalism. They had few concrete policy proposals under the economic cooperation component, but they did emphasize the importance of human-centered development and an active private sector. In the end, participants at the brainstorming meeting appointed a Steering Committee of eighteen members to work out the modalities of how the CSSDCA process should be initiated and sustained, and to continue to advocate for the project.

First Steering Committee Meeting

At its first meeting in Addis Ababa in February 1991, the Steering Committee decided that the principles governing the CSSDCA process should be grouped not under "security," "governance," and "economic cooperation," but in terms of the goals of the process: security, stability, development, and cooperation.[37] To emphasize that the CSSDCA was an African initiative, the committee decided not to use the word "baskets," which the Europeans had employed in referring to the different dimensions of the Helsinki process. Instead, a uniquely African word—"calabash"—was chosen. (Obasanjo said that baskets leaked, whereas calabashes were tight). The Steering Committee decided that the principles of the CSSDCA should be negotiated and then signed by participating member states. After signature, the agreed principles would be incorporated into respective national legislations.

International Roundtable Meeting in Cologne, March 1991

The international roundtable meeting held in Cologne in March 1991 reflected another core idea behind the CSSDCA: that Africans can learn from others' experiences—specifically, from the Helsinki process—and need support and involvement from non-African actors. The meeting, which was organized jointly by the ALF and the German Foundation for International Development, brought together African proponents of the CSSDCA and Europeans who had participated in creating the CSCE. The process was enhanced by the participation of higher-level political figures such as Nigerian foreign minister Major Gen. Ike Nwachukwu, Mozambian foreign minister Pascoal Mocumbi, Ugandan minister of state for foreign affairs Tarsis Kabwegyere, and ANC foreign secretary Thabo Mbeki. Obasanjo saw three main points that came out of the Cologne roundtable:

> The first point was that the European idea started as a private initiative, which was later embraced by governments, and it took time for the idea to take root and for the negotiations to be conducted. The second point was that while Africa could benefit from European process and experience, African process and procedure must be uniquely African. Africa must resist stock-and-barrel importation. Thirdly, although the Helsinki Final Act process as the European Treaty is called had no international secretariat initially, and the hosting country of a conference bears no burden of the meeting being held as the burden is shared among the participating countries, Africa may need to make use of, or supplement, its existing regional organization, the OAU, in advancing and implementing the process.[38]

Several other lessons were also drawn from the Helsinki experience relating to building a consensus, the formula of distribution of costs among the participating members, and the duty to get involved in what is otherwise considered to be within the domain of "internal affairs." Participants at Cologne were largely unsuccessful in their effort to secure a firm commitment to the CSSDCA process from senior European and North American policymakers, being told instead that a significant increase in foreign investments and aid would depend on the performance of African economies and governments.[39]

Consultative Meeting of African NGOs, April 1991

The third conference during this period reflected the CSSDCA's emphasis on popular participation, a central aspect of both the stability and development calabashes. In April 1991, the ALF invited some twenty representatives from African nongovernmental organizations to be informed about and involved in the CSSDCA process.[40] Besides affirming ideas and principles agreed to in Addis Ababa, the participants in Ota offered several specific recommendations on the role of NGOs in the CSSDCA process: that NGOs be invited to the Kampala Forum, that they be appointed to the Steering Committee, and that they be accorded observer status at the OAU meeting in Abuja in 1992 and consultative status at the OAU and the ECA in general. The Ota meeting reaffirmed the roots of the CSSDCA idea in civil society.

The Kampala Forum

On May 19 and 20, 1991, the ALF, the OAU, and the ECA convened the major conference on the CSSDCA. Roughly five hundred participants met in Kampala, Uganda, to agree on the principles of the proposal. Among the participants were five heads of state: Uganda's president Yoweri Museveni, who hosted the conference, Zambia's president Kenneth Kaunda, Botswana's president Quett Masire, Sudan's president Omar Hassan Ahmed al-Bashir, and Mozambique's president Joaquim Chissano. Besides Obasanjo, there were two other former heads of state: Aristedes Pereira from Cape Verde and Julius Nyerere from Tanzania. The rest of the participants were diplomats, scholars, business executives, representatives from students' and women's organizations, and other activists from all sectors of civil society. Nyerere commented on the diversity of the participants, saying, "For the first time you have a combination of views, which is unusual in the Organization of African Unity."[41]

The mix of participants was not the only unique feature of the conference. Observers described the atmosphere of the opening session as one of "unusual candor."[42] According to the ALF director at the time, "The statements were not the usual generalities or platitudes which are common for 'appropriate' courtesies or congratulatory rhetoric that usually dominate many meetings in Africa and elsewhere."[43] Instead, speakers argued that Africa's crisis was mainly a political crisis, and that Africans, not only foreigners, were to blame. Nyerere argued that "the deficit of democracy," and not the deficit of foreign exchange, was Africa's most serious problem. Chissano continued in the same spirit. "We have to face the fact that our institutions are still markedly based on decision making and management practices of vertical societies, and often personified. The tradition of State in our Continent lacks the institutional mechanisms which would allow for a coherent participation of individuals in the political life, promote collective initiatives for the solutions to local problems and pluralism of ideas."[44]

Adedeji told participants that "the systematic economic breakdown in Africa is principally the result of the political and social conditions of the continent—poor governance, lack of public accountability and of popular participation." Before Kampala, statements such as these and related discussions of the governance dimension of Africa's crisis had essentially been taboo at such gatherings.

Not all of the speakers showed the same mood of introspection and will to face the root problems of the continent, however. Kaunda identified the sources of Africa's ills as purely external, claiming that slavery, colonialism, imperialism, and economic exploitation "devastated the continent because African leaders did not have the means to keep at bay and out of the continent these invading forces." Although he referred to the CSSDCA as "a great idea," he did not see any need for greater unity, arguing that the peoples of Africa already were more united than people in other regions. According to Kaunda, Africa's only problem was that its economy was still "a slave of other economies." By avoiding giving Africans any blame for their problems, Kaunda also removed their opportunity to find real solutions. His only suggestion was to have the think tanks of the continent "find some quick and sure ways to build African management of our economies that will lead the continent to economic freedom."[45]

Similarly, al-Bashir argued that "the departure of the foreign ruler was, unfortunately, not the end of exploitation of our resources since it is now apparent that expatriates, advisers, and foreign consultants are today much more among us than before." According to one observer, however, this "familiar recourse to flailing the colonial and the neo-colonial horse did not sit well with the audience."[46] That some leaders would use these kinds of arguments was, however, not unexpected. The conveners of the conference deliberately invited leaders that "may need to be convinced on the desirability of the idea," rather than targeting only like-minded individuals.[47]

After the plenary, participants were divided into four subcommittees to work on the four calabashes of the CSSDCA: security, stability, cooperation, and development. The subcommittees were given issue papers and guidelines for their work and were directed by prominent individuals. The security subcommittee was chaired by Francis Deng, former minister of state of foreign affairs of Sudan, assisted by Akporade Clark, former permanent representative of Nigeria to the United Nations. Eriya Ketegaya, Uganda's first deputy prime minister, chaired the stability subcommittee, assisted by Willie Lamouse-Smith of Ghana. Pascoal Mocumbi, foreign minister of Mozambique, chaired the cooperation subcommittee assisted by Munyua Waiyaki, former foreign minister of Kenya. Jacqueline ki-Zerbo from Senegal, who was adviser to the UN Development Fund for Women (UNIFEM), chaired the development subcommittee assisted by Kasuka Mutukwa of Zambia, who was director of the General East and Southern African Management Institute.

The subcommittee participants developed syntheses of the CSSDCA calabashes, which were subsequently adopted by the full Kampala Forum in an atmosphere of consensus and enthusiasm. Although the principles of the final proposal were similar to Obasanjo's initial ideas, organizers stressed the importance of the contributions from participants at the forum.[48]

Principles and Implementation

The Kampala Document raises several contentious issues in its effort to institute a new normative consensus. Many of these issues gave rise to serious debate, before and after Kampala, and not all have been clearly resolved. Yet even their ambiguity indicates new directions for African norms and practices, and some are resolved in a direction as progressive as the provisions of Helsinki or the OAS.

Sovereignty

The principle of sovereignty is addressed in the Kampala Document in an ambiguous manner that warrants further consideration. The first general principle recognizes the sovereignty of states. The second general principle, however, states that "the security, stability and development of every African country is inseparably linked with those of other African countries" and that "instability in one African country reduces the stability of all other African countries."[49] This principle can of course be interpreted simply as encouraging greater cooperation. In light of the statements made at the opening session of the Kampala Forum, however, it is more likely that the second general principle was intended to modify the principle of sovereignty.

At the Kampala Forum, Museveni argued that sovereignty had become "a sacred cow" in whose name many crimes had been committed. Nyerere claimed that it had been a mistake to build the OAU on the strict rule of noninterference, while Chissano said that while the strategy had been correct, Africa today is faced with new challenges that demand new norms. Obasanjo called for a redefinition of the concept of sovereignty. "In an interdependent world, is there no minimum standard of decent behavior to be expected and demanded from every government in the interest of common humanity?"[50]

In many ways, the second principle challenges the whole notion of sovereignty. Hurst Hannum defines sovereignty as a principle that reserves to each sovereign state the exclusive right to take any action it thinks fit, provided that the action does not interfere with the rights of other states and is not prohibited by international law.[51] It follows from this principle that in all matters falling within the "domestic jurisdiction" of any state, international law does not permit any interference. But if one argues that security, stability, and development are no longer within the exclusive domestic jurisdiction of the state, the concept of sovereignty loses its meaning. Security, stability, and development are such encompassing areas that practically all policy issues in a country can be categorized under one of them. Taken another step, therefore, if no policy decisions are within the exclusive domestic jurisdiction of the state, sovereignty has no meaning whatsoever.

This interpretation of the meaning of the second principle gains support if one looks at a preliminary proposal on the CSSDCA, in which a modification of the recognition of the principle of sovereignty was included:

> Every African State is sovereign and respects the rights inherent in territorial integrity and freedom and political independence of all other African nations and considers as sacred the principle of inviolability of the national borders of others as enshrined in the Charter of the OAU

and the United Nations. *This principle of sovereignty to be adhered to by African countries will take cognizance of the intensifying global interdependence in which a community of interests must be allowed to address common problems which are beyond the capacity of individual nations and invariably transcend national borders.*[52]

Bearing in mind that the fifth general principle of the CSSDCA recognizes that progress in security, stability, and development can only be achieved through collective solutions, this early proposal conveys essentially the same message as the final document. A redefinition of "sovereignty" might have avoided the contradiction between the two principles but was not included. Even so, the following passage offers some guidelines as to the content of a new concept of sovereignty:

> While giving due recognition to the provisions of the United Nations and the Organization of African Unity Charters with respect to the principles of good neighbourliness and non-interference in the internal affairs of states, growing international concern for humanitarian causes and the experience in Africa of civil strives and acts of wanton repression, demonstrates an increasing concern over *domestic conditions pertaining to [a] threat to personal and collective security and gross violations of basic human rights.* The CSSDCA must aim at promoting and strengthening this welcome development to enable African countries to cooperate in ensuring the security of Africans at all levels.[53]

This statement suggests that certain threats to personal and collective security should be considered matters of concern beyond the domestic jurisdiction in a new definition of sovereignty. In the end, though, the Kampala Document remains ambiguous, if not contradictory, on the content of sovereignty.

The Security Calabash

The security calabash was hotly debated at the Kampala Forum for three reasons. First, there was a need to redefine the traditional concept of security, "Gone for Africa and indeed the rest of the world are the days nations erroneously assumed that security came from military power alone and secure national borders."[54] Second, there was the suggestion of implementation measures that would require states to give up a certain degree of sovereignty. Third, security was enlarged to include security of the individual as well as the state, two notions often seen in contradiction.

The Kampala Document employs a broad concept of security to include political, economic, social, and cultural dimensions. The document distinguishes between internal and external security, and between national security and individual security. As Laurie Nathan explains, "Under-development, the lack of self-sufficiency in food and energy, and the abuse of human and peoples rights are regarded as grave threats to the security of people and, since they invariably give rise to conflict between countries, to the security of states."[55] By expanding the traditional concept of security to include people and individuals, and by stating that the security of every African country is inseparably linked with that of other African countries, the document indicates that the security of one African country's individuals is also relevant for other African countries.

The Stability Calabash

The Kampala Document explicitly supports democracy, arguing that security, stability, and sustainable development "can only be brought about by democratic practice and democratic institutions."[56] This was an important shift in principle, since in the past African leaders have typically "opposed the relaxation of authoritarian rule on the grounds that this would lead to chronic instability in ethnically heterogeneous societies."[57] Instead, the Kampala Document blames "monolithic political structures" for past instability and suggests that the institutions necessary for stability will only be viable if they are "derived from a democratic base of governance."[58]

The call for democratization in the Kampala Document seems rooted just as much in a belief that stability, through democracy, will lead to economic development, as in an ideological conviction that democracy is a human right. In discussing the "somewhat monolithic political structure that emerged from the anticolonial struggle," the issues paper presented to the stability subcommittee at Kampala argued that it was "the failure of the political systems to bring a rapid socio-economic change in individual African countries rather than their nature per se which explains the disillusionment that evolved against such systems."[59] (Of course, preceding the call for democratization at Kampala, several treaties and declarations on economics also emphasized the need for democratic societies.)

The Development Calabash

The development calabash emphasizes self-reliance, physical and economic integration, diversification of African economies, popular participation, and responsible leadership as central aspects of the development calabash in the Kampala Document.[60] Many of the ideas of the CSSDCA had already been advanced in other African declarations and forums before the Kampala Forum. The Kampala Document refers to and calls for the implementation of several earlier treaties, including the Lagos Plan of Action (1980), the African Priority Programme on Economic Recovery (1985), Africa's Common Position on the External Debt (1987), the Khartoum Declaration on Human Centered Development (1988), the Mauritius Declaration on Education (1989), and the African Charter for Popular Participation in Development (1990).

The most recent of these documents represented a new perspective on development that emerged as a result of the crisis of the 1980s and reflected a realization that people should be at the center of development. The Economic Commission for Africa passed several declarations that opposed neo-orthodox structural adjustment programs (SAPs) introduced by the World Bank and the International Monetary Fund as anchored to things, not people.[61] The African Alternative to Structural Adjustment Programs (AAF-SAP), published in 1989, was the first document by a UN-affiliated body that publicly linked the continent's economic problems to a "pervasive lack of democracy," followed by the African Charter for Popular Participation in Development.[62] The participants at the 1990 brainstorming meeting in Addis Ababa emphasized the "strong link between democracy and development" and rejected "the notion that economic development could take place on a sustained basis without effective people's participation."[63] The development calabash in the Kampala Document therefore endorses a truly people-centered development, while at the same time, encouraging the pursuit of an "operational common ground" between structural adjustment programs and the African alternative.[64]

The Cooperation Calabash

Unity through cooperation is the broad objective of the CSSDCA, but cooperation among African countries is also to be complemented by cooperation with other countries of the South and by North-South cooperation. The cooperation calabash emphasizes strengthening intergovernmental organizations within Africa but also developing regional and subregional cooperation among private and nongovernmental actors and states that "the need for devolving certain key responsibilities to continental institutions would be imperative."[65] The entire document is open to collaboration across boundaries, returning to the focus that softens sovereignty and challenges old norms.

Implementation

The Kampala Document envisions a process of implementation that starts with a decision by the OAU Assembly of Heads of State and Governments to launch a negotiation process. An OAU intergovernmental process was preferred because "any other arrangement [would] not only be wasteful of scarce financial and organizational resources, but most importantly, [would] pose problems of meshing some elements of the new process with some existing institutions of the OAU which will have to be revitalized to serve Africans better."[66] The purpose of the negotiations, which were recommended to last no longer than two years, was to adopt a convention that is politically binding. After the signing of the convention by African countries, non-African countries "whose actions impact on Africa's security, stability, development and cooperation" should be invited to join the process.[67]

The CSSDCA is described as a process. After individual countries sign the convention, there would be periodic review conferences to "collectively review the progress made in the implementation of the Convention" and to "examine the performance of each member country."[68] The Kampala Document recommends the establishment of a Consultative Secretariat to backstop the negotiations and a Consultative Committee to assist African governments during difficult times of the negotiations. These two support mechanisms would be funded by voluntary contributions from participating states, international organizations, and other donors. The document also suggests that the Consultative Secretariat could form the nucleus of a Permanent CSSDCA Secretariat that would monitor full compliance with the provisions of the convention. Further decisions about the responsibilities, structure, size, and location of the Secretariat are left to the participating states.

Two weeks after the Kampala Forum, in June 1991, the CSSDCA proposal was submitted to the OAU Council of Ministers and the Assembly of Heads of State and Government meeting in Abuja, in Obasanjo's home state of Nigeria, and chaired by its president, Gen. Ibrahim Babangida. Although there were some attempts to stall the document by raising issues of procedure and protocol,[69] no individual country opposed the proposal, and both the Council of Ministers and the OAU summit recognized the importance and necessity of the CSSDCA. Several leaders advised caution in the implementation of the proposal, but their hesitation was "perhaps . . . a reflection of their own domestic situation."[70]

After the discussion at the Council of Ministers, the chairman of the plenary session came to the following conclusion:

> It is evident that the ideas and principles behind the launching of a process of stability, security, development and cooperation are very sound. The fact that several African Heads of State attended the Kampala Forum testifies to the interest, relevance and importance of the subject. Our Continent needs security, stability, development and cooperation. Yet, it is evident that the modalities involved on how to go about the process, as recommended in the Kampala Forum, have to be worked out. In addition, unfortunately the Council does not have the text in all working languages of the Organization.
>
> In order, therefore, to give the matter the importance it deserves and with a view to facilitate the appropriate consultations, both within individual Government machinery as well as within the Institutional Framework of our Organization, I believe it is the consensus of the Council that the consideration of this issue be deferred to a later session of the Council. In the meantime, the General Secretariat should be seized with that Document and Proposals, submit them to all Member States for consideration and comments and then bring the same to the Council of Ministers incorporating whatever proposals and comments made by Member States.[71]

The decision to submit the Kampala Document to OAU member states for additional comments was affirmed by the assembly. It was also decided that the comments should be reflected upon by a group of experts convened by the secretary general of the OAU. The Kampala Document was then to be submitted to the OAU Council in February 1992 and the OAU summit in June 1992 in Dakar.

By the time of the February meeting, however, no communication in response to the substantive issues of the Kampala Document had been received from any OAU member state. This was also true when the OAU Council met again in Dakar six months later, at which point the chairman suggested that a final decision be taken in February 1993. Even then, though, no government had responded, and the CSSDCA proposal was deferred again, this time indefinitely. Despite the frustrations of the OAU process, the ALF deployed its efforts to promote the CSSDCA outside official OAU channels. It organized a conference on the impact of post-apartheid South Africa in September 1991 and a meeting on the African Elders Council portion of the proposal in March 1992. As the CSSDCA initiative continued to be stalled and deferred within the procedures and processes of the OAU, the ALF held off organizing additional meetings.

Obstacles to the CSSDCA

The question of what prevented the OAU from adopting the CSSDCA proposal is crucial to developing a new strategy. The factors that influenced that process are interrelated and hard to differentiate. Still, it is important to ask whether the CSSDCA was a "premature" initiative that OAU member states would never have approved or whether the proposal could have been acceptable if a different strategy had been chosen.

Lack of Political Will?

In 1992 Nathan wrote that "whether a Helsinki-type process in Africa ever gets off the ground, and whether it succeeds in meeting its objectives, ultimately depends on the one critical ingredient missing in previous, similar endeavors: the political will to translate good intentions and lofty ideals into requisite action."[72] The main reason that the CSSDCA was never adopted by the OAU was that a few states were strongly opposed to the proposal, foremost among them Sudan under the Islamic regime of Gen. Omar al-Bashir and Libya under Col. Moammar Qadhafi. These countries perceived the CSSDCA as a threat to their immediate domestic agenda because the principles and ideals that were being presented by the Helsinki process were a threat to their rule.

The request of these two countries at the Abuja meeting to allow member states more time to study the proposal was clearly a tactic to stall the process. At the Council of Ministers six months later, where the CSSDCA again was on the agenda, Libya and Sudan openly and strongly opposed the CSSDCA. A few governments also came out in support of the process, but the negative voices shouted the loudest. In the conventional diplomacy of the OAU, if one head of state feels very strongly about an issue, and speaks out loud, it is very difficult for the others to counter him. It was the OAU's traditional emphasis on sovereignty and consensus that prevented other member states from going against these two strong opponents. The decision to defer the discussion about the CSSDCA was a polite way of killing it. Sam Iboke, head of OAU's Conflict Resolution Division, argues that the problem was that the CSSDCA sought to target the practices of governments of countries, such as Libya and Sudan, but then the only way to find the proposal a greater chance of approval would have been to turn it into a more "neutral" document, devoid of meaning.[73]

Open opposition by some member states does not, however, explain why none of the member states submitted any comments to the OAU Secretariat during the time between the Abuja summit and the Council of Ministers in February 1992. It is likely that the countries opposed to the proposal made their views clear through informal channels, and that this was sufficient to keep other states from following up on the CSSDCA. Felix Mosha, then director of the ALF, argues that the countries that participated in the OAU summit in Abuja can be divided into four groups: states that were genuine in demanding more time; states ("breakers") indifferent to what would happen to the CSSDCA; states ("riders") opposed the CSSDCA but not openly; and states ("derailers") determined to stop the process.[74] The distinction between those that were discreetly opposed and those that were openly opposed suggests that the latter group made their views clear to the others.

Even member states that were not overtly opposed to the proposal, though, had their own reasons for not pushing the CSSDCA forward. Many may have supported the document in principle but felt vulnerable to the impact of its provisions. The most controversial aspects of the CSSDCA were its emphasis on democracy as a prerequisite to economic development and its challenge of the traditional notion of sovereignty. As already discussed, African leaders have often opposed democratization on the grounds that it would lead to chronic instability in ethnically heterogeneous societies. Timothy Bandora, who was a member of the OAU delegation in Kampala, argues that the CSSDCA was premature in its insistence on democratization, because this was a form of rule that was controversial on the continent.[75] Although very few African countries would have rejected the notion of democracy in 1991, there was, and continues to be, much discussion about what "democracy" means in the African context.

Defining "democratization" was one of the tasks confronted by the CSSDCA process. Even among the promoters of the initiative, there were those who shared the rejection of multipartyism by some African leaders as the definition of democracy. In his speech at Kampala, Museveni said that "democracy should take many forms" and argued for a definition of democracy adapted to African traditions. He and others opposed the approach of Western countries who increasingly emphasized a multiparty system as a condition for foreign aid. Some CSSDCA supporters were convinced that multipartyism was not a necessary ingredient for democracy. Others believed that it would be easier to get the CSSDCA accepted if one avoided equating multipartyism with democracy. This approach was highly criticized by those who argued that democracy requires the establishment of at least two different parties. To make an exception for African countries by creating a form of "African democracy," would be, in their opinion, "to give a green light to dictators."[76]

In the end, the Kampala Document recognizes multipartyism as one of many ways to allow plural political structures. "Every country would ensure that there is no hindrance to alternative ideas, institutions and leaders competing for public support. *In the case of multiparty pluralism,* this principle requires that every participating member should ensure the separation of party from the state."[77] Instead of taking a clear stand in the debate about multipartyism, the document lists a set of pillars for democracy, which made some countries still feel vulnerable to the CSSDCA's emphasis on democracy, one of the core principles of the Kampala Document.

However, emphasis on democracy was not the only factor preventing member states from supporting the CSSDCA. Many of the heads of state who were hesitating to accept, or directly opposing, the CSSDCA had already signed earlier declarations and charters recognizing democracy as a prerequisite for economic development. The innovation of the Kampala Document was that it introduced mechanisms for implementation and monitoring compliance. By proposing the establishment of a Council of Elders empowered with a measure of intervention in national security issues and an African Court of Justice, the CSSDCA was clearly challenging the restrictive notion of sovereignty on which the OAU was founded.

According to Bade Onimonde, "obsession with national sovereignty" has been the single most serious internal obstacle to effective regional cooperation.[78] Similarly, J. Isawu Elaigwu argues that "African countries are very suspicious of one another and jealous of their recently acquired sovereignty. The states are therefore unwilling to delegate any real authority to the OAU functionaries."[79] The main reason behind the reluctance to delegate authority to a continental organization is fear that other states may take advantage of such transference. Edem Kodjo, former secretary general of the OAU, however, claims that initiatives to give the OAU a more supranational character have been stalled by "the hostility of certain states whose leaders lack historic perspective or who cling to dated concepts of the nation-state, and believe they can, working within the framework of the present borders of their country, create powerful nations."[80] Elaigwu argues that supranationalism will continue to lose in its battle with nationalism, unless the states of Africa feel more threatened than they do at present.[81] Jonah seems to share the view that the existence of a perceived threat is necessary for states to be willing to give up some degree of sovereignty.

> African states have not experienced the bloody inter-State conflicts that Europe has gone through. It is this bitter experience that has made Europeans understand the absolute necessity for European unity. But even this development would have been insufficient had not the Western European powers perceived a military threat from the Socialist countries in the East. It was this perceived threat that solidified their determination for unity and cooperation.[82]

Even though Africa did not face a similar military threat, the people who initiated and supported the CSSDCA perceived the marginalization of Africa and its causes as threats serious enough to necessitate action, a view not shared by many heads of state. According to Adedeji, further integration in Africa requires the urgent termination of "the costly illusion of the possibility of independent national development. . . . This is possible for only about two countries because of the minuscule size of most African countries, which can hardly support most basic industries. Once the futility of isolated national development is firmly grasped, the stage is set for accelerated African integration."[83]

As a result, though the CSSDCA Steering Committee consulted extensively with many heads of state, the CSSDCA lacked "sponsors" that would follow up on the process at the OAU. One could argue that Uganda, which hosted the Kampala conference, and whose president presented the proposal to the OAU, at times functioned as a sponsor. However, Eloho E. Otobo, a member of the CSSDCA's Technical Committee, claimed that Museveni "played a ding-dong game" with the ALF: "He was uncomfortable with the whole package, and did not come forward in Abuja."[84] The net result, of course, was a lack of political will among those who were needed to approve the proposal.

A Western Initiative?

The provisions on democracy and sovereignty were not the only factors that generated opposition and skepticism among OAU member states. Some states were also hesitant to embrace the CSSDCA proposal because it was modeled on a European experience. According to Sam Iboke, these states looked only at the Helsinki precedent and felt that Western ideas and values were being imposed on them.[85] Kampala did draw its inspiration from Helsinki as an event, as well as sharing its values, but a major reason for referring to the CSCE experience was the belief that it would be easier to get Western support for a process that they recognized.[86] The CSSDCA was driven primarily by the desire to find African solutions to African problems, although the initiative also sought "to attract the support of non-African powers in the realization of Africa's aspiration."[87] This dual purpose created fear among some leaders that involvement of non-African governments would amount to interference.[88]

The CSSDCA Steering Committee gave serious consideration to the possibility of foreign intervention and took precautions to prevent it:

There is a real risk that the CSSDCA process might be scuttled right from the very start in any highly orchestrated manner by the influential non-African powers who will be less keen to see African countries better manage their affairs. CSSDCA is a bold and innovative approach at better self-management of African affairs in the areas of security, governance, economic development, and cooperation. Non-African powers are not famous for encouraging and promoting African initiatives, independence and self-reliance. There is no reason to believe that they will be more altruistic this time.[89]

It was crucial that the proposal be *recognized* as an African initiative to get African states to adopt the Kampala Document. The fact that the CSSDCA Steering Committee named the four dimensions "calabashes" instead of "baskets" symbolizes this awareness. Nevertheless, in some circles, there was still "a feeling that the CSSDCA was externally driven."[90]

A "Take-It-or-Leave-It" Proposal?

In Abuja, there was also confusion over the way the Kampala Document was presented and the nature of the commitment the states would have made if they adopted it. Although the states would have had to accept the general principles of the Kampala Document, the specific principles and the measures for implementation were subject to negotiation. As Obasanjo subsequently explained, "There is no word in the proposal that is sacrosanct or immutable. . . . The proposals are what they are, purely proposals to guide the conduct of negotiations among African governments."[91] Only after an estimated period of two years would the states adopt a convention that would be politically binding. Even though this was clearly written in the Kampala Document, Hans D'Orville, president of the Africa Leadership Foundation, argues that there was still some confusion, saying, "At the OAU, the CSSDCA was perceived as a 'take it or leave it' proposal."[92] Some states thought they would have to agree on all the specific wording of the Kampala Document and were thus reluctant to approve the proposal.

Pressure of Time?

Besides the various political reasons for the failure of OAU member states to adopt the CSSDCA proposal, time may have also played a role. According to an internal memo at the World Bank, the CSSDCA proposal was sent back for further processing through OAU channels as a result of "the speed with which it was prepared and subsequently presented to the Abuja [meeting] of June 3 and 4 1991."[93] There were only a few weeks between the Kampala Forum and the OAU summit, which prevented delegates to the Kampala Forum from consulting and lobbying their governments. The ALF did not have time to produce a clearer and more coherent document or to translate the Kampala Document into all of the working languages of the OAU, thus giving opponents an excuse to defer the issue. According to ALF director Felix Mosha, many OAU leaders at the Abuja meeting felt that they could not adopt something they had not had time to study and were sincere in demanding more time.[94] Countries that were initially positive toward the CSSDCA might have spoken more strongly in favor of the proposal if there had been more time for internal consultation.

Time was also important for broader participation. The ALF was an African NGO rooted in civil society, and its founder was a chicken farmer as well as retired general and former head of state. But other African NGOs were not included in the process until it was too late for them to have any real influence on the future of the CSSDCA. The meeting of NGOs at Ota was held less than two months before the Kampala Document was submitted to the OAU. This gave them very little time to create awareness and gather support that could have influenced the policies of their respective governments.

When asked about possible negative effects of the speed with which the Kampala Document was prepared, one member of the CSSDCA Steering Committee answered, "Of course it went too fast, but it had to."[95] There were several reasons that the ALF considered it necessary, if not crucial, to submit the Kampala Document to the OAU in 1991. First, during the preparations of the proposal, there was an understanding that the outgoing chair of the OAU, President Museveni of Uganda, would present the document before the end of his term at the Abuja summit. The summit was indeed held in the home state of the document's author, but the host, General Babangida, the incoming president of the OAU, was less favorable to the proposal than

Museveni. If the ALF had decided to postpone the proposal, they would have had to find another "presenter" and possibly to go through the whole process again.

Second, along with feelings of opportunity and fear of marginalization driving the process came a sense of urgency. Many leaders and intellectuals feared that they would lose any ability to influence the destiny of the continent if they did not act quickly. As President Nyerere wrote in 1991, "Africa must move quickly—more quickly than Europe did in the lead-up to the Helsinki Agreement. The rest of the world, with which we have to live, is changing with unbelievable speed; its changes will almost certainly make our problems greater and our resources smaller."[96] The urgency brought about by such external factors was intensified by the sweeping political and economic changes taking place internally. There was a sense that the moment could be lost if action was not taken quickly.

Finally, the initiators of the Kampala Movement were also captives of the enthusiasm that the CSSDCA proposal first generated. Participants at the Kampala Forum described the atmosphere there as "euphoric." This engagement and optimism fueled the process but may also have caused some promoters to overlook or underestimate the obstacles the proposal was likely to face. "We were naïve," Mosha commented. "We worked under the assumption that this was something that the African leaders wanted. We thought they were with us."[97]

A Personal Ploy?

The ambitions of individual leaders, and speculations about those ambitions, may have also contributed to the stalling of the CSSDCA proposal at the OAU. The CSSDCA was proposed in the same year as the election of the UN secretary general, and Obasanjo was one of the African candidates. D'Orville argues that the CSSDCA was stalled by powerful people in the OAU who favored other candidates or who were simply jealous of Obasanjo's progress. In his view, both OAU secretary general Salim and its new chairman, Nigerian president Babangida, had personal motives for not supporting Obasanjo. They did not wish to see the successful implementation of a proposal that was considered his brainchild, and thus they refrained from pushing the CSSDCA at the OAU.[98]

Other people involved in the Kampala process have expressed doubts about the impact of possible individual power games, and they argue that individual actors could have done very little given the strong opposition from some member states. Yet even if individual chemistry and the UN secretary general candidacy did not have any direct effect on the CSSDCA process, these factors doubtless had an indirect effect. While the Kampala Document was being discussed at the OAU, there were rumors that Obasanjo's ulterior motive for promoting the CSSDCA was to gain support for his candidacy, and these rumors combined with other factors to prevent the proposal from obtaining sufficient support at the OAU.[99] Obasanjo later denied the accusations against him, saying, "I personally found the coincidence in time of the two issues uncomfortable and not to my liking. It never crossed my mind to tie the CSSDCA to my candidature."[100] Of course, it made little difference whether the rumors were true or not as long as people believed them.

If there is any lesson to be learned from this, it is that tying an initiative too much to one personality can be dangerous. According to P. Olisanwuche Esedebe, individual power games have prevented more extensive cooperation among African countries in the formative years of the early 1960s.[101] Even if all speculations about "power games" were false and did not directly affect the outcome of the Kampala process, the coincidence of the election of a UN secretary general and the CSSDCA proposal did take attention away from the CSSDCA and distracted people from focusing on the passage of the Kampala Document.

A Threat to the OAU Secretariat?

The CSSDCA proposal was resisted not only by African states opposed to its principles but also by the OAU Secretariat. Despite its cosponsorship of the initiative, the Secretariat was opposed to the formation of a regime that threatened to assume many of its own functions.[102] During his speech at the brainstorming meeting in Addis Ababa, as noted, OAU secretary general Salim emphasized that Africa already had a continental institution and warned against duplication. Interestingly, before Salim and his advisers decided upon this speech, they rejected a draft that was far more critical of the CSSDCA initiative. A major part of this first draft argued that the Helsinki process was a unique European experience that was not a suitable model for Africa. It emphasized that Africa already had a framework for cooperation—the OAU—and that first priority should be given to economic integration. It is uncertain who made the decision to write a new speech and the circumstances under which this was done. It is likely, however, that the decision was guided by the advice of Salim's staff "not to show over-eagerness or lack of interest at the same time until the outcome of the exercise is well known."[103]

At the time of the Kampala Forum, the OAU Secretariat seemed to have adopted a much more eager approach. In a letter on May 15, 1991, to Obasanjo expressing regret that he was unable to attend the Kampala Forum, Salim wrote,

> This aside I wish to associate myself fully, as I have done all along, with this timely initiative for a new order for SSDCA, and to assure you of my undivided support for it. As I expect that the proposal will be submitted to the Abuja Council of Ministers and Summit, you can rest assured of my full cooperation in propagating the idea and sensitizing the leaders to the timeliness and the urgent need for such a process in Africa. . . . Please do also convey my sentiments of deep regret to the participants, and assure them that the Kampala Forum and the initiative itself generally has my and the OAU's General Secretariat's unequivocal support.[104]

Whether Salim's words reflected his convictions or were a diplomatic nicety remains a valid question in view of his known earlier concerns. Certainly, other statements and documents indicate that not all of the OAU Secretariat shared his express enthusiasm for the CSSDCA; quite the contrary, some perceived it as a threat and rival to the organization. An internal memo by a member of the OAU delegation to Kampala expressed concern about "whether the ALF tends to accord the exclusive institutional responsibility for the execution and implementation of the said convention to the OAU, or whether its intention is really to sideline and undermine the OAU through the establishment of a completely new rival continental body called CSSDCA."[105]

One of the main causes for this concern was the provision in the Kampala Document calling for a permanent secretariat for the CSSDCA. Obasanjo was aware of the resistance against such a measure. In early 1992, he wrote,

"I have detected some uneasiness especially within the OAU Secretariat that the Kampala Document which recommends implementation and advancement of the proposals through our only continental organization—the OAU—also recommends a small body located either within the OAU or outside it to watch, monitor and help in the advancement of the process."[106] His response was to point to the CSCE "where a number of semi-governmental and nongovernmental organizations show interest in the process and attainment of the process."

Despite these statements, Obasanjo did not fully address the question of the relationship between the OAU and the CSSDCA, and confusion lingered. Although the Kampala Document states that the CSSDCA is a process, and not an institutional structure, lack of clear demarcation of the mandates of new and existing institutions led to concern about "ownership" of different mechanisms and fear of marginalization of the OAU. In the case of the OAU Commission on Mediation, Conciliation, and Arbitration, for example, the Kampala Document calls for revitalization under the CSSDCA. This objective implies that the CSSDCA is to be responsible for the commission, which would no longer operate exclusively under the OAU. At the same time, the Kampala Document stipulates that the Council of Elders is to take "appropriate actions, which may involve arbitration and mediation." Such statements raise questions about the respective mandates of the two bodies and the division of responsibilities between them.

Similarly, for peacekeeping operations, the Kampala Document calls for "a continental peace-keeping machinery as an important instrument for the preservation of peace in instances which potentially or actually threaten the security of states on the African continent. Such arrangements, however, should not preclude UN peace-keeping operations." While the possibility of a UN role is considered, the role of the OAU in international peacekeeping is seemingly precluded. Finally, the Kampala Document says that "the area of stability, in particular governance, democratization, and popular participation will be directly monitored by the permanent secretary of the CSSDCA, and the involvement of the African Commission on Human and Peoples Rights will be sought." Although the ACHPR is an OAU body, the CSSDCA proposal says that it "should be funded separately, not from the OAU budget, drawing upon other independent sources."

OAU criticism of the CSSDCA proposal might have been avoided if there had been more consultation between the OAU Secretariat and the African Leadership Forum. According to the OAU internal memo, when the OAU delegation to the Kampala Forum tried to raise questions about the relationship between the OAU and the CSSDCA, they were "completely silenced by the Chairman of the ALF." Nevertheless, ALF chairman Obasanjo corresponded and met with Salim regularly and assured him from the start of the process that "in whatever shape that the CSSDCA process emerges as it moves forward, I see it as complementary to OAU, ECA."[107] Consultation, therefore, may not have been the issue. The OAU might simply have been waiting to see what kind of support the CSSDCA proposal would receive from member states. If the initiative had gained momentum, further OAU support might have been considered appropriate.

Representatives of the ALF did not feel that they had any problems in their relationship with the OAU Secretariat until April 1992.[108] At that point the OAU was developing its own mechanism for conflict resolution. According to John Tesha, a senior political adviser at the OAU, the organization had already begun to plan the establishment of a more efficient mechanism for conflict resolution at the time of the Kampala Forum. The timing of the CSSDCA proposal was therefore problematic and lent credence to the perception of the document as a poacher on OAU turf.[109] "They tried to steal our mechanism," was the immediate response from an OAU official who had been at Kampala when asked about problems with the CSSDCA initiative.[110]

OAU officials claim that the planning of a new mechanism for conflict resolution started with the 1990 OAU Declaration on the Political and Socio-Economic Situation in Africa and the Fundamental Changes Taking Place in the World.[111] This declaration, however, did not say any more than "we [therefore] renew our determination to work together towards the peaceful and speedy resolution of all the conflicts on our continent." Notably, the internal memo referred to earlier, written in January 1992, contained no information about a new conflict management mechanism within the OAU. For these reasons and others, supporters of the CSSDCA claim that the OAU was stealing from the CSSDCA proposal when it created the Mechanism for Conflict Prevention, Management, and Resolution in 1993.[112]

The speech of OAU assistant secretary general Ahmed Haggag at the Kampala Forum, however, suggests that the OAU had already started thinking seriously about improving its capacity for conflict resolution at that time. According to Haggag, "There is also emerging thinking within the OAU that there is need to devise new procedures and mechanisms for tackling the fratricidal and destructive internal conflicts within the Member States. Therefore, the allocation in the 1991–92 budget of the organization, for the first time, of funds for the purpose of conflict resolution is to be seen in this context."[113]

In the end, therefore, it would seem that the idea for creating a new mechanism for conflict resolution emerged at around the same time in both the OAU and the ALF. Both bodies (and many other observers) identified the same need, but the mechanism for responding to it figures first in the ALF Document. Regardless of the sequence, clearly, the view of many at the time, especially in the OAU, was that the CSSDCA initiative ran contrary to the aspirations of the OAU in the conflict resolution area. Members of the ALF felt that their relationship with the OAU Secretariat became problematic when the OAU came forward with its proposal for a new mechanism for conflict resolution, which was widely believed to have borrowed from the relevant principles of the CSSDCA. Indeed, the establishment of such a mechanism was one of the cornerstones of the CSSDCA, and countries that initially supported the Kampala Document may have lost their incentive for supporting it once the OAU proposal came forward. Even so, it is not necessarily true that the OAU proposal killed the CSSDCA initiative. Possibly, the OAU Secretariat was waiting to see the reaction of member states to the CSSDCA before making its own proposal. Once it become clear that the member states would not accept the CSSDCA, the OAU Secretariat decided not to push it and instead to focus on implementing its most important elements through other means. Subsequent developments and renewed cooperation confirm that any future efforts to pass and implement the CSSDCA proposal will have to address this rivalry and clarify the relationship between the two organizations.

Conclusions

The question remains, was the CSSDCA a premature initiative, or could it have been acceptable if it had been presented in another manner, or at another time, or after more careful consultation? It is clear that the CSSDCA was unacceptable to at least a few heads of state because of the principles it contained. Because these countries were against the proposal in principle, they were not likely to change their positions as a result of more consultation, different formulation of principles, or better timing. The result of more consultation almost certainly would have been to modify the document's content and make it more neutral but also weaken its character. But it is unclear to what extent the proposal would have to have been modified in order to be acceptable to these countries. If the CSSDCA principles were indeed counter to major aspects of these leaders' governance, they would probably not have accepted the proposal until all of its main principles had been eliminated. It is therefore debatable whether a future initiative should seek to satisfy the demands of such countries or should instead attempt to gather more support from the other countries.

The reasons for lack of support among countries that did not have an immediate domestic agenda that ran counter to CSSDCA principles are more controversial. If many heads of state "felt vulnerable" to the provisions of the proposal, perhaps the proposal was "premature." By the same token, paradoxically, perhaps the CSSDCA principles were needed to remedy that very problem. It is possible, however, that no country spoke out in strong support of the CSSDCA simply because it did not know if it would get additional support from other countries. A future initiative may have a better chance of succeeding if proponents focus first on a group of countries that together could function as "sponsors" of the proposal, as the experiences of the CSCE and OAS illustrate. A future initiative also needs to return to the origins of the Kampala Movement in civil society and create modes of support and pressure on governments to join the movement. It may also be more feasible to implement the principles of the CSSDCA in established subregional organizations, rather than at the regional level, because the geographical proximity of countries often creates an interdependence that gives them greater incentive for deepening cooperation and allows for natural ties between neighboring civil societies and regional NGOs to operate.

The perception that the CSSDCA was a Western initiative whose principles and proposals were not open to negotiation could be remedied now that more time is available for consultation and lobbying. Even so, time may not have been the most important influence on the failure of the CSSDCA to gain greater support. According to one participant, "Time was not *the obstacle*. The package was simply not marketable under the circumstances in which we operated."[114] Now, those circumstances may be changing. The proliferation of conflicts in Africa, along with the self-proclaimed "new generation of leaders" and the growth of civil society, may be creating an environment in which the initiative has better chances of succeeding.

Independent of the strategy chosen to seek adoption of the CSSDCA proposal, the implementation of the principles of the CSSDCA necessitates that member states give up a certain degree of sovereignty as it is traditionally defined. To facilitate this process, "sovereignty" must be redefined.[115] Instead of regarding the principle of sovereignty only as something that provides the state with a *right* not to have other states interfere in its internal affairs, sovereignty should be redefined to include *responsibilities* toward citizens. When agreeing to a degree of supranationalism is perceived as sharing responsibilities, rather than giving up rights, states might show more willingness to cooperate and work toward political integration.

5

Beacons and Benchmarks

The essence of the Kampala Movement is the content of the Kampala Document, which stands as a beacon to guide the states of the African continent toward security, stability, development, and cooperation. Waves of conflict and storms of repression crash around this beacon but over a decade have not reduced its light. Yet no statecraft has yet come to be anchored at its base; its principles remain to be attained. Now, in the early twenty-first century, those principles bear re-examination and restatement to make their guidance clear and bright. They also need to be the subject of a strategy for further dissemination and adoption.

The genius of the Kampala principles lies in their universality and in their uniqueness to Africa. In fact, they are an African creation, one of the most important works of statesmanship of the postwar era. Although the primary inspiration for the document comes from the original Helsinki "baskets," their content has not only been adapted to fit African circumstances but has also been enriched by inspiration from African experience. The document establishes a regime of principles, conditions, rights, and obligations drawn from the crossroads of African and world experience and indicates policies that derive from these basic elements.

The most revolutionary aspect of the Kampala principles, starting with security and running through the other calabashes of the document, is their penetration into internal affairs of the state. The Kampala principles break the wall of protective sovereignty and install instead a program of responsible sovereignty. Formerly, state rulers could hide behind the concept of sovereignty as a defense against external interference and a license to do what they would with their own people, but now sovereignty is asserted as an engagement of responsibility for the welfare of one's population. The doctrine also says that a state has a responsibility to help others care for their populations or even to protect others' populations if their state does not exercise its own responsibility.[1] Like much of the rest of the principles, this doctrine has a universal and an African grounding. In universal terms, it is based on the value of human life and Locke's notion of the state as a social contract to protect that value. In African terms, it is grounded in the community's role as the source of guarantees and identity for that human life. Legitimacy is derived from the state's exercise of its responsibility. This theme is part of the fiber of each calabash.

Norms and Africa

Norms have always been important to the organization and functioning of any society. They are observed and they are broken, and both actions are the business of politics. The dramatic paradox is that, in the absence of a legislating and enforcing authority, norms are established (and changed) by the same process by which they are broken—by being tested. Like a muscle, a norm is kept in shape by challenge and exercise. Norms themselves of course do not prevail, since they are not actors; they are made to prevail by the actions of parties who uphold them by sanctioning a violator in a range of ways—from words of condemnation and guidance to acts of opposition and punishment. If such reaction fails too often and the challenge to the norm succeeds too often, the norm is defeated or changed.

Some international relations theory claims that norms do not constrain behavior of states for they observe them or not as their power and interests dictate; even if states do seem to observe norms, they are only doing what they would do anyhow, norms or not.[2] For all its seeming correspondence with reality, such thinking has its limitations. States do not act; people act for them. People follow norms, imperfectly as people do anything. To claim then that people are never constrained by norms is to misunderstand human nature and to build a fantasy world filled with actors called states who do not act like real people. Norms are used to do three things—to make unthinkable acts unthinkable, to correct challenging behavior, and to justify opposition to persisting infractions.

African states were born in an act that challenged the old norm of legitimate colonialism and established a new norm of self-determination.[3] The African nationalist movements did not change the norm overnight. In fact, coming toward the end of the postwar decolonization movement, they largely benefited from the impact of Middle Eastern and Asian states' earlier independence and, before that, from the impact of World War II on the colonizing states. But had they not taken up the movement, it might have been construed to be limited to the Middle Eastern and Asian civilizations, much as the self-determination movement after World War I was restricted to nationalities in Europe.

Independence movements began to bear tangible fruits in the 1950s, with Sudan becoming independent in 1956 and Ghana following a year later. Once independent, African states were important in turning the norm into international law through UN General Assembly resolution A/RES/1215, which stipulated the legitimacy of self-determination by a wide range of methods. The UN General Assembly reinforced the norm with A/RES/2189(XXI), which stipulated that resistance to colonial rule was not to be considered aggression.

In 1963 most of Africa's countries had become independent, and they created the Organization of African Unity (OAU). In article 3 of the OAU Charter, seven guiding principles, which were to form the normative basis of a new system of international relations, were created: sovereign equality of all member states, noninterference in internal affairs, respect for territorial integrity and political independence, peaceful settlement of disputes, condemnation of assassination and subversion, liberation of all colonial Africa, and nonalignment. Some of these were distant ideals rather than effective behavioral constraints. For example, the "unreserved condemnation, in all its forms, of political assassination as well as of subversive activities on the part of neighboring states or any other states" (article 3), the most specific of the seven principles, was a *cri de coeur* of the assembled heads of state upon the elimination of one of the founding members, Sylvanus Olympio of Togo, with the support of Ghana, and one which did not prevent the subsequent assassination of some fifteen heads of state.[4] But other principles had an impressive normative force.

Territorial integrity (article 3.3) was reinforced by a more specific resolution at the 1964 OAU summit, reasserting the principle of *uti possidetis juris,* which guaranteed the borders inherited from colonial rule. Citing the Pandora's box effect as the alternative, African state leaders raised territorial inviolability above the other six norms. [5] Not only did they continually cite the norm in the coming years, but it had a major impact on their policies in several cases. When the Somalis repeatedly asked for support for their irredentist claims against Ethiopia, on the basis of the undeniable fact that ethnic Somalis lived and migrated regularly into eastern Ethiopia, as well as the more debatable claim that Ethiopian rule was colonialism like any other, they could find absolutely no support, even from the enemies of Ethiopia.[6] All Africa, and with it the outside world, turned a deaf ear to their pleas, responding only, "*Uti possidetis!*"

When southern Sudan began to consider the idea of independence on the basis of undeniable cultural and political imperialism from the North, the OAU continued to deny the claim on the basis of *uti possidetis.* The world community joined in disapproving the proposed move, despite its antipathy to the Islamist government of Sudan. When Morocco (and, for a while, Mauritania) laid claim to the western Sahara on the basis of a vote of the territorial assembly and an international agreement with the decolonizing state, Spain, most members of the OAU rejected the claim and supported the national liberation movement's declaration of independence (even though it has not been consummated) and then self-determination by referendum (even though it has not been effected).[7] When Eritrea claimed independence in a referendum in 1993, after having won it militarily in 1991, its existence as a separate colony of Italy was recalled, but when Somaliland also claimed independence in 1991, *uti possidetis* was invoked by the world community to deny it recognition (though it too had been a separate colony of Britain and had even enjoyed independence for four days in 1960).[8] The norm of territorial inviolability has been variously interpreted, but it has not been breached, and it has powerfully affected what is thinkable and what is done by African states.

Another OAU norm referred to the "total emancipation" of all dependent African territories (article 3.6).[9] The words were carefully chosen to cover South Africa as well as European colonies. The norm was the basis of the African states' unrelenting campaign to have South Africa treated as a pariah state (and, less successfully, to be removed from the United Nations).[10] But the OAU Charter has not been the only source of African norms on this matter. A Manifesto on Southern Africa, voted at a summit of thirteen East and Central African states at Lusaka in 1969, carefully considered the South African situation and concluded that if southern African governments continued to oppose change, armed struggle was inevitable. The Lusaka Manifesto and the subsequent South African campaign opened up a vigorous debate among African states over the alternative policy of dialogue, leading to strong condemnation of the dialogue option and restatement of the force option at the 1971 OAU summit.[11] As a result, some pro-dialogue governments were overthrown (Madagascar) or ostracized (Malawi), and the consensus policy prevailed despite some covert dissent until the end of apartheid after 1990.

A final example of the workings of the African normative mechanisms concerns the OAU's 1969 African Refugee Convention, which provides asylum for political refugees.[12] Three decades after signature, Botswana accorded refugee status to members of a dissident group opposing the Namibian government in the Caprivi Strip. When Namibia protested, Botswana cited the convention, which both states had signed as a statement of African refugee norms.

These cases throw light on the sources and strength of normative principles in Africa. First, norms are stronger when they have been put down in writing and strongest when they are contained in a signed and ratified statement. However, the norm of colonial independence was fully observed by Italy, Belgium, Britain, and France, as well as by African national liberation movements, before it could be codified through the action of the newly liberated colonies-turned-states, and it worked to delegitimize the colonialist policies of the hold-outs, Spain, Portugal, and South Africa. Ratified conventions have the force of international law, but declarations of heads of states and their representing ministers are just as powerful when they meet the felt needs of the consenting parties.

Second, norms are stronger when, after being challenged, debated, and contested, they are reaffirmed. Unanimity is not to be expected, but supportive action by the parties to the consensus is. Norms are the basis for action. If they are not strengthened by being defended against internal opposition, they need to be kept alive by being applied to external subjects. Norms left on the shelf may be useful at a later date if someone remembers them, but the strongest norms are those that are continually applied.

Third, norms are the tracks of political relations. They guide action in the paths decided by the framers and subscribers, constrain choices, justify policies, and orient thinking. When relations go off track, the norms indicate where they should be restored and reaffirmed. When the tracks lead where the consensus does not want to go, the tracks can simply, if rarely, be abandoned, or more frequently, the relations can be retracked. In this way the norms serve as a formula for negotiations and a regime for problem solving.[13] As such, they provide order for both ends and means in important relations. It is with this perspective on norms that the principles embodied in the Kampala Document for the promotion of security, stability, development, and cooperation in Africa should be perceived.

Security

Security is the precondition for any positive action and the motivation for any defense. This principle applies to states in the normal considerations of international relations, but it also applies to individuals as they seek to fulfill themselves and make a positive contribution to their community. In between, in the African context, security also applies to groups, whose insecurity leads to conflict, death to the individual, and destruction to the state. Groups, primarily ethnic communities, are important to the fabric of African society, and the 1982 African Charter on Human and Peoples' Rights (ACHPR) covers group as well as individual rights. At all three levels, physical security needs to be complemented by food security, energy security, and security of beliefs. Thus the security of the nation depends on the individual security of its citizens and their composite groups to enjoy peace, the basic necessities of life, freedom and other human rights, and participation in the determination of their own destiny.

The Kampala Document grounds its consideration of security—and indeed, the rest of its principles—on this basic notion. Individual and group security is dealt with in the calabash on stability, whereas interstate relations are dealt with under security, although the document also states that individual and state security are interrelated. The security principles cover two aspects—general precepts (goals) and more specific mechanisms (means). The goals place security within the communitarian context of the African continent, which shares common experiences and identity, and so they are goals of good neighborliness among a community of states, just as Africans individually have traditionally found their identity and well-being within their local community. Security is therefore a nested concept, referring to basic assurances to be enjoyed by the individual within the group within the states within the continent. The nesting works both ways: security at the basic level is the building block for the enjoyment of the same condition at successively higher levels, and security across the continent reflects and ensures the enjoyment of the same value at successively lower levels. This nesting ensures the interrelatedness of the condition, so that when one state no longer ensures the security of its inhabitants or one group no longer feels secure, the security of neighbors is disrupted too.

The means proposed in the Guiding Principles to ensure the condition of security so defined are many. One group of proposals strengthens the capabilities of the OAU at the continental level. The organization lacked a formal mechanism for effecting timely mediation and intervention into situations of conflict, as noted in chapter 3; so the 1993 OAU summit took a leaf from the Kampala proposals and instituted the Mechanism for the Prevention, Management, and Resolution of Conflicts, a reduced Security Council–like organ that could act on the ambassadorial, ministerial, and presidential levels to deal with conflicts between summit sessions. A complementary proposal for a Council of Elders drawn from Africa's distinguished personalities and elder statesmen is designed to anticipate, contain, and even intervene in inter- and intrastate security situations, as a local council of elders would intervene in a community's interpersonal and even family disputes. Though not constituting a council, several former African heads of state have already performed this function in a personal capacity, including Julius Nyerere of Tanzania and, after Nyerere's death, Nelson Mandela of South Africa in Burundi, Canaan Banana of Zimbabwe in Liberia, Ketumile Masire of Botswana in Congo, Amadou Toumani Toure of Mali in the Central African Republic and Zaire, and Olusegun Obasanjo of Nigeria in Sudan.

The continent also needs a peacekeeping machinery, comprising an authorizing body, command and control structures, administrative and logistical support, a funding system, procedures for troop acquisition, and modalities for rapid deployment. Since no international organization has been able to resolve the peacekeeping problem on a permanent basis, this challenge represents the most difficult hurdle of the proposed principles.

Another series of measures begins bilaterally but ultimately calls for some continental coordinating body, whether it be the OAU itself or an agency growing out of the proposed Conference for Security, Stability, Cooperation, and Development in Africa (CSSDCA). One of these involves conventions on confidence and security building measures. These include exchange of information on troop location and movements and on arms imports and exports; joint military training, maneuvers, patrols, and exercises; and joint studies and seminars. Some of these measures have been discussed on a regional level by the Southern African Development Council (SADC) and the Economic Community of the States of Central Africa (CEEAC) but never implemented.[14] Another measure is a continentwide treaty of nonaggression and mutual defense. Such treaties already exist in West Africa, among ECOWAS members and, within ECOWAS, among the members of the Economic and Monetary Union of West Africa (UEMOA), but there are no such treaties applying to the entire continent. A third is the conclusion of a network of bilateral accords delimiting national boundaries with neighbors and at the same time establishing conditions of permeability, immediately complemented by bilateral actions to demarcate these borders and by bilateral commissions to handle the inevitable incidents that arise in transborder intercourse. Such measures are needed to complete the general norm of *uti possidetis* established by the OAU Charter and the 1964 OAU Cairo resolution. A fourth measure is a collective process of lowering military expenditures, as a result of the security and conflict reduction measures already mentioned; a significant proportion of military savings should be diverted to education. This in turn entails coordinated production and purchase of reduced arms supplies, which then feeds back into the confidence and security building measures by introducing greater transparency and limitations on armament policies.

Finally, a third group of measures refers to specific policies and institutions to meet current deficiencies in necessary elements of population security. These include the creation of continental centers for research and development (R&D) in nonmilitary aspects of security. One would focus on agricultural engineering and the development of a "green revolution" for tropical products, much as the International Maize and Wheat Improvement Center (CYMMIT) in Mexico, which developed new grains for the original green revolution. The other R&D center would focus on technologies for the development of renewable energy, including particularly solar and wind energy so plentiful in Africa. A third center could also develop desalinization measures, since large areas of the continent, particularly in the North, South, and East, will be water deficient in the early part of the current century.

Stability

As the security concern focuses on interstate relations within the continent, and their spillover into domestic affairs, the concern for stability refers to intrastate systems of governance. With this concern, the principles step directly into the doctrine of sovereignty as responsibility, for the Kampala Document sets up measures for responsible governance. These include the rule of law, popular participation in governance through political associations, respect for human rights and basic liberties, transparency in public policymaking, and the separation of personal religion from public policy. Such fundamentals are of course not new; they are part of the universalist origins of rising and long-standing concern for good governance. What is new is their explicit expression in a body of principles proposed to govern continental conditions and relations.

The underlying assumption that states find their legitimacy in their conduct of good governance for their people represents a dramatic turn from the contrary postcolonial assumption that the population's needs and identity were incarnate in the state, and that responsibility, if at all, lay in the relation of the people to their state. History shows that stability can indeed be ensured for long periods by a strong, repressive centralized government that controls participation and demands loyalty. Arguably, that assumption was appropriate to an earlier period, when fragile sovereignty needed to be transferred and an object of the social contract established. But now a more normal relation needs to be established in which accountability and responsibility define sovereignty, and stability is found in a reciprocal relationship between governors and governed.

However, the reciprocal nature of this relationship needs emphasis. The notion of participatory government and responsible sovereignty is not simply a reversal of the arrows, replacing upward loyalty with downward accountability. Responsible government needs to earn, but then deserves, the support of its citizens. The debilitating legacy of the previous regimes in Africa has been a permanent confrontation between governors and governed.[15] As a result, government can no longer mediate among constituent groups and choose among competing policies because it is assumed to be the adversary. Stability policies therefore have to overcome a negative legacy as they foster a relationship of ownership by the governed and service by the governors.

In the search for stability, as in the quest for security, a number of means are essential as subsidiary principles to these ends. These can be categorized as structures, processes, rights, and duties. Primary among the structural principles is the establishment of a constitution establishing institutions, procedures, rights, and duties of governance. The constitution should provide for the autonomy of parallel structures along the principle of the separation of powers and allow for the independence of contributing structures such as political parties operating between civil society and the state. Thus the immovability of judges, the protection of organs for monitoring accountability, the assured financing of institutions of adjudication and accountability, and the independence of the civil service need to be guaranteed and protected against political interference.[16] The African Commission on Human and Peoples' Rights needs a broadened and strengthened mandate to monitor and, through an African Court of Justice on Human Rights, adjudicate human rights practices. On the horizontal dimension, political association into parties and governmental access for parties need to be ensured, along with separation of party from state. Within these institutions, procedures necessary for stability include the regular, periodic, secret, universal election of officials and the provision of proportional representation, but also the limitation of elected terms.

In the realm of rights, national constitutional guarantees in a bill of rights are to be backed by the signature, ratification, and implementation of international instruments in the same direction. Governments' performance in the accomplishment of such guarantees needs to be routinely monitored. Legal aid needs to be provided for the defense of the rights for those who cannot afford legal services on their own. *Mandamus* and *habeas corpus* need to be guaranteed, and arbitrary arrest and detention without trial eliminated. Stipulated rights include the right to hold property, the right to the socioeconomic and cultural benefits of society, the right to education, the right to participation in the choice of governing officials, and the right to participation in trade union activities. Women, youth, and labor particularly need to be guaranteed their rights.

Duties are often the other side of rights. They include the citizens' duty to participate and to deliver loyalty to their state. The right to participate without the duty to do so is as empty as the reverse, and the right to demand accountability from the governors is one-sided and meaningless if it is not balanced by a corresponding duty of the citizens to support the accountable state.

Such institutions, processes and rights are the basic ingredients of a responsible, responsive, accountable government exercising sovereignty over its people and territory. By providing stability of governance in states, these practices in turn ensure the security of the states and their constituent groups and citizens.

Development

Africa, long thought of in terms of potential development, has become the underdeveloping continent. The images of improvement and the trends of take-off that prevailed in the 1960s and early 1970s have vanished in a generally dismal performance in meeting the welfare needs of the population. Unfavorable terms of trade and loss of market share for primary products, as well as poor policies of irresponsible borrowing, have taken their toll. But repeatedly, studies have shown that the major cause of this situation has been instability, which destroys a producer ethos and makes long-term calculations and investments overly risky. Leaders eat and run, leaving crumbs for their followers and empty tables for the rest. Underdevelopment breeds insecurity for state and citizen alike. And insecurity compounds the causative instability. The vicious circle has to be broken at all three points along its circumference.

Unlike security, a topic on which little debate among alternative principles occurs, both stability and development are the subject of a vigorous contest between two models, one centralized and the other pluralistic. Along with the open, pluralistic political model chosen for stability goes the open, pluralistic model of economic activity. This notion refers to the social as well as the economic dimension of development, for the two are inseparable, not merely parallel.

But the competitive model of responsibility and participation is also a model of popular ownership of the polity, and this characteristic must also be reflected in developmental efforts as popular ownership of the economy. An economy that is stretched thin across the divide between rich and poor does not engage the full efforts of the lower ranks, just as social status that leaves the bottom levels out of sight of the top does not foster supportive membership in a common society. Development, as opposed to growth, as is well known, does not mean an enriching upper level pulling away from the unimproved lower levels but social promotion and economic betterment across the board.

African development, as prescribed in the Kampala Document, includes another dimension that reflects the African, communitarian spirit of its principles, alongside their universalistic character. In development, it is Afro-centric self-reliance that is emphasized. Self-reliance is not autarky, an impossible illusion in an interdependent globalized world. It does mean collective self-supporting efforts and lowered customs barriers to promote gains from continental trade rather than simply looking to foreign markets and models, and it does mean attainment of food self-sufficiency. Replacement of expatriate technicians, reversal of the brain drain, repatriation of capital, moratorium on foreign debt, inculcation of a development ethos for investment, expansion of R&D investments by universities and businesses, and establishment of continentwide university standards and exchange programs for more integrated and efficient use of university capacities are aspects of self-reliance.

These three conditions—open competition, internal integration and participation, continental integration and self-reliance—are the Kampala Document's characteristics of social and economic development for Africa. The interdependence of these qualities, their ends-and-means relationship, and the circularity of development with security and stability mean that several points of attack are needed to break into the circle. But the front is so broad and the needs so great that it is the application of some good old principles rather than the implantation of new ideas that is required for Africa. As a result, there is a greater emphasis on policies for development, beyond some basic principles, than there is in the other two calabashes, in which principles were the primary focus. Economic matters tend to involve generally accepted principles, conditions, rights, and obligations, but policies implementing these ideas are sharply debated.

Policies for the improvement of human resources and capacity are at the basis of broader socioeconomic development: "People are the means and the desired end of the benefits of development."[17] The elimination of illiteracy, the introduction of science and technology into primary schooling, the expansion of vocational and managerial training, and the development of professional associations are policy goals that reveal an orientation to education. Use of indigenous knowledge, expansion of R&D, and development of Africa-relevant technology for expanded yields from tropical products and for affordable energy from the sun and potable water from the sea are appropriate priorities for efforts at development.

The revalorization of the agricultural sector has begun in recent years, but it requires continued emphasis as the key to African economic growth. Appropriate returns to farmers, increases in intra-African trade in farm products, fully restorative reforestation, promotion of traditional foods, and elaboration of national nutrition policies are ingredients of food self-sufficiency. The reverse trend is evident in industry. In fact, de-industrialization has been taking place. Processing and transformation industries are needed for local consumption and for export.

There is nothing revolutionary about this calabash, which is composed of well-established principles that need to be applied through focused policies. These principles are not matters of institutions, processes, or reciprocal rights but of raised consciousness and implemented measures. The shift from centralized to market economies has at least begun all over the continent and has gone far in many countries, leaving the government an important role as manager, monitor, and regulator.

Cooperation

If security, stability, and development form interlocked rings of values, cooperation is the calabash that holds them all. Cooperation within the African community is the key to efficiency and identity. As such, it too carries an approach that reverses the previous direction of African efforts. Instead of focusing on the state, cooperation requires efforts to be focused on the pool, enabling greater benefits to flow back to all cooperating parties. Reviewing Kwame Nkrumah's dictum that "the independence of Ghana is meaningless unless it is linked to the total liberation of Africa," cooperation maintains that the security, stability, and well-being of any African society is dependent on the security, stability, and development of the African community. Cooperation is therefore not just a matter of relative efficiency or increased payoffs but an absolute condition for benefits to be real and sure.

Cooperation is not obvious. Joint efforts with weaker partners can be a drag; joint efforts with stronger parties can be a drain. Free riders dilute collective benefits; multiple decisionmakers settle to the lowest common denominator. Pooling trade where there is none to begin with produces very small sums; lowering barriers in the absence of comparative advantage diverts rather than creates trade. There is voluminous literature on these drawbacks, and the African experience has afforded ample illustrations of all of them. Yet Africa persists in its pursuit of a form of unity, maybe because it is an island, maybe because of its communitarian spirit, maybe because African unity was the banner under which the continent was divided into states, maybe because it believes in the strength of unity, even or especially among the weak. In any case, the Kampala Document's emphasis on unity as cooperation represents an African longing that is reflected in the communitarian aspects of the previous calabashes.

There are many paths to cooperation, and the document espouses most of them, with the primary exception of the overtly political federative model. Again reversing Nkrumah, the document advises with respect to African unity, "Seek ye first the economic kingdom, and all the rest will be added unto you." The broadest form is the path of continental economic integration. Although a declaration espousing an African Economic Community (AEC) was adopted at Lagos in 1980, there has been no concrete implementation, and the twenty-year period foreseen for the elimination of all tariff barriers is at an end. Kampala calls for another ten years of accelerated implementation of the commitment.

The Kampala Document's preferred path, however, is through the strengthening of regional cooperation within the five economic cooperation organizations established through the ECA (and their four internal competitors)—the Arab Maghrib Union, the Economic Community of West African States (and within it the CFA-based Economic and Monetary Union of West Africa), the Economic Community of Central African States (and within it the CFA-based Economic and Monetary Community of Central Africa), the Southern African Development Community (and within it the Southern African Customs Union), and the Common Market of Eastern and Southern Africa (and within it the Inter-Governmental Authority on Development and the East African Cooperation). These regional organizations of cooperation are smaller and more manageable and based on a closer community of interests, including trade and investment, than the continental AEC. Strengthening each organization would create the pieces for a sort of federation of regional integration efforts at the continental level.

A third path is through geographically based networks and regimes of infrastructure, such as railways, road systems, airlines, and lake and river basins. Africa holds many such institutions, cutting across one another along the lines of their particular transport and infrastructural grids, so as to eventually constitute a system of regimes.

A fourth path involves the many functional and professional associations that unite members of similar vocations across state lines. They form networks of cooperation among individuals, but by their activities they can also work to create standards, coordinate national activities, and strengthen exchanges of ideas and personnel.

A final path is constituted by poles of development that draw neighboring states into zones of cooperation. Stronger states can serve as focal points, attracting and recompensing the cooperation of weaker economies, benefiting from economies of scale, and providing the rational allocation of production sites.

All of these pathways lead to greater benefits, not only to economic development but also to cooperation in building security and stability. They do not preclude cooperation in other directions—South-South and South-North—as is necessary in the interdependent world. But they constitute a primary focus of collaborative means to enhancing welfare for Africans, African communities, and African states.

These values, norms, structures, and policies constitute the scaffolding for the construction of a complex African regime. They would provide a solid orientation toward growth, progress, responsibility and collaboration, overcoming the stagnation, insolvency, autocracy, and conflicts that have been too common on the continent. But they already imply a change of heart and direction as a precondition for the larger changes they would bring. The goal they outline is impressive and promising, but the real challenge is how to create the chicken without first finding the egg, how to bring about the change in both leadership and its support in order to change the orientation and commitment of a continent. Indeed, the first round of efforts in the early 1990s showed that the chicken-and-egg question posed a fatal obstacle to the attempts to build a new regime. But a new millennium lay ahead.

CSSDCA Principles in Recent Initiatives

The Kampala Document has been used as a valuable resource for policy formulation by governments and regional and subregional organizations. While awaiting full enactment on the continental level, it was picked up in bits and pieces in such projects as the African Economic Community, the OAU Mechanism for Conflict Management, and other regional activities.

Perhaps the broadest impact of the Kampala Document could be found in the formulation of the African Economic Community (AEC), which was launched by the OAU Abuja summit of 1991. The design of the AEC drew essentially on the spirit and letters of the cooperation and development calabashes of the CSSDCA. The second principle under the development calabash of the CSSDCA suggested the need for a "rapid physical and economic integration of the African continent as a sine qua non to Africa's economic survival in the 21st Century and prospects for socioeconomic transformation and competitiveness with the rest of the world." The Kampala Document suggested that African countries could not expect to compete or develop individually in the evolving international economic system dominated by regional blocs. The document listed several actions that could deepen and further the overall goal of African economic transformation through economic integration, an approach that had also helped to ground the AEC.[18]

Soon after the decision of the AEC, the OAU Secretariat devised what is known as the secretary general's initiative on conflict management. This initiative was considerably influenced by the security and stability calabashes of the CSSDCA, as discussed in chapter 4. The initiative was formulated at the same time as the CSSDCA, and after a year of study of the Kampala

Document, the OAU Secretariat proposed it in 1992 at the Dakar summit. This mechanism is designed to anticipate potential conflicts and prevent them, with an added proviso that enables the OAU to mediate in actual conflicts.[19] By creating a bureau of eleven members, including the past, present, and future presidents, who would meet in continuous session, the initiative could overcome the blockage to action occasioned by the twelve-month intervals between OAU summits. The initiative was ratified by the Cairo summit the following year.[20] The underlying principles of the CSSDCA were evoked repeatedly as pertinent to Africa's collective security and as guides to the way the OAU could help achieve it.

The first two principles of the security calabash of the CSSDCA stipulated the need to prevent and contain a crisis before it could erupt into violent confrontation. The second principle of the CSSDCA talks about a framework for common and collective continental security. Elements in the security calabash of the CSSDCA were also part of the discussions in the OAU on peacekeeping operations, the need for a continental peacekeeping machinery to deal with potential or actual threats to African security, confidence building measures, nonaggression pacts, and the need to lower military expenditures.

The Entebbe communiqué was issued at the end of the Joint Entebbe Summit for Peace and Prosperity on March 25, 1998, by President Bill Clinton of the United States, Meles Zenawi of Ethiopia, Yuweri Museveni of Uganda, and Vice President Paul Kagame of Rwanda. Drawing on the core principles and guidelines of the four calabashes of the CSSDCA, but without acknowledging the source, the signatories of the communiqué expressed the need for self-sufficiency and economic diversification.[21] The leaders declared that African security interests would be advanced by joint action on transnational problems of terrorism, disease, proliferation of weapons, drug trafficking, and environmental degradation. The communiqué also stated the commitment of the leaders to regional economic integration and the creation of a larger regional market. Increased investment in physical infrastructure was also recognized as essential to sustain regional trade and integration.[22] Unfortunately, the declaration had no follow-up, and the signatories soon found themselves in conflict with one another in the field.

As a prelude to the Southern African Development Community (SADC) Organ on Politics, Defense, and Security, there were several calls for a

Conference on Security and Co-operation in Southern Africa (CSCSA). Experts and political leaders were consistent about the need to apply the core values and principles of the CSSDCA to the subregion.[23] In 1991 former president Frederik Willem de Klerk of South Africa fired the first salvo. He insisted on the need for a CSCSA. D. W. Auret, a senior official of the Department of Foreign Affairs, quoted extensively from the Kampala Document while speaking about future relations in Africa from the South African perspective.[24] Laurie Nathan argued forcefully that, despite its many obstacles, the CSSDCA combines a clear conceptual framework with concrete policy measures and an institutional arrangement to facilitate their implementation.[25] After the fall of the apartheid regime, I. William Zartman proposed a CSCSA by name at a southern African regional security conference in Arusha in June 1994. It was therefore no surprise that the statutory instrument establishing the organ in 1996 drew substantially on the Kampala Document.

Some subregional organizations, though not yet having adopted the Kampala principles by name, have already included Kampala-like declarations and mechanisms in their structures. In December 1999, the Economic Community of West Africa States (ECOWAS), sobered by its experiences in Liberia and Sierra Leone, adopted a defense agreement reflecting the security calabash of the CSSDCA. Earlier efforts in other regions also showed similar partial reflections. The Declaration of Principles on Sudan negotiated by the Inter-Governmental Agency on Development (IGAD) in the Horn of Africa in 1994 included principles of the stability calabash. Even the effort of Laurent Kabila in Congo to convene a regional meeting on security, development, and cooperation in Central Africa in May 1998 to commemorate the one-year anniversary of his takeover of power (to which no one came) was a similar effort in his region. However, these efforts have not been integral adoptions of the Kampala principles, nor have they been based on anything deeper than state foreign policy actions. Still missing is the installation of an effective base in national and regional organizations and groups in local society.

But the critical question is whether the OAU already has a structure, especially in the Mechanism for Conflict Prevention, Management, and Resolution, that can fully implement the CSSDCA principles. Or is it preferable for the CSSDCA to become the all-inclusive structure that could incorporate various initiatives of the OAU? The OAU prefers the former, the founders of the CSSDCA favor the latter to ensure that the comprehensive regime envisaged in the CSSDCA process is established.

Recent Revival

In 1998 the process of promoting the CSSDCA framework received an unexpected impetus from the political events in Nigeria. After the sudden deaths of Gen. Sani Abacha and Chief Mashood Abiola in 1998 and the subsequent election of Obasanjo as president in February 1999, the new Nigerian government made the revival of the CSSDCA process a major point of its foreign policy. President Obasanjo's first major foreign policy appearance came in July 1999, only two months after his inauguration, when he presented the CSSDCA as an important focus of his government at the OAU summit in Algiers and urged his colleagues to refocus their attention on the Kampala Document. At the Fourth Extraordinary Summit of the OAU in Sirte, Libya, on September 8–9,1999, the CSSDCA proposal was again raised by Obasanjo and discussed by attending heads of state. The Sirte Declaration adopted by the Assembly of Heads of State and Government included a resolution to "convene an African Ministerial Conference on Security, Stability, Development and Cooperation in the Continent, as soon as possible." This was a significant victory for the CSSDCA movement and created an unprecedented opportunity to push the process forward. During the UN General Assembly plenary session in New York in September 1999, President Obasanjo repeated his message from Algiers and Sirte that the CSSDCA was to be a principal focus of Nigeria's foreign policy under his administration.

In between these meetings, Obasanjo had convened a small group of ministers and officials from Nigeria, Senegal, Tanzania, Egypt, Mozambique, South Africa, and the ALF, OAU, and ECA on August 28 to discuss reanimation of the CSSDCA process. The group resolved to constitute a Steering Committee to initiate preparations for convening the CSSDCA, mobilizing support for it, and examining pertinent legal and technical issues. At its initial meeting in New York on September 25, 1999, the Steering Committee, comprising Nigeria (chair), Algeria (OAU presidency), Cameroon, Gabon, Mozambique, Senegal, South Africa, Tanzania, Togo, and Uganda, the OAU secretary general, and ALF representation, agreed on steps to push the process forward, including the institutionalization of the initiative within the overall OAU framework, revision of the Kampala Document to reflect changes on the continent since 1991, initiation of negotiations about the CSSDCA principles among ambassadors to the OAU, and distribution of the Kampala Document in all OAU working languages.

The OAU Central Organ formally charged the Steering Committee on October 1 with preparing for the Ministerial Conference as resolved in the Sirte Declaration. The Steering Committee, meeting in Arusha on December 18 and 19, 1999, agreed on the need to situate the CSSDCA initiative within the agenda that the OAU had developed over the decade. In an effort to reinvigorate that agenda, the committee adopted a work program for the early part of 2000 to prepare for the Ministerial Conference. The committee drafted a working document for the conference by a group of experts, which began work in Addis Ababa in February 2000. But at the same time, the OAU was seized by a plan, introduced by Libya's Qadhafi, to turn the organization immediately into an African Union, modeled on the European Union. The plan was approved at the Rome summit in July 2000. The CSSDCA group of experts did not meet thereafter, nor did they meet throughout 2001.

The Next Steps

At this point, the story stops, but the action continues. Although significant progress was made on the OAU front in the year following Obasanjo's July 1999 relaunching of the CSSDCA, it is still too early to tell whether the OAU coalition of "derailers," "brakers," and "riders" of the early 1990s can be overcome even now. It is not the objective of this book to cover comprehensively the steps under way and those that need to be taken toward the full adoption and implementation of the CSSDCA. However, based on the steps so far taken, several observations can be made that might help in conceptualizing and formulating possible alternative approaches to the promotion of the process.

To begin with, while the role of General Obasanjo as the founder of the CSSDCA process and now as president of Nigeria remains pivotal, it is important to institutionalize that process for it to become self-sustaining. Paradoxically, the adoption of the CSSDCA by a single government as a spearhead of its foreign policy has advantages and disadvantages: Kampala gains a strong advocate, but at the same time becomes one (even if the principal) among many foreign policy planks of one (even if the largest) among many African states' foreign policies. It finds competition from other policies within Nigeria and from other states within Africa. Efforts elsewhere to support the movement can be seen—and delegitimized—as attempts at backing another state's foreign policy. In addition, the location of the primary nongovernmental organization behind the process, the ALF, in Nigeria may further portray the movement as a Nigerian initiative rather than a pan-African one.

Second, experience so far indicates that the CSSDCA is a process that requires the engagement of multiple partners at various levels. Although the OAU will remain a central arena, subregional organizations, which have already shown significant initiatives relevant to the framework, need to be involved and effectively utilized. The OAU needs the collaboration of supporting layers of states, acting as sovereigns and collectively as members of a geographic subregion, to underpin its efforts and keep them on track. Otherwise, the OAU resolutions can too easily become a periodic ritual rather than a code of daily conduct.

Third, these various levels of state activity need to be paced by the engagement of civil society, which is where the Kampala Movement began. Unless government efforts are paralleled by the activities of nongovernmental organizations, which can act as implementers and watchdogs, there will be no keepers of the conscience and agents of the principles to keep the movement alive. A regime-building movement—as shown in Helsinki—needs to walk on two feet, one belonging to the states and the other to their people; otherwise, it only hops, tires, and falls. The location of the ALF in Nigeria makes it an agent of the state, whereas it needs local sections throughout Africa, just as various sections of Amnesty International, Transparency, Human Rights League, and democracy movements have appealed to governments to promote new norms related to the Kampala principles.

Fourth, such an ongoing process of negotiation, adaptation, and reformulation of strategies implies flexibility and an eclectic response to needs as they arise. The Kampala Movement must remain alert to developments, take advantage of opportunities as they present themselves, and come up with creative incentives for states to adopt and implement the stipulated principles. Had the Kampala Movement not been kept alive during the latter half of the 1990s while Obasanjo was under house arrest, it would have had to be reinvented on his liberation.

Indeed, the same elements of competition with existing regional organizations or arrangements, dependency on individual leaders or hegemonic governments in the regions, the need for flexibility, creative adaptation, and effective use of opportunities also characterize experiences in the other regions of the world, such as Asia (Association of Southeast Asian Nations), Latin America (Organizations of American States), and Europe (Organization of Security and Cooperation in Europe). The CSSDCA is perceived as an autonomous, organic entity that will negotiate, interact, and cooperate with other organizations or institutional arrangements, but the crucial question of what that entity is envisaged to be remains open. No clear answer can be given to this question, for, while the ALF and a core group of individual and institutional actors have so far nourished, protected, and safeguarded the initiative, the CSSDCA is a movement that is creating owners, promoters, and users over its expanding evolution. It is more appropriate therefore to see it as an eclectic process, whose effectiveness lies in its strategic framework and a variety of actors. Hence the need for elaborating strategies for its future developments.

Strategies for the Future

The initial strategy for the implementation of the CSSDCA, as developed by the ALF and pursued through the 1990–91 meetings, was to strike an alliance between state leadership and nongovernmental organizations (NGOs). This strategy was dictated in part by the European precedent and in part by necessity, since the idea arose primarily in the mind of a sensitized former political figure and needed to be translated through civil society into state action. The Kampala Movement was described as the "voice of Africa," bringing together the many sectors of civil society that its principles sought to protect and enhance. The strategy failed because Africa's many voices were not effective in reaching their own governments, which was the situation that Kampala decried and sought to correct. The process did not get started because the local level was not effectively galvanized and mobilized to reach the government level.

The strategy of the interim, largely by default, was to mobilize expert and civil opinion to keep the idea alive. Rejected by African states and by the African regional organization, and then deprived of its animating figure, the idea needed above all to be kept afloat until better days arrived. During this period, the ALF and friends, working primarily through meetings in Washington, D.C., searched about for a new modus operandi, not daring to expect (despite all hope) the return of its leader. Hardly anyone predicted the sequence of events that led to Obasanjo becoming president of Nigeria in 1999.

The strategy of the twenty-first century, therefore, overcame the disadvantage of the beginning of the decade because responsibility for strategy was placed in the hands of a single, powerful state. But the OAU, toward which the new strategy was directed, became a moving target, just as it was firmly locked in the sights of Nigeria. In its thirty-seventh summit at Lusaka, in July 2001, the OAU transformed itself into a new entity, the African Union. In the excitement and maneuvering of the institutional transformation, the principles and purposes of the Kampala Movement were imperceptibly folded into the new union, put on the agenda in a bowdlerized version for the 2002 summit of the AU in Praetoria. Once again, the battle for a new vision of values on the continental level was transformed by the introduction of a new arena. Other disadvantages must also be overcome by providing the means for various levels above and below the state—national, local, regional, and continental—to communicate with one another. On the "upper" levels, advocates have concentrated on getting the Kampala principles adopted by subregional organizations before turning to the African Union once again. This process of interstate negotiation takes time. On the "lower" levels, advocates have used national and regional think tanks and civic and business groups to generate interest and create pressure for the normative framework. At all levels, the assistance and support of international partners will be important if the CSSDCA process is to be successful.

Faced with hesitation on the level of the African Union and leaving that bastion to the charges of Nigeria, the movement has also been focusing on a more manageable level of international organization—the various subregional groupings. The state groupings in West, Southern, East, Central, and the Horn of Africa were all initially economic in nature and then gradually took on additional security functions, recognizing in practice the interdependent nature of these functions as emphasized in the Kampala Document. This interdependence makes the subregional organizations ready vehicles for the adoption of principles and mechanisms of the movement, which then can be combined at the continental level as part of the overall CSSDCA process.

Current plans are to mobilize local groups as building blocks of a process that moves from local to state to subregional to continental level. Groups promoting clusters of the Kampala principles feed into other groups promoting the Kampala Movement, thus inspiring civil society to hold its government accountable. These efforts are not without their own "derailers" and "brakers," and progress is slow and uneven.

Besides subregional organizations of cooperation, other organizations, even from other continents, are being solicited to include the Kampala Document in their focus of activity and to endorse the CSSDCA process. The National Summit for Africa Movement, an effort to build a grassroots constituency for African policy in the United States, endorsed the CSSDCA in its Statement of Principles and held a special session on the Kampala process at its national convention in Washington, D.C., on February 19, 2000.

In South Africa, the African Center for the Constructive Resolution of Disputes (ACCORD) is probably the leading homegrown institution for the practice and training of peacemaking in its own country and, more broadly, its region. Indeed, it was on a home stopover on his way to ACCORD's African Conference on Peacemaking and Conflict Resolution in March 1995 that Obasanjo was arrested. ACCORD disseminates the Kampala principles through education and practice and works alongside the SADC in many of its activities. In Senegal, the Council for the Development of Social Science Research in Africa is the broadest pan-African institution of research cooperation, working through thematic research networks that cut across linguistic and regional boundaries. Its quarterly, *Africa Development*, is the longest-standing Africa-based journal. At its research planning conference in September 1998 at the University of Witwatersrand, the CSSDCA was prominently highlighted as embodying Africa's own set of principles and mechanisms for conflict management. In Benin, with branches throughout West and Equatorial Africa, the Study and Research Group on Democracy and Economic and Social Development (GERDDES) is an organization for the promotion of principles from the stability and development calabashes of the CSSDCA. The Kampala principles need to be promoted by national sections of the ALF established in African countries, working on their own governments, on regional organizations, and on the new African Union.

Elsewhere, the focus is on using local business groups and chambers of commerce to endorse the CSSDCA principles. More broadly, such groups are also invited to join with local academics, human rights activists, and other civic leaders to form "Councils on Foreign Relations" in the major cities of the continent. At present, such councils do not exist in Africa south of the Sahara except on an ad hoc basis; the closest institutions are foreign relations research academies such as the Nigerian Institute for International Affairs, which has discussed the CSSDCA in its publications. Full plans for the development of such councils are not yet worked out. Most probably, results could only be achieved with outside assistance and encouragement, such as the U.S. Council on Foreign Relations might provide.

To conclude, the CSSDCA may still be a vision, initially conceived by a far-sighted leadership responding to the compelling needs of Africa in the dawn of the post–cold war era. Its aim was primarily to make Africans assume responsibility for the security, dignity, and general welfare of its people within a framework of regional cooperation. But the conference also hoped to create conditions that would win the approval and support of major global partners. Because it is visionary, its adoption and implementation have been problematic and remain aspirations for the future. And yet, the crises of the African continent and their tragic humanitarian consequences continue to challenge not only Africans but also the conscience of humanity throughout the world. Action in response to these compelling conditions cannot be deferred. And so, while the full implementation of the CSSDCA process may be evolutionary, it has to be seen as incremental. Some measures require immediate steps, which the OAU and some of the subregional organizations have already taken. Much more needs to be done urgently to implement the CSSDCA principles. The role of the international community, while complementary or supplementary, is pivotal, not only because African governments for the most part lack the requisite capacity to pursue the objectives of the CSSDCA alone but also because some of them often lack the political will to provide their people with security, physical safety, and protection of human rights and fundamental freedoms. Governments often fail to provide for the general welfare or offer effective assistance when humanitarian tragedies occur. Through regional and international cooperation, African governments can be made to realize that sovereignty entails responsibilities. Governments must meet them or risk forfeiting their sovereignty.

Appendix:
Specific Principles of the Kampala Document

1. The principles of good neighborliness and peaceful resolution of conflicts shall guide African governments individually and collectively.
2. African governments shall initiate, design, and implement policies and strengthen institutions to adjudicate interstate disputes, resolve conflicts, and attenuate the possibility of interstate and intrastate violence.
3. African governments shall undertake appropriate measures to prevent or contain crises before they erupt into violent confrontation.
4. A continental peacekeeping machinery shall be instituted for the preservation of peace in instances which potentially or actually threaten the security of African state(s) or the continent as a whole, and shall operate in cooperation with United Nations peacekeeping operations where necessary.
   4a. An authorizing body for mandating the establishment, extension, and termination of peacekeeping operations; command and control structures; administration and logistic support for operations; finding systems; procedures for acquisition of troops; and modalities for rapid deployment in reaction to situations of aggression against participating member states shall be established.
5. A treaty on mutual nonaggression and mutual defense in the event of external aggression shall be negotiated among all African countries.

6. State boundaries shall be demarcated by bilateral commissions, and conditions of border permeability be established between and among neighbors.

7. Confidence building measures shall be developed between and among African countries to cover, *inter alia*, exchange of information on troop locations and movements; joint military training; joint military maneuvers; joint naval patrols; and joint studies and seminars on subregional, regional, and continental security issues.

8. Military expenditures by member states shall be reduced through ceilings on manpower and limitations on military hardware.

   8a. A collective understanding shall be developed of the type of military equipment justifiable for procurement or manufacture by African countries.

   8b. A collective African effort should be undertaken for the selective manufacturing of desirable military equipment for Africa's defense.

9. An African Peace Council shall be formed of distinguished personalities and African elder statesmen under the OAU, and charged with the task of ensuring that peace and harmony reign in the continent and a state of intra-African and inter-African tranquility is created and maintained, and of effecting a measure of intervention in national security problems of participating member states and determining appropriate actions including reconciliation and mediation or recommendation of deployment of African peacekeeping operations or both.

10. Domestic conditions constituting a threat to personal and collective security and gross violations of human rights lie beyond the protection of sovereignty and are within the domain of actions of all concerned African states.

11. Every individual citizen shall enjoy the security to live in peace with access to basic necessities of life while participating in the affairs of his/her society in freedom and enjoying all fundamental human rights.

12. The rights and freedoms of the citizens of member states shall be promoted and protected.

13. No citizen shall be subject to arbitrary arrest or detention without trial or subject to torture and other forms of inhuman or cruel treatment. Provisions for *mandamus* and *habeas corpus* shall be made in national

bills of rights. Legal aid services for those who cannot secure legal services for themselves shall be funded from public revenue. There shall be no detention without trial.

14. Every state shall have a constitution with a bill of rights promulgated after thorough national debate and adopted by an assembly of freely elected representatives of the people.

15. The individual's right to own property and to enjoy societies' socioeconomic and cultural benefits shall be guaranteed by the constitution.

16. The mandate of the African Commission on Human and Peoples' Rights in accordance with the African Charter on Human and Peoples' Rights (ACHPR) shall be expanded to provide for an annual published assessment of the human rights record of each African country.

    16a. An African Court of Justice on Human Rights within the framework of ACHPR shall be established to adjudicate between governments and peoples' rights. ACHPR should be funded separately by international organizations and other independent sources.

    16b. Every participating state shall sign, ratify, and implement African and other relevant international legal instruments in the field of human rights.

17. Laws shall be legislated by an assembly of freely elected representatives and shall be vigorously enforced by African governments.

18. No one can be exempt from accounting for his/her conduct when a law is breached.

19. Active and genuine participation of the citizens of every country in the governance of public affairs shall be fostered.

    19a. Decisions relating to governance of public affairs shall be freely discussed and choices assessed so that the public will be mindful of the risks and rewards associated with any action of government.

    19b. There shall be no hindrance to alternative ideas, institutions, and leaders competing for public support.

20. Citizens shall have the right to participate in free and fair elections in their countries through an election based on a secret ballot and universal adult suffrage, as stipulated by their national constitutions.

20a. Every citizen of a participating member state shall have the right to stand for election to public office and participate in the affairs of the state.

21. Women shall be fully involved in decisionmaking processes at all levels and assured full access to all factors of production, with special attention to technical assistance and financial resources in rural areas.

22. All laws that discriminate against women shall be abrogated, to be replaced by juridical instruments and mechanisms to guarantee and preserve the rights of women.

23. Political organizations shall be separate from the state and shall not be created on religious, ethnic, regional, or racial basis and considerations and these should not be exploited by leaders.

24. The separation of religion from the state shall be protected, and religion shall remain a personal affair.

25. Governments shall ensure that in making appointments, due regard is given to equitable representation at all levels.

26. Trade union rights shall be guaranteed in accordance with ILO conventions and recommendations.

27. There shall be periodic renewal of the mandate of political leaders. At the same time, the tenure of elected leaders in various branches of government shall be constitutionally limited to a given number of years.

28. The actions of the officers of the bench shall be unfettered by the legislative and executive branches of government, and their tenure shall be guaranteed and provided for in the national constitutions. Decisions relating to the removal of officers from the bench shall be exercised by a Judicial Commission. Independence of the judiciary shall be effected through an inviolate tenure of offices, and through stable emoluments guaranteed by a legislative act.

29. Institutions that promote accountability in public service shall be established and given adequate protection through independent financing and guaranteed tenures. These institutions include boards of audit for public expenditure, code of conduct bureaus for public officials, and ombudsmen.

29a. The financing of organs of adjudication and accountability (courts, audit boards, code of conduct bureaus, or ombudsman) shall be paid from consolidated revenue funds not subject to arbitrary interference by executive fiat.

29b. An independent Civil Service shall be established with guaranteed security of tenure, salary, and pension with members nominated on professional grounds by an independent Civil Service Commission. Removal of a civil servant must be exercised solely by an independent Civil Service Commission.

30. Development shall be based on self-reliance and the internalization of self-sustaining growth, diversification horizontally in broadening the continental production base and vertically in processing and marketing, rapid integration, and popular participation through equal opportunity and access.

31. Meritocracy and incentives and compensations for professionals and civil servants are necessary to curb the brain-drain, to promote the development of professionals to replace expatriate technicians, and to expand endogenous technical institutional capabilities, professional associations, and national consultants.

31a. Policies shall be adopted to achieve the elimination of illiteracy, the promotion of science and technology and of vocational and business training, the continental harmonization of education systems, the improvement of governance capabilities and administrative efficiency, among others.

31b. Educational systems shall incorporate in their curricula teaching in African languages, values, cultures, history, philosophy, etc. Research in African humanities shall be given equal attention with the pursuit of science and technology. All youth shall have the right to the acquisition of basic education.

32. Domestic saving and indigenous investment shall be promoted, to replace the ethos of excessive consumption, as part of a general principle of liberal economic development with government support.

33. Transnational resources and infrastructures such as hydroelectric and hydrocarbon energy sources, waterways, forests, and coastal zones shall be jointly developed.

34. Economic development shall be pursued through agricultural diversification and transformation industrialization.

34a. Policies shall be adopted to achieve increased food productivity and food self-sufficiency, cooperative research for a Green Revolution for tropical products, continental coordination of food and nutrition policy, full and nutritious utilization of traditional foods, among others.

34b. Policies shall be adopted to achieve multinational and national investment in intermediate and capital-intensive industry, national investment in small and medium industry, domestic resource-based manufacturing and processing to meet local needs, among others.

35. Food self-sufficiency for Africa, affordable sources for self-reliance in energy, including renewable sources—notably solar energy—and economical provision of desalinization of water shall be considered as much a security matter as an economic priority.

36. Intra-African trade shall be promoted to foster cooperative development.

36a. Policies shall be adopted to achieve trade preferences for intra-Africa trade in food and agriculture and raw materials and in core and strategic industrial products, to facilitate interstate transportation, communication and payments, and to cooperate in joint ventures to take advantage of economies of scale.

37. Environmental protection is necessary for sustainable development.

37a. Policies shall be adopted to achieve reforestation and management of forestry resources, safe waste disposal and prohibition of foreign toxic waste, and long-term environmental management.

38. African economic integration, joint natural resource development, and continental supranational institutionalization, as well as global interdependence, are necessary conditions for security, stability, and development.

39. Institutions of civil society—including trade unions, chambers of commerce, women's organizations, youth associations, and professional groups—need expanding and strengthening, both within African countries and cooperatively on a regional and continental basis.

40. A structural, functional model of continental integration shall be based on a minimum timetable for an African Economic Community and through revived and accelerated subregional models.

Notes

Chapter 1

1. *The Kampala Document: Towards a Conference on Security, Stability, Development and Cooperation in Africa*, May 19–22, 1991, Kampala, Uganda (New York: Africa Leadership Forum jointly with the secretariats of the Organization of African Unity and the United Nations Economic Commission for Africa), pp. 7–8.

2. In the Nigerian election of 1999, observers, including one of the coauthors, from the National Democratic Institute/Carter Center, International Republican Institute, OAU, Commonwealth, and European Union, among others, monitored the proceedings.

Chapter 2

1. I. William Zartman, ed., *Governance as Conflict Management: Politics and Violence in West Africa* (Brookings, 1996), especially chap. 2, pp. 9–48.

2. I. William Zartman, "Revolution and Development," *Civilisations*, vol. 20, no. 2 (1970), pp. 181–99.

3. Thomas Hodgkin, *Nationalism in Colonial Africa* (London: Mueller, 1956).

4. See Donald Rothchild, *Racial Bargaining in Independent Kenya* (London: Oxford, 1973).

5. C.O.C. Amate, *Inside the OAU* (St. Martin's Press, 1986); Michael Wolfers, *Politics in the OAU* (London: Methuen, 1986); and I. William Zartman, *International Relations in the New Africa*, updated ed. (University Press of America, 1987).

6. Saadia Touval, *The Boundary Politics of Independent Africa* (Princeton University Press, 1970), chap. 4, pp. 82–98.

7. The initials CNS come from the French, "Conférence Nationale Souveraine." See

F. Eboussi Boulaga, *Les conférences nationales en Afrique Nouvelle* (Paris: Karthala, 1993).

8. Samuel Huntington, *The Third Wave* (University of Oklahoma Press, 1991); and Marina Ottaway, *Democracy in Africa: The Hard Road Ahead* (Lynne Rienner, 1997).

9. Alex Gboyega and Adu Boahen, "Nigeria," and "Ghana," in I. William Zartman, ed., *Governance as Conflict Management: Politics and Violence in West Africa* (Brookings, 1996).

10. None of the states was among the seven states, all in Africa, below $200, and Cape Verde, an island state of the region, had a per capita GNP of $1,080 (Washington: Overseas Development Council, 1999), p A54.

11. Global Commission on Africa, *African Social and Economic Trends, Annual Report 1997* (Washington: World Bank, 1998).

12. Ibid.

13. Joan Nelson, ed., *Economic Crises and Policy Choice* (Princeton University Press, 1990).

14. Edmond Kwam Kouassi and John White, "The Impact of Reduced European Security Roles on African Relations," in I. William Zartman, ed., *Europe and Africa: The New Phase* (Lynne Rienner, 1993).

15. The initials come from the French, "Comité Permanent Inter-États de la Lutte contre la Sécheresse dans le Sahel."

16. Saadia Touval, *Somali Nationalisms* (Harvard University Press, 1963), pp. 103, 151.

17. John Markakis, *National and Class Conflict in the Horn of Africa* (Cambridge: Cambridge University Press, 1987), p. 158.

18. Ibid., pp. 106, 110–11.

19. Ibid., p. 112; and Peter Woodward, *The Horn of Africa: State Politics and International Relations* (London: IB Tauris, 1996), pp. 119–21.

20. Markakis, *National and Class Conflict in the Horn of Africa*, p. 165.

21. Woodward, *The Horn of Africa*, p. 121.

22. Ibid., p. 122.

23. Douglas H. Johnson and Gerard Prunier, "The Foundation and Expansion of the Sudan People's Liberation Army," in M.W. Daly and Ahmad Awad Sikainga, eds., *Civil War in the Sudan* (London: British Academic Press, 1993), pp. 125–26.

24. Markakis, *National and Class Conflict in the Horn of Africa*, pp. 178–80, 229–32; and I. William Zartman, *Ripe for Resolution: Conflict and Intervention in Africa* (Oxford: Oxford University Press, 1989), pp. 91–92, 104–08.

25. Woodward, *The Horn of Africa*, pp. 111, 130; and John Sorenson, ed., *Disaster and Development in the Horn of Africa* (Macmillan, 1995), pp. 24–25.

26. Terrence Lyons and Ahmed Samatar, *Somalia* (Brookings, 1995), p. 14.

27. Martin Doornbos, "Changing Perspectives on Conflict and Integration in Uganda," in G. N. Uzoigwe, *Uganda: The Dilemma of Nationhood* (New York: NOK, 1982), pp. 318–19.

28. Thomas P. Ofcansky, *Uganda: Tarnished Pearl of Africa* (Westview Press, 1996), pp. 42–45.

29. Jennifer A. Widner, *The Rise of the Party in Kenya* (University of California Press, 1992), pp. 60-61, 142, 145; and D. Pal Ahluwalia, *Post-Colonialism and the Politics of Kenya* (New Science Publishers, 1996), pp.184–86.

30. Woodward, *The Horn of Africa*, pp. 111–13.

31. Ali Coubba, *Le mal djiboutien* (Paris: L'Harmattan, 1995), pp. 136–40.

32. Markakis, *National and Class Conflict in the Horn of Africa*, chap. 9, pp. 237–71; and Ruth Iyob and Kassam Aneesa, "The Eritrean Struggle for Independence: Domination, Resistance, Nationalism, 1942–1993," *Journal of Modern African Studies*, vol. 37, no. 2 (1999).

33. Sorenson, *Disaster and Development in the Horn of Africa*, pp. 5–9.

34. Global Coalition for Africa, *African Social and Economic Trends, 1997 Annual Report.*

35. Hussein M. Adam, "Comment," in Martin Doornbos and others, eds., *Beyond Conflict in the Horn* (The Hague: The Institute of Social Studies, 1992); "Somali Civil Wars," in Tassier Ali and Robert Matthews, eds., *Civil Wars in Africa* (Montreal: Queens-McGill University Press, 1995); and "Somalia: A Terrible Beauty Being Born?" in I. William Zartman, ed., *Collapsed States: The Disintegration and Restoration of Legitimate Authority* (Lynne Rienner, 1995).

36. Stefan Gunnarsson, "Interstate Cooperation in Locust Control in the Horn of Africa," in Reidulf K. Molvaer, ed., *Environment Cooperation and Confidence Building in the Horn of Africa* (Sage Publications, 1995), p. 154.

37. Doornbos, "Changing Perspectives," p. 322; Babu, "Comment," in Doornbos and others, *Beyond Conflict in the Horn*, p.116; and Christian Potholm and Richard Fredland, eds., *Integration and Disintegration in East Africa* (University Press of America, 1980).

38. Ali Ahmed Saleem, "An Introduction to IGADD," in Doornbos and others, *Beyond Conflict in the Horn*, p. 115.

39. Timothy Shaw, "New Regionalisms in Africa as Responses to Environmental Crises: IGADD and Development in the Horn in the Mid-1990s," in Sorenson, *Disaster and Development in the Horn of Africa,* p. 255.

40. Maina Karaba, "Infrastructural Financial Problems of Regional Cooperation in the Horn of Africa," in Molvaer, ed., *Environment Cooperation and Confidence Building in the Horn of Africa,* pp. 185–89; and Saleem, "An Introduction to IGADD," p. 115.

41. Lionel Cliffe, "Regional Dimensions of Conflict in the Horn of Africa," *Third World Quarterly,* vol. 20, no. 1 (January 1999), pp. 92–93.

42. Mohamed Sahnoun, *Somalia: The Missed Opportunities* (Washington: U.S. Institute of Peace, 1994), pp. 9–11; Woodward, *The Horn of Africa*, p. 188; and Cliffe, "Regional Dimensions," p. 94.

43. Jeffrey A. Lefebvre, "Post-Cold War Clouds on the Horn of Africa: The Eritrea-Sudan Crisis," *Middle East Journal,* vol. 50, no. 3 (Summer 1996), p. 35; and Cliffe, "Regional Dimensions," pp. 96–97.

44. Crawford Young, *Politics in the Congo* (Princeton University Press, 1968), chap. 7, pp. 140–61; Crawford Young and Thomas Turner, *The Rise and Decline of the Zairean*

State (University of Wisconsin Press, 1985); Thomas Callaghy, *The State-Society Struggle* (Columbia University Press, 1984); and Michael Schatzberg, *The Dialectic of Oppression in Zaire* (Indiana University Press, 1988).

45. Gérard Prunier, *The Rwanda Crisis: History of a Genocide* (Columbia University Press, 1995), especially chaps. 2-3, pp. 41–126; and Alison DesForges, *Leave None to Tell the Story: Genocide in Rwanda* (New York: Human Rights Watch, 1999), esp. chaps. 1-2, pp. 1–64.

46. John F. Clark and David Gardiniers, eds., *Political Reform in Francophone Africa* (Westview Press, 1997).

47. The third (1977) and fourth (1978) Congo—actually Zairean—crises were the two successive invasions of Shaba (Katanga) province from neighboring Angola. See I. William Zartman, *Ripe for Resolution: Conflict and Intervention in Africa* (Oxford, 1989), chap. 4.

48. Mohammed Maundi, Gilbert Khadiagala, Kwaku Nuameh, Saadia Touval, and I. William Zartman, *Entry into Mediation* (Washington: U.S. Institute of Peace, 2002).

49. Global Commission for Africa, *African Economic and Social Trends, 1997 Annual Report*.

50. In between, below $200, were Malawi $147, Eritrea $158, Sierra Leone $165, and Gambia $169.

51. Marc-Louis Ropivia, "Failing Institutions and Shattered Space: What Regional Integration for Central Africa," in Daniel Bach, ed. *Regionalization in Africa* (Indiana University Press, 1999), pp. 125–27.

52. Kenneth Grundy, *Confrontation and Accomodation in Southern Africa: The Limits of Independence* (University of California Press, 1993); and Gilbert M. Khadiagala, *Allies in Adversity: The Frontline States in Southern African International Politics, 1975-1993* (Ohio University Press, 1994).

53. Tom Lodge, "The Southern African Post-Colonial State," *Commonwealth and Comparative Politics*, vol. 36 (March 1998), pp. 20–47.

54. Khabele Matlosa, "Democracy and Conflict in Post-Apartheid Southern Africa: Dilemmas of Social Change in Small States," *International Affairs*, vol. 74, no. 2 (1998), pp. 320–22.

55. John Holm, Patrick Molutsi and Gloria Somolekae, "The Development of Civil Society in a Democratic State: The Botswana Model," *African Studies Review*, vol. 39 (September 1996), pp. 43–70.

56. For comprehensive discussion of the FLS see Khadiagala, *Allies in Adversity*; and Khadiagala, "Security in Southern Africa: Cross-National Learning," *Jerusalem Journal of International Relations*, vol. 14 (September 1992), pp. 85–86.

57. James D. Sidaway and David Simon, "Geopolitical Transition and State Formation: The Changing Political Geographies of Angola, Mozambique, and Namibia," *Journal of Southern African Affairs*, vol. 19 (March 1993), p. 24.

58. Liisa Laakso, "Relationship between the State and Civil Society in the Zimbabwean Elections 1995," *Journal of Commonwealth and Comparative Politics*, vol. 34 (November 1996), pp. 218–34. See also Audie Klotz, "Race and Nationalism in Zimbabwean Foreign

Policy," *The Round Table*, no. 327 (July 1993), pp. 255–79.

59. Chris Tapscott, "National Reconciliation, Social Equity, and Class Formation in Independent Namibia," *Journal of Southern African Affairs*, vol. 19 (March 1993), pp. 29–31.

60. Andre du Pisani, "South Africa and SADCC: Into the 1990s," in Alan Whiteside and Gavin Maasdorp, eds., *Towards a Post-Apartheid Future: Political and Economic Relations in Southern Africa* (St. Martin's Press, 1992), pp. 174–86; and Hasu Patel, "The SADCC States, the International Environment, and Change in South Africa," in Whiteside and Maasdorp, *Towards a Post-Apartheid Future*, pp. 45–61.

61. Africa Leadership Forum, *The Kampala Document: Towards a Conference on Security, Stability, Development and Cooperation in Africa* (Kampala, May 1991), pp. 9–10. For discussions of CSSDCA's influence on southern Africa, see Willie Breytenbach, *Conflict in Sub-Saharan Africa: From the Frontline States to Collective Security*, Arusha Papers 2 (Dar es Salaam: Center for Foreign Relations, February 1995), pp. 8–9; and Susan Willet, "Demilitarization, Disarmament, and Development in Southern Africa," *Review of African Political Economy*, vol. 25, no.77 (1998), pp. 413–14.

62. Quoted in Hussein Solomon and Jakkie Cilliers, "The Southern African Development Community and Small Arms Proliferation," in Virginia Gamba, ed., *Society under Siege: Licit Responses to Illicit Arms*, Towards Collaborative Peace Series, vol. II (South Africa: Institute for Strategic Studies, 1998), p. 80. See also Laurie Nathan and Joao Honwana, *After the Storm: Common Security and Conflict Resolution in Southern Africa*, Arusha Papers 3 (Dar es Salaam: Center for Foreign Relations, February 1995), pp. 14–22; and Khadiagala, "Confidence-Building Measures in Sub-Saharan Africa," in Michael Krepon, ed., *A Handbook of Confidence-Building Measures for Regional Security, Third Edition* (Washington: Henry L. Stimson Center, March 1998), p. 106.

63. Solomon and Cilliers, "The Southern African Development Community," *After the Storm*, pp. 80–81; and Nathan and Honwana, pp. 15–27.

64. For accounts of these exercises see Khadiagala, "Confidence-Building Measures in Sub-Saharan Africa," pp. 107–08; "SADC Armies Ready for Peace Keeping Duties," *PanAfrican News Agency*, January 14, 1999; and Tony Lamberti, "SADC Troops Learn to Keep Peace," *Business Day*, April 23, 1999.

65. John Seiler, "Is Military Peacemaking Really Possible?" *Electronic Mail and Guardian*, April 8, 1999.

66. Margaret Novicki, "Interview: Kaire Mbuende, Strengthening Southern Africa," *Africa Report*, vol. 39 (July-August 1994), p. 45.

67. Roger Southall, Petlane Tsoeu, and Colin Murray, "Democratization and Demilitarization in Lesotho: The General Election of 1993 and Its Aftermath," *African Affairs*, vol. 96, no. 382 (1997), p. 136; and David Coplan and Tim Quinlan, "A Chief by the People: Nation versus State in Lesotho," *Africa*, vol. 67, no. 1 (1997), p. 43.

68. Carrie Manning, "The Collapse of Peace in Angola," *Current History*, vol. 98, no. 628 (May 1999), pp. 208–12.

69. Iden Wetherell, "Mugabe Crafts a New Africa Defense Pact," *Daily Mail and Guardian*, April 16, 1999.

70. J. E. Spence, "'Everybody Has Won, So All Must Have Prizes': Reflections on the South African General Election," *Government and Opposition*, vol. 29, no. 4 (1994), pp. 431–44; and Peter Vale and Sipho Maseko, "South Africa and the African Renaissance," *International Affairs*, vol. 74, no. 2 (1998), pp. 271–87.

71. Stephen Chan, "Democracy in Southern Africa: The 1990 Elections in Zimbabwe and 1991 Elections in Zambia," *Round Table*, no. 332 (1992), pp. 183–200; and Lisa Laakso, "Relationships between the State and Civil Society in the Zimbabwean Elections 1995," *Journal of Commonwealth and Comparative Politics*, vol. 34 (November 1996), pp. 218–34.

72. Chisepo J. J. Mphaisha, "Retreat from Democracy in Post One-Party State Zambia," *Journal of Commonwealth and Comparative Politics*, vol. 34 (July 1996), pp. 65–84.

73. Cameron Hume, *Ending Mozambique's War: The Role of Mediation and Good Offices* (Washington: U.S. Institute of Peace, 1994); and Chris Alden, "The UN and the Resolution of Conflict in Mozambique," *Journal of Modern African Studies*, vol.33, no. 1 (1995).

74. Clement Ng'ong'ola, "Managing the Transition to Pluralism in Malawi: Legal and Constitutional Arrangements," *Journal of Commonwealth and Comparative Politics*, vol. 34 (July 1996), pp. 85–110; Jonathan Mayuyuka Kaunda, "The State and Society in Malawi," *Journal of Commonwealth and Comparative Politics*, vol. 36 (March 1998), pp. 48–67; and John Wiseman, "Malawi: The Contested Legacy of the Ngwazi," *Round Table*, no. 346 (1998), pp. 235–49.

75. For interesting perspectives on democratic change see John Saul, "Liberal Democracy vs. Popular Democracy in Southern Africa," *Review of African Political Economy*, no. 72 (1997), pp. 219–36; Saul, "'For Fear of Being Condemned as Old Fashioned': Liberal Democracy vs. Popular Democracy in Sub-Saharan Africa," *Review of African Political Economy*, no. 73 (1997), pp. 339–53; and Kenneth Good, "Accountable to Themselves: Predominance in Southern Africa," *Journal of Modern African Studies*, vol. 35, no. 4 (1997), pp. 547–73.

76. Stephen Chan, "Troubled Pluralisms: Pondering an Indonesian Moment for Zimbabwe and Zambia," *Round Table*, no. 349 (1999), pp. 61–76.

77. Global Coalition for Africa, *African Social and Economic Trends, 1997 Annual Report*.

78. Servaas van der Berg, "Consolidating South African Democracy: The Political Arithmetic of Budgetary Redistribution," *African Affairs*, vol. 97 (April 1998), pp. 251–64.

79. Roland Oliver and Anthony Atmore, *Africa Since 1800,* 2d ed. (Cambridge University Press, 1972), pp. 265–68; Richard Gibbs, "Regional Integration in Post-Apartheid South Africa: The Case Renegotiating the South African Customs Union," *Journal of Southern African Studies*, vol. 23 (March 1997), pp. 67–86; and Colin McCarthy, "SACU and The Rand Zone," in Bach, ed., *Regionalization in Africa*, pp. 159–68.

80. Peter Takirambudde, "The Rival Strategies of SADC & PTA/COMESA," in Bach, ed., *Regionalization in Africa*, pp. 151–58.

81. Africa Leadership Forum, *Kampala Document*, p. 35.

82. I. William Zartman and Victor Kremenyuk, eds. *Cooperative Security: Reducing Third World Wars* (Syracuse University Press, 1995); and David Lake and Patrick Morgan, eds. *Regional Orders: Building Security in a New World* (Pennsylvania State University Press, 1997).

83. Cliffe, "Regional Dimensions," pp. 108–09.

84. Jeffrey Herbst, *States and Power in Africa* (Princeton University Press, 2000); and Paul Henze, "The Economic Dimension of Federalism in the Horn of Africa," in Peter Woodward and Murray Forsyth, eds., *Conflict and Peace in the Horn of Africa: Federalism and Its Alternatives* (Aldershot: Dartmouth, 1994), p. 93.

85. Barry Posen, "The Security Dilemma and Ethnic Conflict," in Michael Brown, ed., *Ethnic Conflict and International Security* (Princeton University Press, 1993); David Lake and Donald Rothchild, eds., *The International Spread of Ethnic Conflict* (Princeton University Press, 1999), especially chaps. 1-2.

86. Wolfram F. Hanreider, "Dissolving International Politics: Reflections on the Nation-State," in Richard Little and Michael Smith, eds., *Perspectives on World Politics* (London: Routledge, 1991), pp. 145–51.

87. Barry Buzan, *People, States, and Fear* (New York: Harvester Wheatsheaf, 1991), pp. 101–03.

88. Zartman, *Collapsed States*, p. 4.

Chapter 3

1. Kao Kim Hourn, *ASEAN-10 Is Born* (Phnom Penh, Cambodia: Cambodian Institute for Cooperation and Peace, 1997).

2. Koro Bessho, "Identities and Security in East Asia," Adelphi Paper 325 (London: Oxford University Press, 1999), pp. 39–51.

3. Amitav Acharya, "Culture and Security: Achieving Regional Security in the 'ASEAN Way,'" in Keith Krause, ed., *Cross-Cultural Dimensions of Multilateral Non-Proliferation and Arms Control Dialogues*, research report prepared for the Non-Proliferation, Arms Control and Disarmament Division, Department of Foreign Affairs and International Trade, Ottawa, Canada, p. 51; and I. William Zartman, ed. *Traditional Cures for Modern Conflict: Africa's Traditional Conflict Medicine* (Lynne Rienner, 2000).

4. Mely Caballero-Anthony, "Mechanisms of Dispute Settlement: The ASEAN Experience," *Contemporary Southeast Asia*, vol. 20, no. 1 (1998), p. 46.

5. Sheldon W. Simon, "Security Prospects in Southeast Asia: Collaborative Efforts and the ASEAN Regional Forum," *Pacific Review*, vol. 11, no. 2 (1998), p. 197.

6. Estrella D. Solidum, "Regional Co-operation and ASEAN: The Philippine Experience," *Asian Journal of Political Science*, vol. 5, no. 1 (1997), pp. 52–59.

7. Dewi Fortuna Anwar, "ASEAN and Indonesia: Some Reflections," *Asian Journal of Political Science*, vol. 5, no. 1 (1997), p. 22.

8. I. William Zartman, *International Relations in the New Africa* (Prentice Hall, 1966; updated, University Press of America, 1987), chap. 1.

9. Michael Welsey, "The Asian Crisis and the Adequacy of Regional Institutions," *Contemporary Southeast Asia*, vol. 21, no.1 (1999).

10. Acharya, "Culture and Security," p. 53.

11. Anwar, "ASEAN and Indonesia," p. 28.

12. Caballero-Anthony, "Mechanisms of Dispute Settlement," p. 58.

13. Ibid., p. 58.

14. Zartman, *Traditional Cures*; and see Richard Stubbs, "Malaysia: Avoiding Ethnic Strife in a Deeply Divided Society," in Joseph V. Montville, ed., *Conflict and Peacemaking in Multiethnic Societies* (Lexington Books, 1991), p. 292.

15. Jeffrey Z. Rubin, Dean G. Pruitt, and Sung Hee Kim, *Social Conflict: Escalation, Stalemate, and Settlement* (McGraw-Hill, 1994); and Joseph A. Camilleri, "Human Rights, Cultural Diversity and Conflict Resolution: The Asia Pacific Context," *Pacifica Review*, vol. 6, no. 2 (1994), p. 32.

16. William Korey, *The Promises We Keep* (St. Martin's Press, 1993).

17. Acharya, "Culture and Security," p. 51.

18. Anwar, "ASEAN and Indonesia," p. 29.

19. Fen Hampson, *Nurturing Peace: Why Peace Settlements Succeed or Fail* (Washington: U.S. Institute of Peace, 1996), pp. 176–79.

20. Simon, "Security Prospects in Southeast Asia," pp. 198–99.

21. Michael Richardson, "Indonesians Plan a Drive to Recover Role in Asia," *International Herald Tribune*, November 6, 1999.

22. Mohan J. Malik, "Myanmar's Role in Regional Security: Pawn or Pivot?" *Contemporary Southeast Asia*, vol. 19, no. 1 (1997), p. 60.

23. Bessho, "Identities and Security," p. 42.

24. As quoted in Acharya, "Culture and Security," p. 62.

25. Ibid., p. 63.

26. William T. Tow, *Subregional Security Cooperation in the Third World* (Lynne Rienner, 1990), pp. 38–41.

27. Acharya, "Culture and Security," p. 59.

28. Tow, *Subregional Security Cooperation*, p. 42.

29. Caballero-Anthony, "Mechanisms of Dispute Settlement," p. 48.

30. Simon, "Security Prospects in Southeast Asia," p. 198.

31. See Camilleri, "Human Rights, Cultural Diversity and Conflict Resolution," p. 41.

32. Mark J. Valencia, "Energy and Insecurity in Asia," *Survival*, vol. 39, no. 3 (1997); Sung-Han Kim, "Human Security and Regional Cooperation in the Asia-Pacific," *Korea and World Affairs*, vol. 23, no. 1 (1999); and Peter Eng, "Transforming ASEAN," *Washington Quarterly*, vol. 22, no. 1 (1999).

33. Narine Shaun, "Institutional Theory and Southeast Asia: The Case of ASEAN," *World Affairs*, vol. 161, no. 161 (1998); and Rosemary Foot, "Pacific Asia: The Development of Regional Dialogue," in Louise Fawcett and Andrew Hurrell, eds., *Regionalism in World*

Politics (Oxford University Press, 1995), p. 228.

34. Ranjit Gill, *ASEAN: Towards the 21st Century* (London: ASEAN Academic Press, 1997), pp. 178–79.

35. Foot, "Pacific Asia," p. 242; and Simon, "Security Prospects in Southeast Asia," p. 205.

36. Simon, "Security Prospects in Southeast Asia," p. 204.

37. Acharya, "Culture and Security," p. 65.

38. Rolf Muetzenich, "Nuclear Weapons-Free Zone in Southest Asia," *Aussenpolitik* 4 (1997), pp. 391–92.

39. Simon, "Security Prospects in Southeast Asia," p. 208.

40. The crises in Indonesia were a result of the brutal mishandling by nationalists in the Indonesian military before and after East Timorese voted overwhelmingly for independence in August 1999 in a UN-sponsored plebiscite organized and sanctioned by the government of President B. J. Habibie. See Michael Richardson, "Southeast Asians Fear a Breakup of Indonesia," *International Herald Tribune*, November 16, 1999.

41. As cited in Eng, "Transforming ASEAN," p. 49.

42. J. Wentges Taylor, "Electoral Monitoring and the OAS/UN International Civil Mission to Haiti," *Peacekeeping and International Relations*, vol. 25, no. 6 (1996), pp. 3–5; and Kent den Heyer and Jeremy King, "Security and Peacekeeping: The Experience of the OAS," *Peacekeeping and International Relations*, vol. 25, no. 3 (1996), pp. 15–16.

43. Javier Corrales and Richard E. Feinberg, "Regimes of Cooperation in the Western Hemisphere: Power, Interests, and Intellectual Traditions," *International Studies Quarterly*, vol. 43, no. 1 (1999), pp. 5–9.

44. Tom J. Farer, "The Role of Regional Collective Security Arrangements," in Thomas G. Weiss, ed., *Collective Security in a Changing World* (Lynne Rienner, 1993), p. 163.

45. Viron P. Vaky, "The Organization of American States and Multilateralism in the Americas," in Viron Vaky and Heraldo Muñoz, *The Future of the Organization of American States* (New York: Twentieth Century Fund, 1993), p. 33.

46. Hal Klepak, "Cross-Cultural Dimensions of the Non-Proliferation and Arms Control Dialogue in Latin America," in Krause, ed., *Cross-Cultural Dimensions*, p. 139.

47. G. Pope Atkins, *Latin America in the International Political System* (Westview Press, 1989), pp. 209–11; and Vaky, "The Organization of American States," pp. 116–17.

48. Atkins, *Latin America in the International Political System*, pp. 205–09.

49. Vaky, "The Organization of American States," pp. 9–10.

50. Ibid., p. 10.

51. Heraldo Muñoz (translated by Mary D'León), "The Right to Democracy in the Americas," *Journal of Interamerican Studies and World Affairs*, vol. 40, no. 1 (1998), p. 5.

52. Muñoz, "The Right to Democracy in the Americas," p. 6; and Farer, "The Role of Regional Collective Security Arrangements."

53. As cited in Muñoz, "The Right to Democracy in the Americas," p. 7. At that time, the OAS had no provision for expulsion. See Atkins, *Latin America in the International Political System*, pp. 212, 223–24.

54. Andrew Hurrell, "Regionalism in the Americas," in Louise Fawcett and Andrew Hurrell, eds., *Regionalism in World Politics* (Oxford University Press, 1995), pp. 254–55.

55. Vaky, "The Organization of American States," p. 12.

56. Corrales and Feinberg, "Regimes of Cooperation in the Western Hemisphere"; and Joaquin Tacsan, "Searching for OAS/UN Task-Sharing Opportunities in Central America and Haiti," in Thomas Weiss, ed., *Beyond UN Subcontracting: Task-Sharing with Regional Security Arrangements and Service-Providing NGOs* (Macmillan, 1998), pp. 91–114.

57. Madeleine Korbel Albright, "The OAS and the Road to Santiago: Building a Hemispheric Community in the Americas," *U.S. Department of State Dispatch*, vol. 9, no. 2 (1998).

58. Klepak, "Cross-Cultural Dimensions of the Non-Proliferation and Arms Control Dialogue in Latin America," pp. 138–39. See also Atkins, *Latin America in the International Political System*, p. 215; and Tacsan, "Searching for OAS/UN Task-Sharing Opportunities," p. 95.

59. Tacsan, "Searching for OAS/UN Task-Sharing Opportunities," p. 96.

60. Commission on Global Governance, *Our Global Neighborhood: The Report of the Commission on Global Governance* (Oxford University Press, 1995).

61. Tacsan, "Searching for OAS/UN Task-Sharing Opportunities," p. 103.

62. Ibid., pp. 96–97.

63. Michael Shifter, "The Challenge of Multilateralism: Intervention and Aid in the Americas," *Brown Journal of World Affairs,* vol. 4, no. 2 (1997), p. 87.

64. Jack Child, *Geopolitics and Conflict in South America: Quarrels among Neighbors* (Praeger, 1985).

65. Paul Wehr and John Paul Lederach, "Mediating Conflict in Central America," in Jacob Bercovitch, ed., *Resolving International Conflict* (Lynne Rienner, 1996), pp. 58–59.

66. Hampson, *Nurturing Peace*, pp. 130, 137.

67. Muñoz, "The Right to Democracy in the Americas," p. 3.

68. Hurrell, "Regionalism in the Americas," pp. 254–55.

69. Edward J. Laurence, "Small Arms, Light Weapons, and Conflict Prevention: The New Post-Cold War Logic of Disarmament," in Barnett R. Rubin, ed., *Cases and Strategies for Preventive Action* (New York: Twentieth Century Fund, 1998), p. 139.

70. Klepak, "Cross- Cultural Dimensions of the Non-Proliferation and Arms Control Dialogue in Latin America," p. 146; Shifter, "The Challenge of Multilateralism"; and Jeanne Kirk Laux, "Human Contacts, Information, Culture and Education," in Robert Spencer, ed., *Canada and the Conference on Security and Co-operation in Europe* (University of Toronto, 1984), p. 259.

71. Tacsan, "Searching for OAS/UN Task-Sharing Opportunities," p. 98.

72. As cited by Muñoz, "The Right to Democracy in the Americas," p. 8.

73. AG/Res. 1080 (XXI-0/91), Resolution on Representative Democracy adopted at the fifth plenary session of the Organization of American States held on June 5, 1991.

74. Richard Bloomfield, "Making the Western Hemisphere Safe for Democracy? The OAS Defense-of-Democracy Regime," *Washington Quarterly,* vol. 17, no. 2 (1994), p. 158.

75. Muñoz, "The Right to Democracy in the Americas," p. 5.

76. Vaky, "The Organization of American States," p. 20.

77. Ibid., pp. 19–20.

78. Manuel Pastor Jr. and Carol Wise, "The Politics of Second Generation Reform," *Journal of Democracy*, vol. 10, no. 3 (1999), pp. 34–48; and Peter Hakim and Abraham F. Lowenthal, "Latin America's Fragile Democracies," in Larry Diamond and Marc F. Plattner, eds., *The Global Resurgence of Democracy* (Johns Hopkins University Press, 1993), pp. 293–306.

79. Klepak, "Cross-Cultural Dimensions of the Non-Proliferation and Arms Control Dialogue in Latin America"; Steven Levitsky, "Fujimori and Post-Party Politics in Peru," *Journal of Democracy*, vol.10, no. 3 (1999), pp. 78–92.

80. Klepak, "Cross-Cultural Dimensions of the Non-Proliferation and Arms Control Dialogue in Latin America," p. 145.

81. Victor-Yves Ghebali, *Le diplomatie de la détente: la CSCE, d'Helsinki à Vienne (1973-1989)* (Brussels: Établissements Emile Bruylant, 1989); and Philippe Schoutheete, *La coopération politique européenne* (Brussels: Labor-Nathan, 1980).

82. John J. Maresca, *To Helsinki: The Conference on Security and Cooperation in Europe 1973-1975* (Duke University Press, 1985).

83. Arie Bloed, ed., *The Conference on Security and Co-operation in Europe: Analysis and Basic Documents 1972-1993* (Kluwer Academic Publishers, 1993).

84. Ghebali, *Le diplomatie de la détente*, p. 62 (translation).

85. Bloed, *The Conference on Security and Co-operation in Europe*, p. 50.

86. Merja Pentikäinen and Martin Scheinin, "A Comparative Study of the Monitoring Mechanisms and the Important Institutional Frameworks for Human Rights Protection within the Council of Europe, the CSCE, and the European Community," in Arie Bloed and others, eds., *Monitoring Human Rights in Europe* (Martinus Nijhoff, 1993), p. 110.

87. Thomas Burgenthal, "The CSCE Rights System (Excerpt)," *CSCE ODIHR Bulletin*, vol. 1 (1993), p. 6.

88. Arie Bloed, "Monitoring the CSCE Human Dimension: In Search of Its Effectiveness," in Bloed and others, eds., *Monitoring Human Rights in Europe*, pp. 42–43; and S. Lehne, *The CSCE in the 1990s: Common European House or Potemkin Village?* (Vienna: Braumüller, 1991), pp. 170, 188.

89. S. Lehne, *The Vienna Meeting of the Conference on Security and Cooperation in Europe, 1986-1989* (Westview Press, 1991), p. 152.

90. Lehne, *The CSCE in the 1990s*, p. 155.

91. Richard Weitz, "Pursuing Military Security in Eastern Europe," in Robet O. Keohane, Joseph S. Nye, and Stanley Hoffman, eds., *After the Cold War: International Institutions and State Strategies in Europe: 1989-1991* (Harvard University Press, 1993), p. 353.

92. Ibid., p. 346.

93. Weitz, "Pursuing Military Security in Eastern Europe." See also Bloed, *The Conference on Security and Co-operation in Europe*, pp. 116–18.

94. William H. Courtney and Janice Helwig, "1999 OSCE Summit Held in Istanbul,"

CSCE Digest, vol. 22, no. 12 (1999), p. 109.

95. I. P. Blischenko and A. H. Abashidze, "National Minorities and International Law," in Allan Rosas and Jan Helgesen, eds., *Human Rights in a Changing East-West Perspective* (Pinter, 1990), pp. 205–06; Arie Bloed, "The CSCE and the Protection of National Minorities," *CSCE ODHIR Bulletin*, vol. 1, no. 3 (1993), p. 1; Commission on Security and Cooperation in Europe, "The OSCE/ODHIR Seminar: Human Rights: The Role of Field Missions," report prepared by the staff of the Commission on Security and Cooperation in Europe (Washington,1999); and Ann-Catherine Blank, "Three Years after Dayton: Lessons Learned in Bosnia and Herzegovina," report by working session rapporteur, Organization for Security and Cooperation in Europe, Working Session I, May 17, 1999.

The Copenhagen Report (IV: 32) (CSSCE, 1990) provides that "to belong to a national minority is a matter of a person's individual choice and no disadvantage shall arise from the exercise of such choice." It also allows that persons belonging to a national minority may "establish and maintain unimpeded contacts among themselves within their country as well as contacts across frontiers with citizens of other States with whom they share a common ethnic or national origin, cultural heritage or religious beliefs" (IV:32.4). However, both the problems relating to the collective enjoyment and protection of minority rights and the definition of the concept "national minority" remain. Also, several escape clauses condition the obligatory character of many provisions, for example, the Copenhagen Report only calls on participating states "to note" the possible use of autonomous administrations of minorities.

96. Shaun, "Institutional Theory and Southeast Asia."

97. Todd Eisenstadt and Daniel Garcia, "Colombia: Negotiations in a Shifting Pattern of Insurgency," in I. William Zartman, ed., *Elusive Peace: Negotiating an End to Civil War* (Brookings, 1995), pp. 265–98.

Chapter 4

1. Letter from the Africa Leadership Forum to Mrs. Mullen, May 1991.

2. "Inaugural Programme of the African Leadership Forum," *The Challenges of Leadership in African Development*, booklet (New York: Africa Leadership Forum, 1988), p. 2.

3. Quoted in "Dramatic Proposals from Obasanjo," *Africa Recovery*, 1987.

4. Olusegun Obasanjo, *Africa in Search of Common Values* (New York: Africa Leadership Forum, 1989), p. 1.

5. Africa Leadership Forum, *The Challenges of Leadership in African Development: Report on the Inaugural Programme of the African Leadership Forum* (New York, 1988), p. 4.

6. Olusegun Obasanjo, "Africa in the 90s: The Challenges of Economic Reforms," address to the Fourth Africa Leadership Forum Meeting, Washington, September 1989 (New York: Africa Leadership Forum), p. 1.

7. Adebayo Adedeji, *Africa within the World: Beyond Dispossession and Dependence*

(Atlantic Highlands, N. J.: Zed Books in association with African Center for Development and Strategic Studies, 1993), p. 5.

8. Thomas M. Callaghy, "Africa and the World Economy: Caught between a Rock and a Hard Place," in John W. Harbeson and Donald Rothchild, eds., *Africa in World Politics* (Westview Press, 1991), p. 43.

9. "Africa: The Scramble for Existence," *Time*, Chicago, September 7, 1992.

10. Olusegun Obasanjo, "Africa in Today's World," in *Africa in Today's World and the Challenges of Leadership* (New York: Africa Leadership Forum, 1988), p. 12.

11. Vice President Edward Jaycox of the World Bank, quoted in Obasanjo, "Africa in the 90s," p. 2.

12. Obasanjo, "Africa in Today's World," p. 16.

13. "Issues Paper for the Security Committee of the Kampala Forum: Collective Continental Security for Stability and Sustained Socio-Economic Transformation in Africa," in Olusegun Obasanjo and Felix G.N. Mosha, eds., *Africa: Rise to Challenge: Towards a Conference on Security, Stability, Development and Cooperation in Africa* (New York: Africa Leadership Forum, 1993), p. 217.

14. Obasanjo, "Africa in the 90s," p. 7.

15. Callaghy, "Africa and the World Economy."

16. Terrence Lyons, "Can Neighbors Help? Regional Actors and African Conflict Management," in Francis M. Deng and Terrence Lyons, eds., *African Reckoning: A Quest for Good Governance* (Brookings, 1998), p. 71.

17. I. William Zartman, "Strengthening of the OAU: Perspectives and Possibilities," in Ralph Onwuka, 'Layi Abegunun, and Dhanjoo Ghista, eds., *African Development* (Brunswick, 1985).

18. Former executive secretary of the OAU, William Eteki, quoted in J. Isawa Elaigwu, "Toward Continental Integration: Supranationalism and the Future of Africa," in Timothy M. Shaw, ed., *Alternative Futures for Africa* (Westview Press, 1982).

19. See Obasanjo, "Africa in the 90s," p. 1.

20. Francis M. Deng, "African Policy Agenda: A Framework for Global Partnership," in Francis M. Deng and Terrence Lyons, eds., *African Reckoning: A Quest for Good Governance* (Brookings, 1998), p. 142.

21. Commission on Security and Cooperation in Europe, Joint Hearing Report on the CSSDCA, CSCE-102-1-7 (Washington, July 30, 1991), p. 2.

22. See "Africa: The Scramble for Existence," note 26.

23. Obasanjo, "Africa in Today's World," p. 12.

24. Olusegun Obasanjo, *Africa Forum*, January 1991.

25. Callaghy, "Africa and the World Economy," p. 42; see also Donald Rothchild, "Regional Peacemaking in Africa," in Harbeson and Rothchild, *Africa in World Politics*, p. 286.

26. Obasanjo, "Africa in the 90s," p. 6.

27. Adedji, *Africa within the World*, p. 47. The author is the former secretary general of the UN Economic Commission on Africa.

28. See Obasanjo, "Africa in Today's World," p. 19.

29. Quoted in Mark Huband, "Africa Ill-Prepared for Challenge from Europe," *Financial Times Limited*, Financial Times (London), November 16, 1989.

30. Sadig Rasheed, "Africa at the Doorstep of the Twenty-First Century: Can Crisis Turn to Opportunity?" in Adedeji, *Africa within the World*, p. 47.

31. Quoted in Jane Perlez, "Africa Fears Its Needs Will Become Secondary," *New York Times*, December 27, 1989.

32. Only one European minister attended the joint ministerial council meeting in Fiji in March 1990. See John W. Harbeson and Donald Rothchild, "Africa in Post-Cold War International Politics: Changing Agendas," in Harbeson and Rothchild, *Africa in World Politics*, p. 10.

33. Interview with Hans D'Orville, president of the African Leadership Foundation, New York, June 1998.

34. Felix Mosha, "The Origins of the CSSDCA," in *Implementation of the Helsinki Accords: Joint Hearing before the Commission on Security and Cooperation in Europe and the Subcommittee on Foreign Affairs* (Government Printing Office, 1992), p. 4.

35. Ibid.

36. All the speeches from the opening session are published in "Report on a Brainstorming Meeting for a Conference on Security, Stability, Development and Cooperation in Africa, November 17–18, 1990," in Obasanjo and Mosha, *Africa: Rise to Challenge*.

37. The report from the meeting is published in Obasanjo and Mosha, *Africa: Rise to Challenge*, pp. 361–62.

38. Olusegun Obasanjo, *Africa in Search of Common Values*, booklet (New York: Africa Leadership Forum, n.d.), p. 3.

39. Laurie Nathan, "Towards a Conference on Security, Stability, Development and Cooperation in Africa," *Africa Insight*, vol. 22 (1992), p. 216.

40. "Report of the Meeting of African NGOs on CSSDCA, April 15–16, 1991," in Obasanjo and Mosha, *Africa: Rise to Challenge*, p. 377.

41. All the speeches from the opening session of the Kampala Forum are published in Obasanjo and Mosha, *Africa: Rise to Challenge*.

42. *Africa Report*, July-August 1991, p. 8.

43. See Mosha, "The Origins of the CSSDCA," p. 7.

44. All the speeches from the opening session of the Kampala Forum are published in Obasanjo and Mosha, *Africa: Rise to Challenge*.

45. *Africa Report*, July-August 1991, p. 8.

46. Ibid.

47. Obasanjo in a letter to Salim, March 7, 1991.

48. "What we took to Kampala was largely accepted, but the Forum provided . . . input, and did not just accept. It was truly a document adopted by the Forum." Interview with Felix Mosha, New York, September 1998.

49. *The Kampala Document: Towards a Conference on Security, Stability, Development and Cooperation in Africa*, May 19–22, 1991, Kampala, Uganda (New York: Africa Leadership Forum jointly with the secretariats of the Organization of African Unity and the

United Nations Economic Commission for Africa), p. 7.

50. Speeches from the opening session of the Kampala Forum in Obasanjo and Mosha, *Africa: Rise to Challenge.*

51. Richard B. Lillich and Hurst Hannum, eds., *International Human Rights: Problems of Law, Policy, and Practice* (Little, Brown and Company, 1995).

52. Felix Mosha, "Change for Survival and Progress in Africa: Preliminary Proposals on the Issues to be Embodied in the Declaration of Binding Principles under CSSDCA and the Process for Implementation," in Obasanjo and Mosha, *Africa: Rise to Challenge*, p. 200. Emphasis added.

53. *Kampala Document*, p. 10. Emphasis added.

54. "Issues Paper for the Security Committee," in Obasanjo and Mosha, eds., *Africa: Rise to Challenge*, p. 216.

55. Laurie Nathan, "Towards a Conference on Security, Stability, Development and Cooperation in Africa," *Africa Insight*, vol. 22, no. 3 (1992), p. 212.

56. *Kampala Document*, p. 15.

57. Nathan, "Towards a Conference on Security, Stability, Development and Cooperation in Africa," p. 212.

58. "Issues Paper for the Stability Committee of the Kampala Forum: Collective Continental Stability: A Critical Necessity for Sustained Development in Africa," in Obasanjo and Mosha, *Africa: Rise to Challenge*, p. 232.

59. Ibid., p. 228.

60. *Kampala Document*, p. 21.

61. Adebayo Adedeji as quoted by Michael Barratt Brown, *Africa's Choices: After Thirty Years of the World Bank* (Westview Press, 1996), p. 170.

62. Salim Lone, "Africa Moves Towards Radical Restructuring of Political Framework," *Africa Recovery*, vol. 5 (June 1991), p. 10.

63. Obasanjo and Mosha, *Africa: Rise to Challenge*, p. 358.

64. *Kampala Document*, p. 25.

65. Ibid., p. 33.

66. Issues Paper for the Ota meeting of the Steering Committee.

67. *Kampala Document*, p. 41.

68. Ibid., p. 40.

69. *Africa Report*, July-August 1991, p. 10.

70. Olusegun Obasanjo and Felix G. N. Mosha, "Introduction," in Obsanjo and Mosha, *Africa: Rise to Challenge*, p. ii.

71. Report of the OAU Secretary-General on the Implementation of the Consensus Reached by the Fifty-Fourth Session of the OAU Council of Ministers, meeting in Abuja, on the Conference on Security, Stability, Development and Cooperation in Africa (CSSDCA).

72. Nathan, "Towards a Conference on Security, Stability, Development and Cooperation in Africa," p. 217.

73. Interview with Sam Iboke, Addis Ababa, September 1998.

74. Interview with Felix Mosha, New York, September 1998.

75. Comment by Timothy Bandora to John Tesha in a phone conversation in September 1998.

76. Interview with Ould-Abdallah, July 1998.

77. *Kampala Document*, p. 15. Emphasis added.

78. Bade Onimonde, "African Cooperation and Regional Security," in Obasanjo and Mosha, *Africa: Rise to Challenge*, p. 153.

79. Elaigwu, "Toward Continental Integration," p.138.

80. Edem Kodjo, *Africa Today* (Accra: Ghana Universities Press, 1989), p. 42. Kodjo is former secretary general of the OAU.

81. Elaigwu, "Toward Continental Integration," p. 132.

82. James O. C. Jonah, "Problems of Security in Africa," in Obasanjo and Mosha, *Africa: Rise to Challenge*, p. 32.

83. Adebayo Adedeji, "Africa in a World in Transition: Laying the Foundation for Security, Stability, Structural Transformation and Cooperation," in Obasanjo and Mosha, *Africa: Rise to Challenge*, p. 8.

84. Interview with Eloho E. Otobo, Addis Ababa, September 1998.

85. Interview with Sam Iboke, Addis Ababa, September 1998.

86. Interview with Ould-Abdallah, July 1998.

87. Olusegun Obasanjo, "Chairman's Summary of Conclusions and Recommendations at the Cologne International Roundtable, March 20–21, 1991," in Obasanjo and Mosha, *Africa: Rise to Challenge*, p. 369.

88. Obasanjo, *Africa in Search of Common Values*, p. 9.

89. Issues Paper for the Ota meeting of the Steering Committee.

90. Comment by Timothy Bandora to John Tesha in a phone conversation in September 1998.

91. Obasanjo, *Africa in Search of Common Values*, p. 8.

92 . Interview with Hans D'Orville, New York, June 1998.

93. According to the internal World Bank memo, "The Kampala Document contains some language that could be improved upon."

94. Interview with Felix Mosha, New York, September 1998.

95. Interview with Ould-Abdallah, July 1998.

96. Julius K. Nyerere, "Foreword," in Obasanjo and Mosha, *Africa: Rise to Challenge*, p. VII.

97. Interview with Felix Mosha, New York, September 1998.

98. Interviews with Hans D'Orville and Eloho E. Otobo, Addis Ababa, September 1998.

99. Interview with Sam Iboke, Addis Ababa, July 1998.

100. Obasanjo, *Africa in Search of Common Values*, p. 10.

101. P. Olisanwuche Esedebe, *Pan-Africanism; The Idea and Movement, 1776-1991* (Howard University Press, 1994), p. 194.

102. Nathan, "Towards a Conference on Security, Stability, Development and Cooperation in Africa."

103. *Africa Management*, vol. 22, no. 3 (1992).

104. Letter to Olusegun Obasanjo from Salim Ahmed Salim, May 15, 1991.

105. Confidential document.

106. Obasanjo, *Africa in Search of Common Values*, p. 10.

107. Letter from Obasanjo to Salim, November 19, 1990.

108. Interview with Eloho E. Otobo, Addis Ababa, September 1998.

109. Interview with Mr. Tesha, Arusha, September 1998.

110. Interview with Adwoa Coleman, Chief Research and Early Warning, OAU's Political Office, September 1998.

111. Interview with Mr. Tesha, Arusha, September 1998.

112. Interview with Eloho E. Otobo, Addis Ababa, September 1998.

113. "Statement by Ambassador A. Haggag at the Kampala Forum, 19-23 May 1991," in Obasanjo and Mosha, *Africa: Rise to Challenge*, p. 305.

114. Interview with Felix Mosha, New York, September 1998.

115. Francis Deng and others, *Sovereignty as Responsibility: Conflict Management in Africa* (Brookings, 1996).

Chapter 5

1. Francis Deng, Sadikiel Kimaro, Terrence Lyons, Donald Rothchild and I. William Zartman, *Sovereignty as Responsibility: Conflict Management in Africa* (Brookings, 1996), especially chap. 1, pp. 1–33.

2. Susan Strange, "*Cave! Hic Dragones*: A Critique of Regime Theory," in Stephen Krasner, ed., *International Regimes* (Cornell University Press, 1983).

3. Donald Puchala and Raymond Hopkins, "International Regimes: Lessons from Inductive Analysis," in Krasner, ed., *International Regimes*, pp. 61–91; and David Gordon, *Self Determination and History in the Third World* (Princeton University Press, 1971).

4. C.O.C. Amate, *Inside the OAU* (St. Martin's Press, 1986), p. 62.

5. W. Scott Thompson and I. William Zartman, "The Development of Norms in the African System," in Yassin el-Ayouty, ed., *The OAU after Ten Years* (Praeger, 1975).

6. I. William Zartman, *Ripe for Resolution: Conflict and Intervention in Africa* (Oxford University Press, 1989), chap. 3.

7. Ibid., chap. 2.

8. Saadia Touval, *Somali Nationalism* (Harvard University Press, 1963), p. 108.

9. Amate, *Inside the OAU*, p. 63.

10. Ibid., pp. 391–93; and Audie Klotz, *Norms in International Relations* (Cornell University Press, 1996).

11. Michael Wolfers, *Politics in the OAU* (London: Methuen, 1976), pp. 36–45; and Klaus van Walraven, *The OAU* (University of Leiden Press, 1996), pp. 216–24.

12. Amate, *Inside the OAU*, pp. 459–75.

13. I. William Zartman and Maureen Berman, *The Practical Negotiator* (Yale Univer-

sity Press, 1982); and Bertram I. Spector, Gunnar Sjöstedt and I. William Zartman, eds., *Negotiating Post-Agreement Regimes* (U.S. Institute of Peace, 2002).

14. *New Vision [Kampala]*, November 12, 1994; and *Jeune Afrique* 1707, September 23, 1993, p. 28.

15. I. William Zartman, ed., *Governance as Conflict Management* (Brookings, 1996).

16. INTOSAI, *Lima Declaration of Guidelines on Auditing Precepts* (Lima: International Organization of Supreme Audit Institutions, XI Congress, 1977); INTOSAI, *Draft Accords* (Uruguay: International Organization of Supreme Audit Institutions, XVI Congress, 1998) [www.intosai.org/2_URUACe.html]; P. Langseth, J. Pope, and R. Stapenhurst, *The Role of A National Integrity System in Fighting Corruption* (World Bank, 1997); and U. Mbanefo, *Strengthening African Supreme Audit Institutions* (Washington: World Bank, 1998).

17. *The Kampala Document: Towards a Conference on Security, Stability, Development and Cooperation in Africa*, May 19–22, 1991, Kampala, Uganda (New York: Africa Leadership Forum jointly with the secretariats of the Organization of African Unity and the United Nations Economic Commission for Africa), p. 21.

18. Ibid., pp. 32–37.

19. T. A. Imobighe, "Conflict Management Mechanisms in West Africa: Relationship between Regional and Sub-regional Mechanism" (OAU/ EECOWAS, ANAD) in Olu Adeniji, ed., *Conflict Management Mechanism in West Africa* (Lagos: AFSTRAG, 1997), pp. 84–95.

20. See "The Report of the Secretary General on Conflicts in Africa: Proposals for an OAU Mechanism for Conflict Prevention and Resolution," CM/1710 (LVI), Council of Ministers, Fifty-Sixth Ordinary Session, June 1992, Dakar, Senegal.

21. Communiqué issued at the end of the consultative meeting of East and Southern African leaders with President Bill Clinton, 1998, p. 3.

22. Ibid., p. 4.

23. Dennis Ventner, "The Discourse On Regional Security in Southern Africa," in Edmond J. Keller and Donald Rothchild, eds., *Africa in the New International Order* (Lynne Rienner, 1996).

24. D. W. Auret, "Regional Cooperation in Southern Africa: Current and future prospects," paper presented at the *Conference on Southern African Security Relations Towards the Year 2000*, Defence Institute of Southern Africa/Institute for Strategic Studies, University of Pretoria, November 1991.

25. Laurie Nathan, *Towards a Conference on Security, Stability, Development and Cooperation in Africa*, Southern African Perspectives Working Paper Series (Cape Town, South Africa, May 1992).

Index

Abacha, Sani, 9, 12, 18, 20, 105
Abboud, Ibrahim, 26
Abiola, Mashood, 12, 20
Abubakar, Abdulsalami, 12
Adedeji, Adebayo, 111, 116, 128
Africa in global economy, 110–11; leadership, 67, 71; norms of state behavior, 140–44; nuclear nonproliferation efforts, 84 post–cold war political development, 2–5, 107–09; recent history, 1–2; regional relations, 2. *See also specific country; specific geographic region*
Africa Democratic Rally, 23–24
Africa Leadership Forum (ALF) activities, 5, 6; CSSDCA implementation, 124, 130–31, 135 CSSDCA origins, 110, 115 goals, 105, 107 in Kampala Forum, 115–116 in Kampala movement, 11, 160–61 OAU and, 135, 136; during Obasanjo imprisonment, 11; origins, 5, 105–06, 108, 110; Paris conference, 110–11
Africa Leadership Foundation, 129
African Center for the Constructive Resolution of Disputes, 56, 162

African Charter for Popular Participation in Development, 4
African Commission on Human and Peoples' Rights, 148
African Economic Community, 152, 154
Agriculture, 146–47, 151. *See also* Food production
Ajello, Aldo, 48
al-Bashir, Omar Hassan Ahmed, 10, 115, 116, 125
ALF. *See* Africa Leadership Forum
Amin, Idi, 27, 29, 39, 63
Angola, 49; civil war, 50, 52–53; economic development, 50; regional relations, 40–41, 53, 60
Aptidon, Hassan Gouled, 30
Argentina, 84
Arias, Oscar, 84
ASEAN. *See* Association of South East Asian Nations
Asia-Pacific Economic Cooperation, 75
Association of South East Asian Nations (ASEAN), 66, 98; civil society involvement, 76–77; confidence building measures, 76; conflict management,

73–74, 77; core principles, 69–72; decisionmaking mechanism, 69–70; distinguishing features, 68, 99; evolution, 67, 69; future prospects, 77; member relations, 70–72, 100; membership, 68; post–cold war challenges, 74–77; purpose, 68, 69; Regional Forum, 75–76; security regime, 69, 72–74, 76, 99–100; significance of, as regional organization, 99–100, 102; structure and functioning, 68–69
Auret, D. W., 156

Babangida, Ibrahim, 10, 19, 20, 123, 130
Banana, Canaan, 145
Banda, Kamazu, 54–55
Banda, Kamuzu, 49
Bandora, Timothy, 126
Barre, Siad, 4, 29, 63
Benin, 19, 21, 162; economic development, 22; regional relations, 24
Biya, Paul, 44
Bokassa, Jean-Bedel, 40
Bongo, Omar, 42, 43
Border and boundary issues, 146; *uti possidetas* principle, 142, 146
Botswana, 143; economic development, 58; political development, 49, 53, 55; regional relations, 52, 59, 60
Brazil, 84, 86, 88
Brunei, 68
Buhari, Muhammadu, 20
Burkina Faso, 18, 21, economic development, 22; regional relations, 24
Burundi, 12, 46; economic development, 44; living conditions, 45; political development, 62; regional relations, 40–41, 43, 47; Tutsi-Hutu conflict, 39–40, 41
Bush, George H. W., 81
Buyoya, Pierre, 41

Calabashes of CSSDCA, 7, 13, 113, 117. *See also specific topic*
Cambodia, 68, 71, 72
Cameroon, 12, 46; economic development, 44, 45, 46; living conditions, 45; political development, 40, 44, 46; regional relations, 47
Campaore, Blaise, 21
Canada, 78, 96
Cape Verde, 22–23
Carnegie Corporation, 11
Carter, Jimmy, 81
CEAO. *See* West African Economic Community
Cedras, Raoul, 85
Central African Economic Union, 47
Central African Republic, 18, 41, 46; economic development, 45; living conditions, 45; political development, 42, 43; regional relations, 40–41, 47
Central African states cooperation among, 46–48; economic development, 44–46; Kampala Movement in, 38–39, 48; political stability, 43–44, 45–46; regional characteristics, 46–47; security conditions, 40–43
Chad, 18, 40; economic development, 44, 45; living conditions, 45; political development, 43–44; regional relations, 40–41, 47; UN interventions, 46
Chile, 84, 88
Chiluba, Frederick, 54, 55–56, 58
China, ASEAN and, 74–75
Chissano, Joaquim, 115, 118
Civil society: in ASEAN decisionmaking, 76–77; business sector in Kampala Movement, 162–163; in CSSDCA origins, 115; in Kampala movement, 5, 11, 130, 137, 159; in OAS, 81–82; recent emergence of, 16; in West African political development, 19–20

Clark, Akporade, 117

Clinton, Bill, 155

CNS. *See* Sovereign national conference (CNS) movement

Cold war, 1, 2; ASEAN development after, 74–77; CSSDCA origins in, 107–09; formation of regional organizations, 66–67; OSCE after, 89, 95–98; political development in Africa after, 2–5, 14, 107–09; trends toward regionalism, 66

Colombia, 88, 101

Colonial period, 141; economic legacy, 15; political legacy, 14, 15

Common Market for Eastern and Southern Africa, 33, 153

Common Market of Eastern and Southern Africa, 47; Goals; 60; membership, 60; SADC and, 60

Common Position on External Debt, 3

Conference on Security, Stability, Development, and Cooperation in Africa (CSSDCA), 6, 7, 8–9, 12, 48, 100; calabashes, 7, 13, 113–14, 117–22; civil society in, 115; cold war origins, 107–09; conflict resolution mechanisms, 135–36; Consultative Secretariat, 122–23, 133–34; development goals, 112; goals, 163; historical milieu, 105–11; implementation, 160; Kampala Forum, 115–17; lessons from other regional efforts, 114 OAU and, 156–57; obstacles to OAU adoption, 10–11, 124–38; origins and development, 13, 104, 105, 111–15, 122–24; OSCE and, 88, 102; perception of Western influences in, 128–29, 137–38; principles and norms, 111–12, 113; recent initiatives, 154–58; security regime, 154–55; sovereignty principles, 117–19, 127–28, 138. *See also* Kampala Movement

Conference on Security and Cooperation in Europe, 6, 67, 89, 90–91, 93, 128. *See also* Organization for Security and Cooperation in Europe

Conference on Security and Cooperation in Southern Africa, 155–56

Confidence building measures, 69–70, 76, 87, 146

Congo, Democratic Republic of, 38, 46, 156; economic development, 44, 57; political development, 39, 43–44; regional relations, 40–41, 41, 42, 48, 53, 60

Congo-Brazzaville, 41, 46; economic development, 44, 45–46; political development, 42, 43, 45–46; regional relations, 47

Conté, Lansana, 22

Cooperation, 5; among Central African states, 46–48; among Horn of Africa states, 26, 32, 33, 34–38; among Southern African states, 50–51, 59–61; among West African states, 23–25; economic context, 152–53; future development and, 64–65; importance of, 151–52; Kampala principles, 7, 9, 117, 122, 151–54; OSCE norms, 91; pathways for, 152–53; regionalism and, 61–62, 153; sovereignty and, 117–18, 127–28

Council for the Development of Social Science Research, 162

Council on Security and Cooperation on the Asia-Pacific, 77

CSSDCA. *See* Conference on Security, Stability, Development, and Cooperation in Africa

Cuba, 80

Customs and Economic Union of Central Africa, 47

Dallaire, Romeo, 46

Deby, Idris, 44

Decisionmaking and problem-solving mechanisms in ASEAN, 69–70, 73–74, 77; in CSSDCA, 135–136; need for continental institutions in Africa, 145–146; in OAS; 79, 82, 83–84; in OAU, 107; 135–36, 154–55, 156–57; in OSCE, 91, 93–94, 96–97; recent initiatives, 154–55

de Klerk, Frederik Willem, 156

Democratic institutions and processes, economic development and, 56, 106, 121, 127; in Horn of Africa states, 28–29, 30; inadequacy of Western model, 63, 126; Kampala principles, 7–8, 120–21, 126; multipartyism and, 126; OAS goals and implementation, 78, 80, 81, 84–86; OAU goals and efforts, 86; objections to CSSDCA implementation, 126; recent development in Nigeria, 12; recent history of Africa, 1–2, 4–5, 11–12, 16, 63; security and, 8; social fragmentation and, 63; in southern Africa, 53–56; stability and, 8, 120; in West Africa, 18, 19–22

Deng, Francis, 11, 117

Desert Locust Control Organization, 34

Development, 5; causes of underdevelopment, 149; in Central African states, 44–46; competition and, 149–150; conditions for, 8–9, 149–51; CSSDCA principles, 112; democratic functioning and, 106, 121, 127; in Horn of Africa states, 31–33; Kampala principles, 6–7, 8–9, 56, 117, 121, 150–51, 154; self-reliance and, 150; social context, 150–51; in Southern African states, 49–50, 56–59; stability and, 45–46; in West Africa, 22–23

Development assistance, to Central African states, 45; global competition for, 110–11; to Southern African states, 58, 59

Diouf, Abdou, 21

Djibouti, 26; economic development, 31, 32; political development, 29, 30; regional relations, 27, 36

Doe, Samuel, 4, 19, 63

Dominican Republic, 80

D'Orville, Hans, 129, 131

Doussou, Robert, 19–20

Drug trade, 74, 101

East African Common Market, 46–47

East African Common Services Organization, 34, 46–47

East African Community, 26, 34, 46–47

East Timor, 71–72, 74, 77, 100

ECA. *See* United Nations, Economic Commission for Africa

Economic and Monetary Community of Central Africa, 47, 153

Economic and Monetary Union of West Africa, 146

Economic Community of the Great Lakes Countries, 47

Economic Community of the States of Central Africa, 47, 48, 146, 153

Economic Community of West African States (ECOWAS), 4, 24–25, 15; security actions, 17, 19, 24

Economic functioning: African competition with Europe, 110–11; business sector in Kampala Movement, 162–63; challenges for ASEAN countries, 74; colonial legacy, 116–17; cooperation among Central African states, 46; cooperation among Southern African states, 59–61; cooperation among West African states, 24–25; cooperation in, 152–53; Entebbe communiqué, 155; food production, 3; globalization, 108; governance and, 56, 116; international interest in Africa, 2; Kampala goals and princi-

ples, 7, 9; OAU reform efforts, 3–4; in postcolonial period, 16; recent history of Africa, 1–2, 2–3, 105–06, 108, 109; stability and, 8; structural adjustment programs, 121; trade balances, 3. *See also* Development
ECOWAS. *See* Economic Community of West African States
Educational system: Central African states, 45; in West African states, 23
Elaigwu, J. Isawu, 127
El Salvador, 84
Entebbe communiqué, 155
Environmental regime, 146–47
Equatorial Guinea: economic development, 44; living conditions, 45
Eritrea, 142; economic development, 32; political development, 31, 62; regional relations, 26–27, 31, 32, 36–38
Esedebe, P. Olidanwuche, 132
Eteki, William, 107
Ethiopia, 29, 71, 142; economic development, 31, 32; political development, 30–31, 62, 63; regional relations, 26, 27, 32, 35–38
Ethnicity, politics and, 63–64
European Union, 110
Eyadema, Gnassigbe, 21

Food and Agriculture Organization, 34, 57
Food production, 3, 106; Central African states, 44; Southern African states, 57; West African development, 22
Formation and development of regional organizations, generally, 66–68, 99; role of norms in, 140–144
France, 96; in postcolonial Central Africa, 48; in postcolonial West Africa, 24
Frontline States, 49–50, 50

Gabon, 12, 40; economic development,
44, 45, 46; living conditions, 45; political development, 43, 46
Gambia, 22
Garang, John, 27, 36
Ghana, 11, 18, 141; economic development, 22, 23; health and mortality, 22, 23; political evolution, 20–21
Globalization, 108
Grenada, 80
Guatemala, 80
Guellah, Ismail Omar, 30
Guinea, 18, 22; health and mortality, 22; regional relations, 24, 25
Guinea-Bissau, 17, 19; economic development, 22; health and mortality, 22; regional relations, 24
Gulf War, 32

Habyarimana, Juvenal, 4
Haggag, Ahmed, 136
Haiti, 86
Hannum, Hurst, 118
Health and mortality; in Central African states, 45; in Horn of Africa states, 35; in West Africa states, 22
Helsinki Document for Europe and North America, 6, 10, 128
Helsinki Final Act, 88–89, 91–93, 94
Horn of Africa states, cooperation, 26, 33, 34–38; economic development in, 31–33; political stability, 28–31; security regime, 26–27. *See also specific state*
Houphouet-Boigny, Felix, 21
Human rights: challenges for ASEAN countries, 74; CSSDCA principles, 113; Kampala principles, 7–8; of minority populations, 97–98; OAS regime, 80, 85, 86–87; OSCE principles and programs, 89–90, 92, 93–95, 97–98, 102; protections in Southern African states, 56; security and, 120,

144; structural and procedural protections, 148–49

Iboke, Sam, 125, 128
IGADD. *See* Inter-Governmental Authority on Drought and Development.
Income, individual, 106; Central African states, 44, 45; per capita national product, 3; West African development, 22
Indonesia, 67, 68, 70, 71–72, 73, 77, 99, 100
Infant mortality, in West African states, 22
Inter-American bank, 79
Inter-Governmental Agency on Development, 156
Inter-Governmental Authority on Development, 26, 37, 153
Inter-Governmental Authority on Drought and Development (IGADD), 35–37
International Monetary Fund, 59, 121
International relations: domestic politics and, 63–64;foreign organizations in CSSDCA implementation, 162; post–cold war political development in Africa, 2; trends in Africa, 2
Interstate relations in Africa; Central African states, 40–43; Horn of Africa states, 26, 32; Kampala principles, 6–7; OAU principles, 141; postcolonial development, 15; recent developments in Africa, 4–5; Southern African states, 51–53; West African states, 17–19. *See also* Cooperation
Islamic movements, 28, 31, 36, 37
Israel, 27
Ivory Coast, 11, 18, 19, 86, 110; economic development, 22, 23; health and mortality, 23; political evolution, 21; regional relations, 24

Japan, ASEAN and, 74–75

Kabbah, Ahmed Tejan, 19
Kabila, Laurent, 39, 41, 48, 53, 156
Kabwegyere, Tarsis, 114
Kagame, Paul, 155
Kampala Document: implementation, 11–12, 61–63, 122–38, 154–57; preparation of, 5–6, 104, 115–17; principles and declarations, 6–9, 117–22, 139–40, 164–69
Kampala Movement, 13, 91; as African movement, 139; business sector in, 162–63; in Central Africa, 38–39, 48; experiences of similar movements, 13, 66–68, 98–103; future prospects, 12, 67, 157–63; initial responses to, 9–11, 104; in Nigeria under Obasanjo, 12; OSCE and, 92; outcomes, 61–63, 154, 160; regionalism as basis of, 61; in southern Africa, 48–49, 61; sovereignty concepts in, 139–40; subregional organizations in, 161–62; in West Africa, 16–17, 20. *See also* Conference on Security, Stability, Development, and Cooperation in Africa (CSSDCA); *Kampala Document*
Kaunda, Kenneth, 10, 49–50, 54, 56, 58, 115, 116
Kennedy, John F., 80
Kenya, 11; economic development, 32–33, 45, 46; living conditions, 45; political development, 29–30, 40, 46; regional relations, 26, 27, 34, 35, 36–37, 47
Kenyata, Jomo, 30
Kerbit, Makonnen, 35
Kerekou, Mathieu, 19, 21
Ketegaya, Eriya, 117
Khama, Seretse, 49
Khartoum Declaration on Human Centered Development, 3

Kiplagat, B. A., 110
ki-Zerbo, Jacqueline, 117
Kodjo, Edem, 127
Konan Bedie, Henri, 21
Konare, Alpha Oumar, 21

Lagos Plan of Action, 3
Lamouse-Smith, Willie, 117
Laos, 68, 75
Leadership: African Leadership Forum
    goals, 105; ASEAN, 71; for CSSDCA
    implementation, 158–59, 161; Kam-
    pala Forum, 115–17; of regional
    organizations, 67, 99
Lesotho: political development, 49, 52;
    regional relations, 59, 60
Letsie III, 52
Liberia, 11, 18, 156; civil war, 17, 18–19;
    economic development, 22, 23; politi-
    cal development, 63; recent political
    history, 4; regional relations, 25
Libya, 10, 125; regional relations, 27,
    40–41
Life expectancy: Central African states,
    45; West African states, 22–23
Lissouba, Pascal, 41, 42

Mainasara, Ibrahim Bare, 18
Malawi: economic development, 58;
    political development, 49, 54–55;
    regional relations, 60
Malaysia, 68, 72, 76
Mali, 18, 21; economic development, 22;
    health and mortality, 22; regional rela-
    tions, 24
Mandela, Nelson, 43, 54, 145
Mariam, Mengistu Haile, 30
Masire, Ketumile, 49, 145
Masire, Quett, 115
Mauritania, 18, 22; economic develop-
    ment, 22; regional relations, 24
Mauritius, 60

Mauritius Declaration on Education, 3–4
Mbeki, Thabo, 48, 54, 114
Mbuende, Kaire, 52
Mechanism for the Prevention, Manage-
    ment and Resolution of Conflict, 10,
    16
Mobutu Sese Seko, 39, 43, 47
Mocumbi, Pascoal, 114, 117
Mogae, Festus, 55
Moi, Daniel arap, 30
Mokhehle, Ntsu, 52
Morocco, 142
Mosha, Felix, 5, 125, 130
Mozambique, 49; economic develop-
    ment, 50, 58; political development,
    50, 53, 54; regional relations, 60
Mswati III, 55
Mubarak, Hosni, 37
Muduuli, David, 35
Mufakat, 70
Mugabe, Robert, 50, 53, 56, 59
Muluzi, Bakili, 54–55, 58
Museveni, Yoweri, 29, 36, 39, 41–42, 43,
    115, 118, 126, 128, 130–31, 155
Mutukwa, Kasuka, 117
Myanmar, 68, 72

Namibia, 143; economic development,
    57; political development, 50, 53, 54,
    55; regional relations, 40–41, 53, 59,
    60
Nathan, Laurie, 156
National Endowment for Democracy, 11
National Institutes for Strategic and
    International Studies, 76–77
Nationalist movements, 14–16
National Summit for Africa Movement,
    162
NATO. See North Atlantic Treaty Organi-
    zation
Ndadaye, Melchior, 44
Ndayikengurukive, Jean-Bosco, 41

Nguema, Macias, 40
Nguesso, Denis Sassou, 42
Nicaragua, 81, 84, 85
Niger, 18; economic development, 22; health and mortality, 22; regional relations, 24
Nigeria, 12; economic development, 22, 23; Kampala Movement in, 9–10, 157, 158–59; leadership role in Africa, 67, 71, 89, 158–59, 161; Obasanjo administration, 12, 20, 105, 157, 161; political evolution, 18, 20, 63; regional relations, 24, 25
Nimeiri, Gaafar, 28, 63
Nixon, Richard, 80, 90
Nkrumah, Kwame, 152
Nongovernmental organizations: in CSSDCA implementation, 130, 137; in planning Kampala Initiative, 6
Noriega, Manuel, 85
North Atlantic Treaty Organization, 90, 95, 96
Ntibantaunganya, Sylvestre, 41
Nuclear nonproliferation, 84
Nujoma, Sam, 50, 55
Nwachukwu, Ike, 114
Nyangoma, Leonard, 41
Nyerere, Julius, 42–43, 49–50, 115, 116, 118, 131, 145

OAS. See Organization of American States
OAU. See Organization of African Unity
Obasanjo, Olusegun, 5, 9–10, 11, 108, 145; ALF and, 105, 106, 107, 110; origins and development of CSSDCA, 105, 112, 114, 115, 118, 129, 131, 132, 135, 157–58, 161; presidency of Nigeria, 12, 20, 105, 157, 161
Obote, Milton, 27, 29
Oil economy: Central African states, 44, 45; Sudan, 33; in West Africa, 23

Okello, Tito, 27
Olympio, Sylvanus, 141
Onimonde, Bade, 127
Organization of African Unity (OAU), 5, 6; Abuja meeting, 10; accomplishments, 106; African Leadership Forum and, 135, 136; ASEAN and, 100; conflict resolution mechanisms, 135–136; CSSDCA development and implementation, 10–11, 123–36, 156–58, 159; democratization efforts, 86; early response to Kampala Movement, 9–11, 104; economic reform efforts, 3–4; future of Kampala Movement and, 161; Kampala Forum, 115; limitations, 106–107; member relations, 71; norms and principles, 141; OAS and, 101; in postcolonial period, 15; refugee policy, 143; security regime, 4, 10, 37, 42, 145, 154–55; similar regional regimes, 98, 102–03; Sirte Declaration, 157; South Africa and, 142–43; U.N. and, 46
Organization for Security and Cooperation in Europe (OSCE), 68; future challenges, 102–03; human rights regime, 89–90, 92, 93–95, 97–98, 102; member relations, 91; origins and development, 67, 88–91, 92–93, 101–02; postcold war mission, 95–98; principles and norms, 91–93; security regime, 89, 91, 95–96, 102; structure and procedures, 96–97
Organization for the Development of the Senegal River, 25
Organization of American States (OAS), 66, 68, 98; accomplishments, 79–80, 81, 102; cold war, 79; democratization efforts, 80, 81, 84–86; future prospects, 78, 101; human rights regime, 80, 85, 86–87; member relations, 78–79, 80–81; origins and

development, 67, 78–82, 100–01; principles and norms, 78, 82, 83; security regime, 82–84, 87–88, 100; significance of, for OAU, 101, 102; status, 78; structure and functioning, 79, 81–82; United Nations and, 81–82

OSCE. *See* Organization for Security and Cooperation in Europe

Otobo, Eloho E., 128

Panama, 80, 85

Papua New Guinea, 75

Patassé, Ange, 42

Pereira, Aristedes, 115

Permanent Interstate Committee for Drought Control in the Sahel, 25

Peru, 88

Philippines, 68, 71–72

Politics and governance: colonial legacy, 14–15; development in Central Africa, 38–40; development in Southern Africa, 49, 50; economic reform and, 23; ethnicity and, 63, 64; foreign influences, 2; internationalization of, 63–64; Kampala principles, 8; military governments, 18, 19, 20–21, 28–29, 62–63, 87–88; nationalist trends, 14–16; norms of state behavior in Africa, 140–144; obstacles to CSSDCA implementation by OAU, 124–28, 131–36; post–cold war, 2, 107–09; postcolonial period, 16, 23–24; prospects for reform, 64; recent history of Africa, 1–3, 4–5, 62–63. *See also* Democratic institutions and processes; Stability

Portugal, 50, 52

Preferential Trade Agreement of Eastern and Southern Africa, 47

Priority Program for Economic Recovery, 3

Privatization, 2–3, 58

Qadhafi, Moammar, 125,158

Ramos, Fidel, 71

Rasheed, Sadig, 110

Rawlings, Jerry, 20–21

Refugees, 143

Regionalism, 61–62, 66; post–cold war trends, 109; subregional organizations for CSSDCA implementation, 161–62

Rhodesia, 49

Russia, 75

Rwanda, 39, 46; economic development, 44, 45; living conditions, 45; political development, 62; recent political history, 4; regional relations, 38, 40–41, 47, 53; Tutsi-Hutu conflict, 39–40, 41, 42; UN intervention, 46

SADC. *See* Southern African Development Community

Sahnoun, Mogamed, 42

Salim, Salim Ahmed, 111, 131, 132, 133, 135

Sankoh, Foday, 19

Savimbi, Jonas, 41, 52–53

Security: ASEAN regime, 69, 72–74, 76, 99–100; in Central Africa, 40–43; CSSDCA peacekeeping role, 134; CSSDCA principles, 112, 113, 119–20, 155; democratization and, 8; Horn of Africa states, 26–27; Kampala principles, 6–8, 53, 117, 144–47, 154–55; need for continental institutions in Africa, 145–47; nuclear nonproliferation, 84; OAS regime, 82–84, 87–88, 100–01; OAU regime, 10; OSCE regime, 89, 91, 95–97, 102; of peoples, security of governments and, 8, 120, 144–45, 146–47; in postcolonial period, 15; recent developments in Africa, 4, 154–57; regionalism and, 61;

in Southern Africa, 51–53; sovereignty and, 119; in West African states, 17–19, 24, 25

Selassie, Haile, 27, 30

Senegal, 11, 19, 162; economic development, 22; health and mortality, 22; political evolution, 21; regional relations, 24

Senghor, Sedar, 21

Seychelles: economic development, 57; regional relations, 60

Sid'Ahmed Taya, Maaouya Ould, 22

Sierra Leone, 12, 18, 156; civil war, 18–19; economic development, 22, 23; Liberia and, 17; regional relations, 25

Singapore, 68, 71

Sirte Declaration, 157

Sobhuza II, 49

Social unrest: democratic institutions and, 63; economic reform and, 23; in Sudan, 28–29; in Swaziland, 55; in Zimbabwe, 59

Soglo, Christopher, 21

Somalia, 36, 142; economic development, 31; recent political history, 4; regional relations, 26, 27, 35

Somaliland, 142

South Africa, 1, 48, 162; apartheid regime, 108, 142–43; economic development, 57, 60; leadership role in Africa, 71; political development, 48, 53–54; regional relations, 47, 48, 49, 50, 51–52, 53, 59, 60

Southern African Customs Union, 59

Southern African Development Community (SADC), 42, 47, 48, 50–51, 153, 155–56; membership, 60; programs, 60; security regime, 51–52, 53, 56

Southern African Development Coordination Conference, 50–51

Southern African Development Council (SADC), 146

Southern African Human Rights and NGO Network, 56

Southern African states; colonial legacy, 49; cooperation, 50–51, 59–61, 155–56; decolonization, 49; economic development, 49–50, 56–59; future prospects, 61; Kampala Movement and, 48–49, 61; political development, 49, 50; political stability, 53–56; security conditions, 51–53, 56, 155–56

South West Africa, 49

Sovereign national conference (CNS) movement, 4, 16; in Central Africa, 39, 40, 43–44, 44 in West Africa, 18, 19–20, 21–22

Sovereignty: Kampala principles, 6, 117–19, 127–28, 138, 139–40; OAU principles, 141–42; stability and, 147–48

Soviet Union, 89–90, 92–93, 95–96

Stability, 5; causes of instability, 62, 63–64; Central African states, 43–44, 45–46; CSSDCA role in monitoring, 134; determinants of, 8, 148; governance and, 147–48; Horn of Africa states, 28–31; Kampala principles, 6–7, 8, 117, 120–21, 147–49; Southern African states, 53–56; West African states, 19–22

Structural adjustment programs, 121

Study and Research Group on Democracy and Economic and Social Development in Africa, 162

Sudan, 10, 26, 124–25, 141, 142; economic development, 33; political development, 28–29, 63; regional relations, 26–27, 35–38, 40–41, 42

Suharto, Mohammed, 71, 99

Sukarno, Ahmed, 71

Suu Kyi, Aun San, 72

Swaziland: economic development, 57, 59; political development, 49, 55; regional relations, 59, 60

Tanzania, 29, 39; economic development, 44, 50, 57; political development, 40, 43; regional relations, 34, 42–43, 47, 49–50, 60

Taylor, Charles, 19, 25

Terrorist activity, in Sudan, 37

Tesha, John, 135

Thailand, 68, 71, 76

Togo, 21; economic development, 22, 23; health and mortality, 22–23; regional relations, 24

Toure, Amadou Toumani, 18, 145

Trade, international; Central African states, 45; challenges for ASEAN countries, 74; Kampala principles, 9; recent trends, 3; Southern African economies, 57

Trade, intraregional; among Central African states, 47–48; among Horn of Africa states, 32; among Southern African states, 60

Tunisia, 11

Uganda, 12, 26, 39; economic development, 31, 32, 44, 45; living conditions, 45; political development, 29, 41–42, 43, 62, 63; regional relations, 27, 34, 35, 37–38, 40–41, 47, 53

United Nations, 37, 131, 132; Angolan intervention, 53; ASEAN and, 76; CSSDCA peacekeeping and, 134; Economic Commission for Africa (ECA), 3, 5, 46, 115, 121, 152–53; inadequacy of African interventions, 46; OAS and, 81–82; security actions, 19; Southern Africa interventions, 50

United States, 67; ASEAN and, 74–75; in OAS, 78, 80, 101; OSCE and, 89, 90, 96; Sudan and, 37

Universal Declaration on Human Rights, 86

van der Stoel, Max, 98

Vietnam, 68, 75

Violent conflict; among Horn of Africa states, 26, 30–31, 37–38; in Central Africa, 39–42; in Horn of Africa, 32; Kampala principles, 7–8; need for peacekeeping institutions in Africa, 145–146; in OAS region, 80; recent developments in Africa, 4, 62; in Southern Africa, 50, 51–52; in West Africa, 17, 18–19, 25

Wade, Abdoulaye, 21

Wahid, Abdurrrahman, 72

Waiyaki, Munyua, 117

Weapons of mass destruction, 84

West Africa: development in, 22–23; interstate relations, 23–25; Kampala Movement in, 16–17, 20; stability, 19–22. See also specific nation

West African Economic and Monetary Union, 24

West African Economic Community (CEAO), 24, 25

Wifaq, 70

World Bank, 58, 121, 130

Yemen, 27

Yugoslavia, 96, 97

Zaire: political development, 39; UN intervention, 46; War of Succession, 17, 38, 40–41, 42, 46, 53. See also Congo, Democratic Republic of

Zambia, 10, 11; economic development, 50; political functioning, 53, 55–56; regional relations, 49–50, 53, 60

Zartman, I. William, 156

Zenawi, Meles, 155

Zimbabwe, 11; economic development, 58–59; political development, 50, 54, 56; regional relations, 40–41, 48, 51–52, 52, 53, 60